Dream Destinations
EUROPE

Dream Destinations
EUROPE

ABOUT THIS BOOK

Spectacular volcano landscapes, the longest and deepest fjords in the world, pristine national parks, mysterious monuments from the Stone Age, windswept coastlines, formidable cathedrals, splendid castles and palaces, serene monasteries, gentle lakes and rivers, cosmopolitan cities, romantic vineyard towns, the largest and most exciting museums in the world, medieval hamlets, dark forests and rugged mountains, idyllic fishing villages, ancient temples, island paradises in the Mediterranean…Europe!

This book presents the most fascinating destinations on the "old" continent, many of which are protected UNESCO World Heritage Sites. Breathtaking images take you to paradisical locations that everyone should have the pleasure of seeing at least once.

In addition to the absolute must-see sights such as Venice, London or Paris, you will see landscapes and places that are simply begging to be discovered in person. The Island of Skye in Scotland, the romantic Duero Valley in Spain…these are both dream destinations that are all worth a visit.

Read, look, dream…travel.

I wish you an exciting journey,

Wolfgang Kunth

The pictures on the previous pages show a fresco of a dancer from between the 13th and 7th century BC. It was originally in a former palace in the ancient city of Tiryns (Peloponnese) and is now in the Archeology Museum in Athens. The next photo shows a salmon fisherman at Hraunfossar Falls in the west of Iceland, which eventually flow into the Hvítá River.

CONTENTS

The square in front of St Peter's Basilica in Rome (below) is simply awe-inspiring. Bernini's elliptical complex, built between 1656 and 1667, is 240 m (790 ft) long and framed by a 17-m-wide (60-ft) colonnade comprising 284 individual columns.

KRAFLA

Situated just to the north-east of Mývatn, the countryside around Krafla, an active, 818-m (2,684-ft) volcano (above and main picture), is tectonically one of the least stable regions in Iceland. Believed for almost 2,000 years to be extinct, Krafla suddenly exploded to life at the beginning of the 18th century, smothering the region under a thick layer of lava and ash. What remained was a sparkling, emerald-green crater lake measuring 320 m (1,050 ft) across at its widest point.

In the year 1975, Krafla erupted yet again, this time for almost a decade. Its sulfur mud pots have been bubbling and steaming ever since and are now a popular tourist attraction as well as the most visible icon of Iceland's continuing volcanic activity.

GODAFOSS

About 40 km (25 mi) to the east of Akureyri, traveling from the Sprengisandur gravel and lava desert toward the ocean, the Skjálfandaðfljót River thunders over a 10-m-high (33-ft) cleft in the terrain. The Goðafoss (right, top) owes its name, Waterfall of the Gods, to Thorgeir, speaker of the Althing, Iceland's parliament. In the year 1000, he is said to have thrown the statues of the former pagan gods into the river because the Icelandic parliament had decreed that Iceland should become Christian. The decision followed a threat from Norwegian King Olaf to stop the trade in timber, a move that would have endangered a vital industry for Iceland, shipbuilding.

DETTIFOSS

The Dettifoss (right) in Iceland's north-eastern corner is an impressive 100 m (328 ft) wide and 44 m (144 ft) high waterfall, with a flow of up to 1,500 cu m (52,972 cu ft) per second, the most powerful waterfall in Europe.

MÝVATN

Roughly 30 km (17 mi) east of Goðafoss is "Mosquito Lake" (right), formed by the escaping lava from volcanic eruptions as recently as about 2,000 to 3,500 years ago. The lake covers an area of 37 sq km (14 sq mi) but it is only 4 to 5 m (13 to 16 ft) deep and fed by hot springs. Hardly anywhere else on the planet does such a diversity of fauna and flora exist at such northern latitudes. A great variety of mosses, grasses, ferns, herbs and birches grow along the lakeshore and on its numerous islands. During the summer months, huge swarms of mosquitoes buzz, giving the warm waters their name. Together with the insect larvae in the water, they provide nutrition for rich stocks of fish as well as several thousand waterfowl that nest in the network of bays.

The Mývatn also counts as one of Iceland's most spectacular landscapes due to its location in a zone of extreme volcanic activity. Strolling along the well-marked footpaths you will see an array of unusual lava formations. Especially bizarre are the Dimmuborgir (Dark Castles), a series of fantastic formations that feature small caverns and arches.

You can get the best view of the pseudocraters in and around Mývatn from the rim of Hverfjall, an ash cone that rises roughly 170 m (558 ft).

SKAFTAFELL

Skaftafell National Park, founded in 1967 and part of the Vatnajökull National Park since June of 2008, stretches from the center of the Vatnajökull, Iceland's largest glacier, to the south as far as the Ring Road. Signposted footpaths lead through dense forests (for example, near Núpsstadaskógar), along extensive swamps, moorlands and meadows to farms – some no longer in use, some still operational – and a grand waterfall surrounded by lava columns. The waters of the Svartifoss – or Black Waterfall – tumble over an impressive basalt cliff shaped like an amphitheater (main picture).

VATNAJÖKULL

This national park covers a vast area of roughly 12,000 sq km (4,632 sq mi) and has a variety of attractions: moors, swamps, birch groves, scree fields and sandy terrain all against the magnificent backdrop of the Vatnajökull, or Water Glacier (top), which consists of a larger volume of ice than any of the glaciers in the Alps. Above: Glaciers reflected on a lake in the national park.

Since June of 2008, the Skaftafell and Jökulsárgljúfur parks have also been integrated into the protected area, which now constitutes the largest national park in Europe.

The great attraction at Iceland's so-called South Cape are the bird rocks on the Dyrhólaey Peninsula near Vík. Many common species of North Atlantic waterfowl live on several different levels of the landscape here: at the top are the puffins, which dig their corridors into the grassy knoll; below, on the rocky ledges, are the kitti wakes and northern fulmars. You can reach the black sand and lava beach by boat where the rock formations rise a good 120 m (394 ft) above the strand. A lighthouse marks a famous viewpoint.

STAVANGER

Stavanger, on the Boknafjord, is the capital of the county of Rogaland. Around the year 872, King Harald Fairhair united the still fractured parts of the Norwegian realm here. Monumental Viking sword sculptures in the Hafrsfjord commemorate the event.

The Romanesque cathedral, begun in 1125, is the most intact medieval religious stone building in Norway. The Norwegian Canning Museum (Norsk Hermetikkmuseum), located in a former canning factory, documents the industry that dominated life in the town from the 1840s. In the middle of the 20th century, fifty sardine canning factories were based in Stavanger; in 2002, the last one shut its doors.

During its rapid development as a center for the oil and gas industries (since 1971), Stavanger also celebrated its origins: Gamle Stavanger, the lovingly restored old town of wooden houses, is a protected historical monument.

With more than 150 wooden houses dating back to the 18th and 19th centuries, the Old Town (Gamle Stavanger) is one of the largest collections of wooden houses in the world (above: a view of the port).

LYSEFJORD

East of Stavanger, the Lysefjord cuts through roughly 40 km (25 mi) of the Ryfylkeheiene mountain region. Thrills for hikers are guaranteed, from the famous boulder wedged into a crevasse on the Kjerag to the sheer cliffs of the Prekestolen, or Preacher's Pulpit, which can be accessed via a rather narrow, unsecured rock path – the platform at the top of the cliff has no security railings.

If, however, you prefer admiring the scenery from the safer lower reaches, then take a boat through the Lysefjord. From Forsand at the mouth of the fjord, a car ferry takes visitors to Lysebotn at the end of the fjord, where one of the most spectacular serpentine roads in Norway begins. At the Lysefjordsenteret information center near Oanes at the national road bridge at the mouth of the fjord, you can find out more interesting facts about this myth-enshrouded natural wonder and its mountainous surroundings. The center also has information on interesting hiking and climbing routes.

Above: At the Kjerag wedged rock, the Ryfylkeheiene mountains plunge up to 1,000 m (3,281 ft) down to the Lysefjord.

The Prekestolen rock platform, also known as the Preacher's Pulpit, towers at a dizzying height of nearly 600 m (1,969 ft). It measures 25 by 25 m (27 by 27 yds) and is unhindered on three sides. The views across the Lysefjord to the Ryfylkeheiene mountain region are breathtaking.

BERGEN, GEIRANGERFJORD, SOGNEFJORD

Dalsnibba (1,476 m/4,843 ft) offers amazing panoramic views of the Sunnmøre mountain region (main picture) into which the Geirangerfjord slashes a more than 1,000-m-deep (3,281-ft) valley. You can also reach the mountain by car on a 5-km (3-mi) toll road.

BERGEN

From the 14th to the 16th centuries, it was mostly German merchants who controlled business dealings in the trading and port town of Bergen, Norway. The Germans ran the salt trade, an important ingredient needed to conserve the fish catches from the Norwegian Sea. In those days, salted fish was sold as far away as the Mediterranean and, thanks to its extensive commercial ties, Bergen eventually became one of the most important towns in the Hanseatic League.

On the Tyske Bryggen Quay – which means German Bridge and plainly reveals its use among Hanseatic merchants – gabled warehouses still bear witness to the former prosperity of this once mighty trading port. The 58 wooden houses that have been carefully preserved in the historic district, however, are not actually left over from medieval times. They were rebuilt in the original style after a fire in 1702. Fires have caused continuous damage in Bergen, which is still an important Norwegian port. The most recent fire was in 1955.

GEIRANGERFJORD

If statistics are proof, then the Geirangerfjord is one of the most impressive landscapes on the planet: The innermost arm of the Storfjord is roughly 120 km (75 mi) long and visited by more than 150 cruise ships from around the world each year. From the ship you will be able to see three famous waterfalls, among other things: Seven Sisters (above), Suitor and Bridal Veil. In summer, the Hurtigruten ships also dock in Geiranger, a village of about 250 people at the end of the fjord. The Ørneveien pass (or Eagle Road), from the Geirangerfjord to the Norddalsfjord farther north, is one of the most breathtaking roads in all of Scandinavia featuring hairpin turns and stunning vistas. The most spectacular viewpoint, however, can only be reached on foot at 1,112 m (3,648 ft) above the fjord: the nearly vertical Flydalshornet.

The Marina and the Old Town (left) are among the loveliest attractions in Bergen, Norway's second-largest city. Situated on the Byfjord, Bergen enjoys a mild climate as it is sheltered from the colder inland temperatures by mountains reaching up to 2,000 m (6,562 ft).

SOGNEFJORD

The Sognefjord (top) is not only Europe's longest fjord at 204 km (127 mi), but also the deepest on earth at 1,308 m (4,292 ft). Both Nærøyfjord (above left), flanked on both sides by rock cliffs up to 1,800 m (5,906 ft) high, and Aurlandfjord (above right) are arms at the south-eastern end of Sognefjord.

URNES

The Vikings traveled down the Lustrafjord to the stave church on the Urnes promontory (main picture) to pray in the naves. Reconstructions made after the Reformation damaged the original appearance, but the richly carved decor has been well preserved.

Norway's stave churches are unique among religious Christian buildings: the framework of the medieval wooden structures comprises staves reminiscent of ships' masts, which is why these religious buildings are also known as "mast churches". Their interiors are usually very cramped; the main room, to which side aisles were only very rarely added, is considered the architectural successor of the Old Norwegian king's hall concept. Typical features include the steep tiered roofs, open access balconies and porches.

Out of the just under thirty Norwegian stave churches still preserved today, the one in Urnes, located on a promontory in the Lusterfjord, is considered by far the oldest. It was built in the 12th century, and its prominent features are the Viking-style carved ornaments depicting an array of mythical creatures, scorpionfish, closely intertwined animal figures and snake-like forms. They are found on the cushion capitals of the interior as well as on the powerfully designed reliefs at the entrances.

BORGUND

Norway's most lovingly preserved stave church can be visited by making a short detour inland along the E16 after passing through the long Lærdal Tunnel. Built around 1150, the church is known for its elaborate carvings and the pagoda-shaped bell tower that stands next to it.

The stave church in Borgund near Borlaug in the inner Lærdal is more than 850 years old and dedicated to the Apostle Andrew.

HEDDAL

The Telemark village of Heddal is home to the world's largest preserved stave church – with its three-tiered roof and towers it is also considered the most beautiful. This "cathedral" of stave churches was built in the 12th/13th centuries and reconstructed in the 1950s so that it today largely matches the original. According to legend, the builder was a troll named Finn, who is said to have eventually fled the town because he could not bear the noise of the bells. The faithful laid down their weapons in front of the church, which was dedicated to the Virgin Mary in 1242, before entering the "ship".

Like all stave churches, Heddal was also not built in a city, but rather in a desolate location with unique scenery.

Urnes, probably the oldest stave church in Norway (left), is considered a perfect example of Scandinavian wooden architecture from the end of the Viking age.

The Melkevollbreen Glacier flows down a steep valley into Lake Oldevatnet on the edge of Jostedalsbreen National Park. It is just one arm of the largest glacier in mainland Europe, the Jostedalsbreen.

JOSTEDALSBREEN

Jostedalsbreen is the largest glacier in mainland Europe. From the interior arms of the Sognefjord, this plateau glacier stretches about 100 km (328 mi) into the north-east at widths of up to 15 km (9 mi). The ice is 500 m (1,640 ft) thick in places.

In the middle of the glacier stands the Høgste Breakulen, a 1,957-m (6,421-ft) glacial cone covered in ice. Only a few rocky islands break through the ice cover, the highest of these being the Lodalskåpa at an impressive 2,083 m (6,834 ft). You can take Route 604 to the Jostedalen Valley, which runs for 50 km (31 mi) and contains a network of valleys with glacial fingers stretching toward the east. Brigsdalsbreen is the best-known glacier arm on the sunnier northwest side.

Guided glacier tours (above) offer added security during your discovery of this icy realm. They start at the visitor center, which was built to resemble a crevasse.

DOVREFJELL-SUNNDALSFJELLA

Dovrefjell-Sunndalsfjella National Park combines expansive Vidda plateaus (top right) and the glacial high mountain range of the Snøhetta. In the steep tributary valleys of the Sunndalsfjord, the plateau tumbles down an impressive series of 100-m-high (328-ft) rock formations (top).

The animal world is as diverse as the spectacular landscape here. At thirteen degrees latitude, in the south it is hardly distinguishable from that of Central Europe, while the mountain plateaus and the northern reaches have a more Arctic feel. The muskox (above), the iconic animal of the Arctic,

has been reintroduced all the way from Greenland to the tundra Dovrefjell. Above middle: A white-tailed eagle during a precision catch. Above bottom: A reindeer.

JOTUNHEIMEN

Jotunheimen National Park, home to Northern Europe's highest summits, is the most easily accessible hiking and mountain sports region in all of Norway. Galdhøpiggen, at 2,469 m (8,101 ft), is the highest peak in Scandinavia and more than two hundred other summits surpass the 2,000 m (6,562 ft) mark in this glacial mountain range.

On the Vestland side the area is characterized by an alpine ruggedness while the Østland side features much gentler, undulating landscapes. Overall, approximately 1,151 sq km (444 sq mi) of these central highlands are protected by the national park.

NORTH CAPE

The rocky promontory on the north side of Magerøya Island, also known as North Cape, has for centuries wrongly been regarded as mainland Europe's northernmost point (main picture). Admittedly, the actual northernmost point is not far away: the next rocky spit of land, Knivskjellodden (above). Jutting about 1.5 km (0.9 mi) farther northward into the sea, it is comparatively flat and not quite as spectacular as its more famous neighbor, a tall headland protruding 307 m (1,000 ft) into the Norwegian Sea. It was Englishman Richard Chancellor, chief navigator of a fleet of seven ships undertaking the first journey in search of the North-East Passage between 1553 and 1554, who spotted this impressive rocky bluff and, believing it to be the northern tip of the continent, named it the "North Cape".

LOFOTEN

VESTERÅLEN

The Lofoten chain of islands, part of the county of Nordland and separated from the mainland by the Vestfjord, is actually a submerged mountain range whose tips poke out of the sea. Aust-vågøy is the largest island and has the highest peaks in the Higrav-tinden (1,161 m/3,809 ft). On Moskenesøy Island you will find the Lofoten villages of Reine (top) and Sakrisøy (bottom) with fish-ermens' houses up to 100 years old built on piles.

The Vesterålen archipelago off the coast of Troms extends over an area of 150 km (93 mi), and in the south merges almost seamlessly into the Lofoten archipelago. The Raftsund strait and the Trollfjord on the Lofoten side are seen as the dividing line. The overall landscape resembles that of Lofo-ten: fjords, straits, bays, skerry islands, rivers, lakes, moors, val-leys, plains, alpine summits and sandy beaches like those in the south. The main islands are Hin-

nøya, the largest island in Norway covering 2,205 sq km (851 sq mi), Langøya and Andøya.
In 2003, the lakes and highlands on Hinnøya island were made into the Møysalen National Park (above). The 51-sq-km (20-sq-mi) area extends from Indrefjord to the Møysalen (1,266 m / 4,154 ft), the highest peak on the Vester-ålen. Administratively, only a part of Hinnøya is in Troms, despite its geographical proximity. The rest belongs to Nordland.

SVALBARD (SPITSBERGEN)

In 1194, Vikings landed on an archipelago that they subsequently named Svalbard (Cold Coast). This name was then given to the Norwegian administrative district comprising ten larger and countless smaller islands, and which is around 600 km (373 mi) north of the mainland. About 36,502 sq km (14,090 sq mi) of the archipelago, which covers roughly 61,022 sq km (23,554 sq mi), are covered in ice. The main town and seat of government is Longyearbyen on Spitsbergen, the largest of the islands and the only one inhabited year round. Nomen est omen: Having set out in 1594 from Amsterdam with two ships to find the north-eastern passage to Asia, it was

actually the island's mountain peaks that inspired Dutch sailor Willem Barents to name this significant Arctic Ocean island "Spitsbergen" three years later in 1597.

Above: The slender Liefdefjord with the Monaco Glacier in the north-west of Svalbard is one of the best tips for travelers. Large quantities of ice from the Monaco

Glacier regularly break off into the sea, and the surrounding tundra is frequently visited by polar bears.

The polar bear (main picture), a close relative of the brown bear, only became concentrated in the Arctic coasts and edges of drift ice in geologically recent times – some 50,000 years ago. The near-white color of its extremely thick, water-repellent fur allows the bear to largely blend in with the landscape. These creatures are also excellent swimmers and divers.

The capital of Sweden, Stockholm (main picture), has just under 800,000 inhabitants and is spread across fourteen islands at the south-eastern end of Lake Mälar on the east coast. The region has numerous skerry island formations where freshwater and saltwater come together.

DROTTNINGHOLM

Completed in around 1700, Drottningholm Palace (or Queen Island) is majestically located on Lovön Island in Lake Mälar, on the site of an earlier building dating back to the 16th century. Commissioned in 1662, by Hedwig Eleonora, wife of the late King Charles X Gustav, it is the largest baroque palace in Sweden and widely regarded as the most important work by architect Nicodemus Tessin.

The main façade of the rectangular structure faces the water. The palace was enlarged after 1750, and numerous rooms were furnished in the lavish style of the rococo. When the palace was increasingly used for state visits, starting in 1777, some of the important rooms were remodeled in elegant neoclassical style. King Gustav III (1771–92) had the gardens laid out in English landscape style.

Aside from the splendid rooms from a range of style periods, visitors are especially fascinated these days by the China Pavilion and the Drottningholm Theater, one of very few rococo theaters still in use.

Drottningholm Palace, residence of the Swedish royal family, is surrounded by several gardens and has been delightfully incorporated into the aquatic scenery around Lake Mälar (left).

STOCKHOLM

Founded in 1252, and the capital since 1634, Stockholm has long been a dynamic and international city, and its wonderful mix of grandiose buildings, parks, waterways and bridges give the vibrant metropolis a unique ambience.

All of the major sights can easily be visited on foot during a stroll through the Old Town (Gamla Stan), and overall there are roughly one hundred museums. In addition to the Nationalmuseet, which has the country's most important art collection, and the Moderna Museet, with contemporary art, it also features Skansen, the world's oldest open-air museum, and the Vasamuseet. The latter exhibits the Vasa, King Gustav II Adolf's flagship, which sank upon its launch in 1628.

The main picture shows Riddarholmen Island with the steeple of Riddarholmskyrka church. This former place of worship is now a museum and the last resting place of the Swedish kings.

ÖLAND, VISBY (GOTLAND), FÅRÖ

Gotland and Öland are Sweden's largest islands and were originally settled by the Vikings. Gotland's capital is Visby, whose fortifications extend for 3.4 km (2 mi). During the time of the Hanseatic League, it was considered one the most important trading ports in the entire Baltic.

ÖLAND

Öland, Sweden's second-largest island after Gotland, features steep, jagged cliffs on its western side, while the eastern side enjoys a more gentle descent toward the sea. The south-east possesses soil deposited by glaciers and is the only part of the island that can be cultivated. The rest of Öland's plateau to the south is dominated by sandstone, slate and chalk.

The Stora Alvaret area, a 40-km (25-mi) stretch of treeless limestone heathland, acquired its present appearance from centuries of overgrazing and deforestation that exposed bare limestone in some areas. Despite these difficult topographic and climatic conditions, humans have been able to inhabit South Öland for at least 5,000 years.

South of the Mysinge hög, the largest Bronze-Age burial mound in Sweden, is a passage grave where thirty people were buried roughly 4,000 years ago. Numerous burial fields from the Iron Age and several ring fort refuges from the time of the Great Migration even indicate permanent settlement.

VISBY (GOTLAND)

The main town on Gotland's north-western coast was settled as early as the Stone Age. In the 12th century, Visby served initially as a stopping point for German merchants in their highly lucrative trade with Novgorod, but soon it became the launch pad for an extension of the Hanseatic League cities into the east.

In the 13th century, Visby was regarded as probably the most important trading town in the north of the European continent aside from Lübeck in Germany. It even minted its own coins, and it was here that the so-called Visby Rules were agreed, an international maritime treaty binding for the entire Baltic region. This golden age came to a relatively abrupt end, however, when Gotland was conquered by Danish King Waldemar IV in 1361.

Today, the mighty fortifications still bear witness to the town's former prosperity. Thirty-eight historical defense towers have been preserved, but the port of Visby has since silted up.

Herbs, grasses and flowers flourish on Öland, including the pasqueflower (left). The large stones, which probably mark burial places (far left with windmill in the background) indicate at least one prehistoric settlement, possibly during the last Ice Age.

FÅRÖ

The most famous inhabitant of Fårö was Swedish director Ingmar Bergmann, who was buried here after his death on July 30, 2007. Separated from Gotland only by a narrow sound, this tiny island is a quiet summer paradise with lovely beaches that are popular among visitors from the mainland. There is a ferry from Fårösund on Gotland and the island's military installation has been shut down since the mid-1990s.

Highlights in the countryside are the nature reserve of Ullahau in the north with its sand dunes, and the limestone stacks (left) of Digerhuvud, Gamle Hamn and Langhammars, given their bizarre shapes by wind and erosion.

Since Denmark and Sweden were connected by the ambitious Öresund Bridge, it has become even easier to travel between the two "united kingdoms". One of the strangest, and yet somehow still accurate, travel recommendations for Denmark came from the much-loved and down-to-earth Queen Margrethe II: "No country is as much Denmark as Denmark itself." Indeed, it is an ideal travel destination for people who love the sea. Where else can you find 7,400 km (4,598 mi) of mostly undeveloped and freely accessible coastline combined with a choice of the blue shimmering Kattegat, the mild Baltic, the rough Skagerrak or the tidal North Sea?

And in Copenhagen, which has been the capital of Denmark since 1443, visitors encounter history and tradition around virtually every corner. The ambience is at once cosmopolitan and pleasantly tranquil, and most of the sights can be comfortably visited on foot.

The city on the Öresund experienced its first period of prosperity back in the late Middle Ages as a trading port. A new golden age developed in the 16th and 17th centuries, in particular under King Christian IV, who did a lot to expand and further enhance the capital.

NYHAVN

The Nyhavn Canal district (above) is particularly charming with its old wooden sailboats and a slew of cafés. Canal and harbor cruises begin here and take visitors to the popular Little Mermaid (Lille Havfrue, Copenhagen's most famous icon, main picture) on a rock in the bay. The statue was sculpted by Edvard Eriksen, based on the main character in the eponymous fairytale by Hans Christian Andersen. As models for the piece he used both his wife and the prima ballerina who danced the part of the mermaid in a ballet based on the fairytale. The statue was donated by Carl Jacobsen, a brewer and patron of the arts, and was finally unveiled in the year 1913.

AMALIENBORG SLOT

FREDERIKSKIRKE

CHRISTIANSBORG SLOT

North of Nyhavn is the Amalienborg, city palace of Danish Queen Margrethe II commissioned by King Frederick V and completed between 1749 and 1760. It was based on designs by Nicolai Eigtved and has been the residence of the Danish royal family since 1794.

Many visitors to Frederikskirke are reminded of St Peter's Basilica in Rome when they see its dramatic cupola (33 m/108 ft in diameter). Also known as the Marble Church, it was designed by Nicolai Eigtved, begun in 1749, and not completed until 1894.

Today, the Folketing, the 179-member Danish Parliament, holds its sessions in the former royal palace, which did not take on its present form until 1928. It was built on the site of two former structures, both of which were destroyed by fire.

As a former capital, Roskilde has great symbolic significance for Danish people. Several Danish kings and queens were buried in Roskilde Cathedral from the 15th century onward (main picture).

JELLING

Located in front of Jelling church is Denmark's most impressive royal tomb. The burial remnants found here document the great power of the Vikings, who gained control of the northern seaways in the early Middle Ages. The entire complex – two massive grave mounds with diameters of 60 and 77 m, respectively (197 and 253 ft), with a church and two rune stones in between – is also a historic document of the Christianization of Denmark, which saw the country join the fold of other European states. The still heathen King Gorm (presumably 860 to 940) and his wife Tyra were originally entombed in the northern part of both grave mounds while the couple's son, the first Christian Danish King Harald Blåtand (ca. 940-986, baptized 960), later had his remains moved into the newly built church.

The inscription on the older of the two rune stones was a dedication by King Gorm to his wife Tyra. The larger rune stone from approximately 980 shows Scandinavia's oldest depiction of Christ.

ROSKILDE

Until the Reformation in the 16th century, Denmark's ecclesiastical center was focused in Roskilde, a city on the island of Sjælland, some 30 km (19 mi) west of the capital, Copenhagen. As a royal residence, Roskilde was also the capital of Denmark until 1443.

Copenhagen was originally founded by Bishop Absalonthe, architect of the first romanesque-Gothic brick church in Scandinavia. He erected his church on the foundation walls of two former smaller churches in

The cathedral towers over the buildings of Roskilde's old town. It was started in romanesque and finished in gothic style, primarily emphasized by the spires (above).

1170, in order to give the royal residence a correspondingly dignified place of worship.

The cathedral was largely given its present-day look when the great spires were added in the 14th century. The interior of the cathedral, which was expanded with porch structures and side chapels until well into the 19th century and which is considered an important example of Danish church architecture, is home to the lavishly adorned tombs of thirty-seven Danish kings and queens who were buried here from the 15th century onwards.

The rune stones of Jelling (left and far left), a town near Vejle in the eastern part of Jutland, are some of the largest of their kind. They show animal motifs and a depiction of Christ.

HELSINKI

Roughly 500,000 people live in Finland's capital, a city originally founded by King Gustav I of Sweden in 1550. After a series of fires, Czar Alexander II commissioned Berlin architect Carl Ludwig Engel with the neoclassical reconstruction of Helsinki. Twenty of the monumental edifices from that time, 1820 to 1850, are still standing today and, along with other famous buildings in styles from Art Nouveau to modern, they lend the capital on the Gulf of Finland a unique urban landscape.

Worth seeing are Engel's Senate Square with the cathedral and the statue of Czar Alexander II (main picture), the Government Palace, the main university building and the university library, as well as the Orthodox Uspenski Cathedral, built in 1868 and boasting rich interior flourishes. Other attractions include the market square and the historic market building on the south side where the ferries dock that take visitors to the island fortress of Suomenlinna and the skerry islands. Numerous Art Nouveau buildings can be seen on Luotsikatu, one of Helsinki's most elegant streets. The Esplanade, the capital's pedestrian zone, is bordered by parks. This is also where you will find Stockmann's flagship department store, the largest of its kind in all of Scandinavia.

The best panoramic view across Helsinki can be enjoyed from the Katajanokka Peninsula.

SAIMAA

With its countless fingers, bays and satellite lakes, the Saimaa region forms the largest connected lake district in Finland. Saimaa Lake itself (above, with Loikansaari Island) is also known as the "lake of a 1,000 islands". Up to 90 m (295 ft) deep in parts, it covers a vast area of about 1,300 sq km (502 sq mi), not including the islands. Spread out over several lakes is Savonlinna, the region's main town.

SAVONLINNA

KOLI

Sights in the lovely little town of Savonlinna include the provincial museum, which is located in a former grain storehouse on Riihisaari Island in front of the gates of the castle; the converted museum ships "Mikko", "Savonlinna" and "Salama"; the market square with its docks for boat excursions into the Saimaa lake district; and the 100-year-old wooden villa Rauhalinna a short way outside of town.

Olavinlinna (above), an impressive fortress that can be reached via pontoon bridge, dates from the year 1475. It is considered Finland's most beautiful and most intact medieval castle complex. For more than thirty years it has played host to the Savonlinna Opera Festival, the country's largest regular cultural event.

From the modest summit of this 347-m (1,139-ft) granite rise in Karelia, Ukko Koli, there are superb views of Lake Pielinen (above). Finnish artists saw the juxtaposition of granite rock formations, conifer and deciduous trees, and majestic lakes as a leitmotif of the Finnish natural landscape. Koli National Park invites you to explore its extensive hiking trails, but be careful of the national animal, brown bears (below).

OULANKA

North of the city of Kuusamo near the Arctic Circle, Oulanka National Park covers an area of some 270 sq km (104 sq mi) and protects a diverse region characterized by the river landscape of the Ouloankajoki (below) and its many branches, an area that had long been settled by the Sami before the first Finns arrived toward the end of the 17th century. The park is a popular place for hikers, particularly in fall when the foliage is very colorful.

URHO KEKKONEN

This national park covers approximately 2,550 sq km (984 sq mi) of land in Finland's extreme northwest near the Russian border. It was named Urho Kekkonen after the long-time Finnish prime minister. Originally also home to the semi-nomadic Sami people, the rich flora and fauna of this fascinating woodland, moor and fjäll (fell) landscape today attracts droves of hikers and nature enthusiasts.

The vast array of wildlife in Oulanka National Park also includes the golden eagle, here snatching up its prey from the cold snow. These proud hunters, with their dark brown and glinting gold feathers, eat animals ranging in size from rock squirrels to ibex fawns.

In Finland's northern regions, the fauna has adapted to the harshest of living conditions. Clockwise from top left: Brown bear, reindeer, red-throated diver, great grey owl.

This Baltic town was founded by Danes and developed into a center of the Hanseatic League in the Middle Ages. Many of the patrician houses and churches still bear witness to this time of prosperity, such as St Olav's Church, which dominates the city (below, seen from Cathedral Hill, with fortification towers in the foreground).

After being severely damaged in World War II, the historic center of the Estonian capital was rebuilt in the style of the 18th century. Originally called Reval (a Latin reference to the surrounding area) by the Swedish, Danish and the Germans, the city has been known as Tallinn since 1920, a name whose meaning is debated. The Old Town is on Cathedral Hill.

Sites worth seeing include St Mary's Cathedral (from 1230), the Church of the Holy Spirit (12th/13th centuries), St Nicholas' Church (13th to 14th centuries), and St Olav's Church (13th century) with its 123-m-tall (404-ft) steeple that for many years served as a lighthouse. St Mary's Chapel was built from 1512 to 1523. The trade guilds here also commissioned grand buildings for themselves as symbols of civic pride. The Great Guild, for example, supplied the members of the municipal council and moved into its hall in 1410. The two-story town hall, built in the early 15th century, is surrounded by well-preserved medieval homes. The baroque Kadriorg Palace was built as a royal summer residence in the years between 1717 and 1725.

The historic center of Tallinn resembles other small medieval towns in Central Europe. The narrow alleyways, dominated by the towers of St Nicholas' Church (far left) and the town hall (center), create a romantic atmosphere especially at night. Far left: Raekoja Square.

The magnificent House of Blackheads stands on Town Hall Square (main picture). It was once a meeting place for unmarried foreign merchants. They were named "blackheads" after their patron saint, Mauritius, who was often represented as a Mauritanian.

Riga is situated on the Baltic Sea at the mouth of the Daugava River. Among the many important churches in the city, the cathedral, which was begun in the year 1211 and only completed in its present form in 1775, stands out along with the octagonal wooden steeple of the Lutheran Jesus Church (1819–22). Of the once-mighty fortifications, the 14th-century Powder Tower and the 13th-century Ramer Tower have been very well preserved. The Citadel was begun in 1760, while the area was under Swedish rule, and the Swedish Gate also dates back to that time.

The Guildhall is the only remaining medieval administrative building in Riga. The Small Guild, built around the middle of the 14th century and remodeled in 1866, is one of the most prestigious buildings in the city. The Latvian Stock Exchange was built between 1852 and 1855 in the style of a Venetian palazzo with a playful façade. Other architectural delights include splendid patrician houses such as the Reutern House, begun in the year 1683, and some outstanding Art Nouveau buildings by Mikhail Eisenstein.

You can enjoy beautiful panoramic views of Riga's Old Town from the left bank of the Daugava River (left). The skyline here is dominated by the towers of the cathedral (in the center) and St Peter's Church (on the right).

ANNO 1334   RENOV. ANNO 1999

VILNIUS

Like many medieval cities, the Old Town of this former trading settlement spreads out from the base of Vilnius Castle, on the left bank of the Neris River near its confluence with the Vilnia River. The city experienced its heyday in the 15th and 16th centuries as a mediator between the cities of the Russian czardom and what were then strongholds of the Hanseatic League. As a result of its location, the Lithuanian capital features some remarkable urban architecture that mirrors the turbulent history of this small nation. Among the older buildings, a number of late-Gothic churches such as St Anne's Church, St Nicholas' Church, and St Bernhard's Church, as well as some baroque era noblemen's palaces are of particular historical interest. The 17th-century Church of Saints Peter and Paul is also baroque in style.

The center of the Old Town, however, is dominated by St. Stanislaus Cathedral, which received its present appearance between 1783 and 1801. Neoclassical in style, it resembles a Greek temple. The cathedral's bell tower was originally the defensive tower of the Lower Castle, which was built in the 13th century. During the Soviet period, the church was used as a large exhibition space. Vilnius Town Hall was also later remodeled in neoclassical style.

The neoclassical Vilnius Cathedral (main picture) was consecrated in 1801. As is typical for many churches in the Baltic states, it has a separate steeple. The upper story of the 16th-century "Gates of Dawn" has a chapel dedicated to the "Blessed Virgin Mary Mother of Compassion" (right).

LONDON

The whole world in one city – not just a great advertising slogan but a reality. London is truly a global city, created and defined by people from all over the world who have brought their cultures with them to create the unique urban mélange that is the British capital. The diversity of the city, however, is not solely a result of the interplay between different cultures, which among other things has given London a great variety of cuisines and some of the most exciting restaurants in Europe, for example. No, what also makes London special is its spirit of innovation and creative energy, which in turn contributes enormously not only to European but also world culture and business in general. The world comes to London, and London welcomes the world with open arms.

BUCKINGHAM PALACE

Built in 1703 as a residence by John Sheffield, the first Duke of Buckingham and Normandy, Buckingham Palace came into royal family ownership in 1761 under King George III and, has been the residence of the English kings and queens since 1837. Buckingham Palace, Westminster Abbey and the Palace of Westminster – better known as the Houses of Parliament – are historical landmarks in the United Kingdom and it is here, in the center of the City of Westminster borough, where the political heart of the United Kingdom beats. Both the lower house (House of Commons) and the upper house (House of Lords) meet here at the British seat of government. The Queen has also inherited a position in the House of Lords and she attends during important events such as the Queen's speech. In personal union law, Elizabeth II is the Queen of the United Kingdom of Great Britain and Northern Ireland as well as of the member states of the Commonwealth of Nations. As head of state in the United Kingdom, however, she fulfils a purely ceremonial function.

BIG BEN

The clock on Big Ben is the largest in Britain. Each of its four faces measures 8 m (26 ft) in diameter. Although the bell tower of Westminster Palace itself is commonly referred to as Big Ben, this is in fact the name of the largest of the tower's five bells, which has become known simply as the Great Bell instead.

WESTMINSTER

The Thames is London's lifeline. The river (above) connects historical sights such as Big Ben at the Palace of Westminster with modern attractions like the giant London Eye Ferris wheel.

Construction of the Palace of Westminster and Westminster Abbey began in 1045, under King Edward the Confessor (1003–1066). The church, which was replaced by a Gothic cathedral in the 13th century, served as a burial place for Edward and subsequent rulers until 1760. It is still used as the coronation church of the monarchs. Royal weddings and funerals also take place in Westminster Abbey. Right: The 30-m-long (98-ft) main aisle.

In 1097, the Palace of Westminster, begun by Edward the Confessor, was enlarged by William II. In 1547 it became the seat of the English parliament. The complex was rebuilt between 1840 and 1888 by Charles Barry following a fire in 1834 that had destroyed the Palace and only spared Westminster Hall and St Stephen's Chapel. Its current neo-Gothic design was intended to match the façade of nearby Westminster Abbey, which is dominated by Big Ben to the north.

Many of the palaces rooms were partially renovated in the 19th century. St Margaret's Church built and consecrated in the 11th century, is the parish church of parliament and received its present look as early as the beginning of the 16th century.

View of Big Ben from Trafalgar Square. In the foreground are two of the four lions at the foot of Nelson's Column.

LONDON

During construction of the neo-Gothic Tower Bridge, the towers were clad with limestone from the Isle of Portland for aesthetic reasons as well as to hide the steel used in the bridge's substructure.

THE TOWER OF LONDON

After his successful invasion of England in 1066, William the Conqueror commissioned the Tower of London as a fortified residence and observation post for the boats and barges plying the Thames. It was given its present appearance in the 13th century.

The Tower remained the royal residence of English monarchs until the year 1509, when the fortress was transformed into the state prison. Many famous citizens were held here, among them Thomas More, two of Henry VIII's wives, and the future Queen Elizabeth I.

The building is primarily a museum these days and has an extensive collection of European military items and torture devices. The Jewel House contains the crown jewels.

London's oldest church, the Norman Chapel of St John from 1080, is also on the grounds. Prisoners executed in the Tower, including two wives of Henry VIII (Anne Boleyn and Catherine Howard) and the Queen For Nine Days Lady Jane Grey, were buried in the St Peter Royal Chapel, restored in 1512 after a fire.

TOWER BRIDGE

Tower Bridge opened in 1894, and combines bascule and suspension bridge design. It is not only one of London's most famous landmarks, but is also an important testimony to the already advanced engineering capabilities of the time.

Originally, steam engines were used to operate the hydraulics, which allowed the bridge to be opened within just a few minutes. Today it is operated by electricity.

Both towers contain exhibitions on the structure's history, and from the glassed-in walkway high above the bridge you can get spectacular views of the city.

The castle complex, also known as the "White Tower" (left), is Britain's best-preserved fortress. With walls up to 3 m (10 ft) thick, it prevented breakouts as much as break-ins.

ST. PAUL'S CATHEDRAL

II's coronation in 2002. In 1981, Lady Diana Spencer and Prince Charles were married at St Paul's. Built between 1675 and 1710 on the site of a previous cathedral that was destroyed in the Great Fire of 1666, St Paul's is considered Christopher Wren's most important work.

St Paul's Cathedral rises above the city about 300 m (328 yds) north of the Thames. It is the main church of the Anglican Diocese of London and the venue for important state occasions, from the funeral of Lord Nelson in 1806 to the festivities celebrating the Golden Jubilee of Queen Elizabeth

FINANCIAL DISTRICT

London is one of the world's most important centers of business and finance. The prosperity of the city is reflected in its innovative architecture, for example in Richard Roger's Lloyd's building (above), which has all its service tracts, stairways and elevators on the outside of the structure.

HAMPTON COURT PALACE, WINDSOR CASTLE, ROYAL BOTANIC GARDENS

HAMPTON COURT PALACE

Situated in the south-west of London on a bend in the Thames, Hampton Court Palace is one of the most attractive of the English royal palaces. The central structure dates back to a 14th-century country estate that was enlarged as a Tudor palace between 1514 and 1520 according to plans by Harry Redmann on the orders of Cardinal Thomas Wolsey (1475–1530), archbishop of York and Lord Chancellor under Henry VIII. When Wolsey refused to approve the annulment of the king's marriage with Catherine of Aragón, he fell into disfavor and was stripped of both office and property. Subsequently, Hampton Court was re-modeled twice – once on the orders of Henry VIII himself, who had it expanded and added the Royal Tennis Court, and once again at the end of the 17th century by Christopher Wren, the most important English architect of his day. Hampton Court Palace served as royal residence through the reign of George III (1727–1760), but he mostly lived in London.

WINDSOR CASTLE

Windsor Castle (above: Waterloo Chamber), the main residence of English and British rulers since the Middle Ages, stands in the Thames Valley west of London. Dating back to the 12th and 13th centuries, the building was changed and expanded several times, serving alternatively as a garrison, a fortress or a prison, depending on the particular politics of the day.
Windsor Castle is the largest private and the oldest continuously inhabited palace in the world. Every year, the Queen spends many weekends there with her family.

According to legend, two of Henry VIII's (left) wives, Jane Seymour and Catherine Howard, are still said to haunt Hampton Court Palace (far left). The palace was often modified to incorporate architectural elements of the Tudor style, which can be found next to those from the English Baroque.

ROYAL BOTANIC GARDENS

The history of the present-day Royal Botanic Gardens in Kew, a south-western district of London, began with a herb garden that was laid out in 1759. Before that, a complex of gardens and parks with many buildings existed there, including Kew Palace (1631), which was built in the Dutch style. The gardens were not converted for scientific purposes until 1773, when famous botanist Sir Joseph Banks, who had sailed around the world with Captain Cook, became its director. The best-known landmark in the gardens is the Palm House (above), which was completed in 1848, by the architects Richard Turner and Decimus Burton. It is 20 m (66 ft) high and contains one of the largest collections of palm trees in the world.

LEEDS, BODIAM, SISSINGHURST, HEVER, STOURHEAD GARDEN

Bodiam Castle (main picture), a fortress completely surrounded by the waters of the castle moat, was built during the Hundred Years' War between England and France and is one of the best-preserved medieval castles in England.

LEEDS CASTLE

In the heart of the county of Kent, just under 6 km (4 miles) south-east of Maidstone, stands moated Leeds Castle, on two islands in the river Len and surrounded by an extensive park. For many, Leeds, which was first mentioned in documents from the year 857, is the epitome of a medieval castle. Yet it owes its present appearance largely to the Tudor-style additions in the 19th century. At least the gatehouse, however, is a testimony from the 13th century, when Edward I had the former manor house enlarged as a royal palace. Henry VIII, too, is said to have enjoyed staying there – a 16th-century bust inside the palace remembers the king.

Leeds Castle's main claim to fame, however, were its female residents. Many queens and widows of kings made this their home and thus provided the epithet "Lady's Castle". The grand interior is often used as a film location, for example in "Kind Hearts and Coronets" (1949).

BODIAM CASTLE

Built in 1385, on the orders of Sir Edward Dalyngrigge, a former knight of Edward III, Bodiam Castle is one of the most romantic castles in England.

Originally, the fortress was built to defend against an attack by French troops that never materialized. The castle did not see any battle action until the English Civil War, which was fought between followers of King Charles I and parliament between 1642 to 1649. In order to prevent the king, who was later beheaded in London, from using the fortress as a stronghold, parlia-

Bodiam Castle, guarded by eight towers, rises like a fairy-tale palace from the castle moat.

mentary troops destroyed the roof and parts of the castle's interior. Since that time, Bodiam Castle has remained uninhabited.

It was not until 1919 that Lord Curzon, a member of the British parliament who had also made a name for himself as Viceroy of India, had the beautiful castle restored and donated it to the nation. Since 1926, the National Trust has been taking care of the upkeep and maintenance of the facility.

Leeds Castle was the favorite residence of Edward I, who had given the palace to his wife, Eleanor of Castile. The Banqueting Hall (left) testifies to its earlier glamour. Far left is a view of the exterior.

SISSINGHURST, HEVER, STOURHEAD GARDEN

If you are unaware as to why the British are considered passionate gardeners, make sure you visit Sissinghurst Castle in Kent. Created by Vita Sackville-West and her husband, who lived there from 1930, the gardens offer beautiful wide open spaces and feature attractions such as geometrically shaped hedges or enchanted corners that seem like miniature biospheres.

The parks of Hever Castle, also in Kent, welcome visitors with the artful topiary of their hedges,

The English art of horticulture at its most refined: Stourhead Garden (top), Hever Castle (above) and Sissinghurst Castle (right, top to bottom).

lavish flowerbeds and a labyrinth of yew hedges. "Nature abhors a straight line", proclaimed English landscape gardener William Kent, summing up the basic principle of English horticulture. This is exemplified at Stourhead Garden farther west in Wiltshire, a unique "landscape painting" created between 1741 and 1780 with lakes, streams, woods and small temples all harmoniously set in a breathtaking setting.

SALISBURY

Salisbury's early-Gothic cathedral (main picture) was mostly built between 1220 and 1258. The bell tower at 123 m (404 ft) is the highest church steeple in England. With its tall arched windows, the church is an outstanding and very rare example of the English Gothic style, which is characterized by its minimalism. It is also referred to as "Early English".

CANTERBURY

One of England's oldest cities plays host to the mother church of the Anglican Communion, Canterbury Cathedral, which was begun as a Norman structure in the year 1070, and achieved infamy only 100 years later when Archbishop Thomas Becket was assassinated there by followers of the king in 1170. The archbishop was buried in the cathedral and canonized just three years later. As a result, the church became a popular destination for a steady stream of pilgrims. Having mostly burned down in 1174, it was rebuilt by architect William of Sens. The church's tower rises to 75 m (246 ft) and is known as "Bell Harry Tower" after the large bell. It was not added to the structure until 1504. The cupola under the bell tower as well as the superb cloisters were built between 1396 and 1420 and possess an almost unearthly beauty.

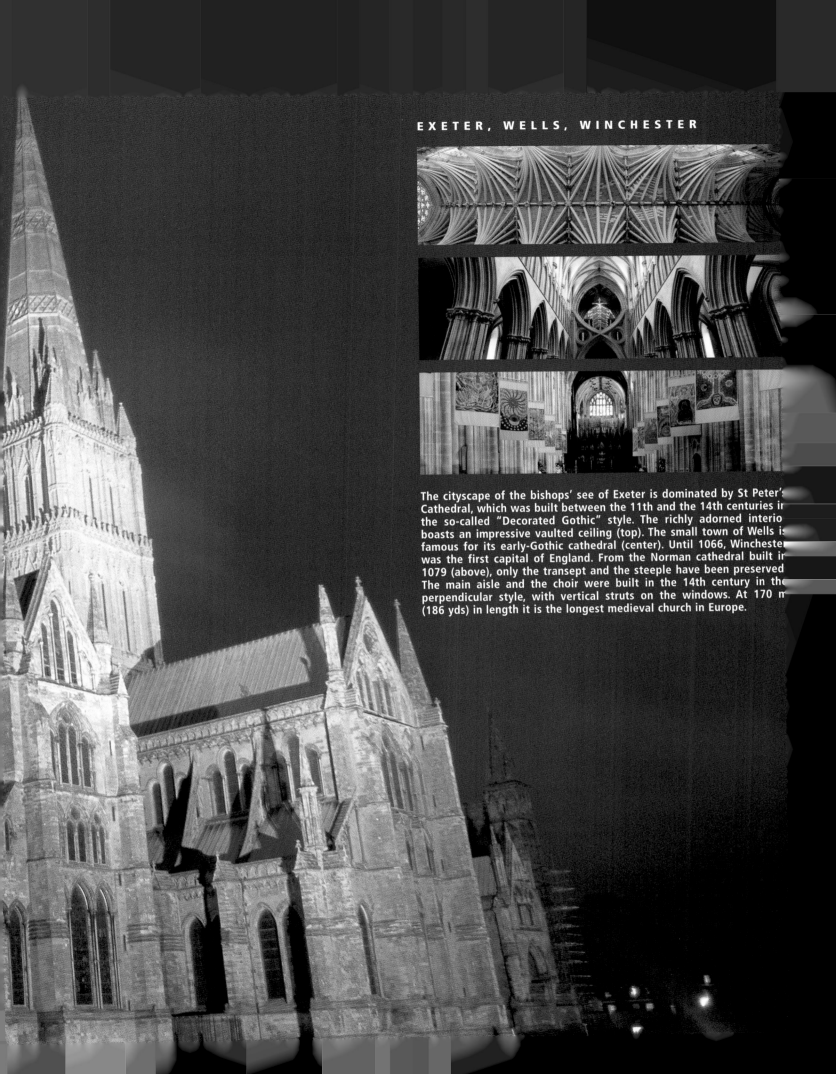

The cityscape of the bishops' see of Exeter is dominated by St Peter's Cathedral, which was built between the 11th and the 14th centuries in the so-called "Decorated Gothic" style. The richly adorned interior boasts an impressive vaulted ceiling (top). The small town of Wells is famous for its early-Gothic cathedral (center). Until 1066, Winchester was the first capital of England. From the Norman cathedral built in 1079 (above), only the transept and the steeple have been preserved. The main aisle and the choir were built in the 14th century in the perpendicular style, with vertical struts on the windows. At 170 m (186 yds) in length it is the longest medieval church in Europe.

The seaside resorts along the English Channel coast are in constant competition to outdo each other with their impressive Victorian pier pavilions. The one in Eastbourne (main picture), from the 1870s, is one of the most attractive.

"JURASSIC COAST"

The 150 km (93 mi) of coastline that stretch between Old Harry Rocks near Swanage and Orcombe Point in Devon is like an open history book of the Mesozoic period, with layers of deposits dating from the Triassic, Jurassic and Cretaceous periods. It is basically an uninterrupted view of the three layers of what could be considered the Earth's Middle Ages. Geomorphologists first took note of this coastline in the year 1810, when Mary Anning, an eleven-year-old girl, discovered a "dragon" in the rocks near the fishing village of Lyme Regis (now Dorset). In fact, it was the first complete fossil imprint of an Ichthyosaurus and resembled a cross between a giant fish and a lizard. Since then, ever new finds are being made along the Dorset and East Devon coasts as erosion of the rocky landscape continues to take place at breathtaking speed - geologically speaking of course. A relaxing stroll along this wild coast becomes a journey of discovery taking you through the different stages of evolution and the Earth's history.

EASTBOURNE

Originally built east of the Bourne, a small stream, Eastbourne declared itself the "Sunshine Coast" and began attracting visitors with a promise of more hours of sunshine than anywhere else in England. It wasn't long before grand hotels shot up along the elegant beach promenade to service holidaymakers from the cities.

BRIGHTON

In the middle of the 18th century, Doctor Richard Russell described the positive benefits of seawater, and in particular the water off of the coast of Brighton, in curing certain diseases. His endorsement sparked unexpected popularity for the fishing village. In 1786, when Prince Regent and future King George IV built the faux-Oriental Royal Pavilion, it was tantamount to giving the village a royal seal of approval and increasing numbers of people began visiting. Brighton is still a popular destination for daytrippers thanks to its proximity to London. Brighton Pier (left) was built in 1899 and juts far into the sea. Its official name was originally "Brighton Marina Palace and Pier". The pavilion (below) was remodeled in 1815, by John Nash in the style of an Indian Mogul's palace.

Superb views of the coast in Dorset and East Devon can be enjoyed on a walk along the South West Coast Path, which follows the lovely cliffs (left). With its fossil remains, the coast offers a unique overview of around 185 million years of the earth's history.

CORNWALL

ST MICHAEL'S MOUNT

According to legend, a fisherman saw the archangel Michael appear on this tidal rock island in the year 495. Since then the island has been known as Michael's Mount, and a church was built there in the 15th century. A monastery was also built here before it was transformed into a country mansion by subsequent owners. At low tide, the island can be reached on foot via a causeway. Historians assume this to be the island of Ictis, which was an important center for local trade in tin during the Iron Age.

LAND'S END

The westernmost point in England features a number of archeological sites including tombs from the Iron and Bronze Ages, stone circles, Celtic crosses and entire villages from the time before the birth of Christ, all of which bear testimony to thousands of years of settlement in the area. The waves of the Atlantic crash incessantly against the peninsula, which was given the name Belerion by the Romans, or "seat of storms". From Land's End to John O'Groats in northern Scotland it is 1,406 km (900 mi) overland – the farthest distance between any two points in the United Kingdom.

ISLES OF SCILLY

About 40 km (25 mi) off the coast of southwest Cornwall are the 140 Isles of Scilly, which you can reach by ferry from Penzance. Some 2,000 people live mostly from tourism and flower exports and are spread out over five inhabited islands, each with steep granite cliffs, white sand beaches and turquoise bays that are great for exploring on foot or by bike. The mild climate even allows palm trees and exotic plants to flourish here. A collection of exotic plants that are indigenous to these islands can be seen at the Abbey Garden in Tresco.

ST IVES

St Ives has a history of attracting painters and sculptors looking for inspiration in the enchanting light and landscapes here. Small, grey granite houses characterize this former fishing village that is home to one of Cornwall's most attractive beaches.
Towering above Porthmeor Beach in the north, the Tate Gallery has opened a museum featuring the works of local St Ives artists. They include, for example, the pictures of Patrick Heron and Ben Nicholson, who lived here with his wife, artist Barbara Hepworth.

Lighthouses like this one built in 1859 on Godrevy Island are common along Cornwall's wildly romantic coast.

DARTMOOR

Dartmoor is most famously known as the location where Sir Arthur Canon Doyle's Sherlock Holmes encounters the Hound of the Baskervilles. The landscape is virtually untouched and can be very romantic as well as a bit spooky, especially when it is cloaked in the typically dense fog. The so-called "tors", enormous granite towers that have managed to withstand the forces of erosion, are typical of the area. Dartmoor National Park, which covers more than 950 sq km (367 sq mi), is noted for its vast meadow and moor landscapes.

STONEHENGE AND AVEBURY

The megaliths of Stonehenge near Salisbury are arranged in a circle of pillars connected by capstones (main picture). The stones of the inner circle came from the Preseli Hills in Wales, some 400 km (249 mi) away.

Stonehenge, an inspiring arrangement of megaliths in the county of Wiltshire, is still a mystery to us today. How were these giant stones transported? And what was the true purpose of the formation? The stones each weigh in at several tons and tower to heights of up to 7 m (23 ft) while an impressive trench 114 m (374 ft) wide surrounds the entire site.

During the final phase of construction, in roughly 2000 BC, the monoliths were transported hundreds of miles to this location, some having come from what is now Wales. They were then apparently oriented toward certain heavenly bodies, giving rise to the theory that the complex may have served both religious as well as astronomical purposes over the millennia.

The stone circle of Avebury east of Bath has the same orientation as Stonehenge and was built between 2600 and 2500 BC. According to an 18th-century British scholar, the Neolithic sanctuary was a druid temple, later destroyed under orders from the Church during the 1300s. Many of the megaliths were then used to build homes in the region.

The sun and the moon were probably the orientation points for the sanctuary at Stonehenge. Seen from the central altar stone, the sun once rose in between two sarsen stones, exactly aligned with the Heel Stone. Since then, it has shifted slightly with the gradual shift in the Earth's axis.

Of the former 154 stones at the Avebury site, only 36 have been preserved. Of those, 27 formed part of the large outer stone circle (left); they were inserted into the ground to a depth of 15 to 60 cm (6 to 24 in). In the 1930s, members of the National Trust began to re-erect the stones in their original positions.

BATH

Pulteney Bridge (main picture) is reminiscent of Palladio's architectural designs for the Rialto Bridge in Venice. It has traversed the river Avon in Bath since 1773. Designed by Robert Adam, it is one of only four bridges in the world with shops along both sides of its span.

Bath is located in the county of Somerset, not far from Bristol, and is England's most important spa town. The Romans set up spa facilities and baths near the thermal springs, but the curative waters here are actually said to have been discovered much earlier, by the Celts. According to legend, the Celtic King Bladud, who suffered from leprosy, was healed by the hot springs. The Romans eventually built a bath complex and an accompanying temple in 100 BC. The greenish water typical of these springs still gurgles its way to the surface at around 46 °C (115 °F).

Bath, a bishops' see since the 10th century and the center of the textiles trade in medieval times, became England's most popular spa resort in the 17th century and indeed the most important social center outside of London. The town owes its largely Georgian cityscape primarily to the late-18th-century projects of architects John Wood and Son. The streets lead to neoclassical masterpieces such as the Assembly Rooms, the Royal Crescent and Pulteney Bridge, which was designed in the year 1770.

The Royal Crescent of 1775, a terrace of Georgian houses laid out in a half-moon formation (left), can be ascribed to John Wood the Younger. The uniform façades conceal terraced homes of varying designs and one of the houses is now home to a museum.

At the center of Bath stands the abbey church (top), begun in 1499 in the late-Gothic style. The Roman open-air bath complex (around 65–75 BC) is located close to the abbey church and was rediscovered in 1870. The 19th-century terrace is adorned with ornate sculptures (above).

OXFORD

Oxford is home to the oldest university in the United Kingdom dating back to the 12th century. It is a town dominated by student life. The numerous colleges and prestigious institutions such as the Bodleian Library, one of the most important literature collections in the world with roughly four million volumes, combine to create an environment that motivates students to attend their lectures. But you can also follow in the footsteps of a now-famous magician's apprentice: the Great Hall of Christ Church College and the Bodleian Library were used in the Harry Potter films.

The University of Oxford was formed from a number of different schools dating back to as early as the beginning of the 12th century. Many were originally run by monasteries.

All Souls College (top) was founded in 1438 while the circular Radcliffe Camera building dates from the 18th century and is today a reading room.
Hertford Bridge (above), on New College Lane, is known as the Bridge of Sighs because of its similarity with the bridge in Venice of that name.

CAMBRIDGE

Also known as "Silicon Fen", Cambridge has become a center for modern technology and science. Its rich history began in 1220, when some scholars defected from Oxford. The oldest college, Peterhouse, was founded in 1284. Nine Nobel Prize winners studied at the venerable St John's College. Margaret Beaufort, mother of Henry VII, was an avid supporter of the institutions here during her lifetime and, in 1511, it was indeed the trustees of her estate who founded St John's. Among its graduates are writers William Wordsworth and Douglas Adams as well as Maurice Wilkes, a pioneer in the field of information technology.

The most magnificent college in Cambridge is King's College (top), founded in 1441. The main picture shows King's College Chapel, completed in 1547. The Old Library of Trinity Hall (above) contains numerous valuable manuscripts and rare volumes.

At King's College, students at times feel like gondoliers in Venice, punting their boats on the river Cam.

A statue of the Earl of Pembroke guards the entrance to the Bodleian Library in Oxford (main picture). However, it was the scholar and diplomat Sir Thomas Bodley who made the original donations of money and books to the library named after him in 1598. Its catalogue from the year 1605 is the oldest printed library catalogue in England.

BLENHEIM PALACE

The Great Hall (main picture, center) introduces the visitor to the overwhelming splendor of the palace. The Saloon (below) is used for Christmas dinner each year. The other rooms of Blenheim Palace (far right) are equally extravagant.

Britain's largest private residence is also the most attractive and expressive example of baroque architecture in England. In 1704, the English government gifted this magnificent complex in Oxfordshire to John Churchill, the first Duke of Marlborough, a token of gratitude for his successful campaign against French and Bavarian troops near Blindheim (known in England as "Blenheim") on the Danube. Eighteen years later, Blenheim Palace was completed under the supervision of architect Sir John Vanbrugh. The three wings of this two-story baroque palace were arranged around a large courtyard. The extensive gardens – originally created by Henry Wise based on the model of Versailles – have been redesigned several times over the years.

General John Churchill (left, a painting by Adriaen von der Werff from 1705) was ennobled as First Duke of Marlborough by Queen Anne immediately after her coronation in 1702. Blenheim Palace (far left) was also the birthplace of Britain's future prime minister Winston Churchill (1874–1965).

CHESTER

Chester, known in ancient times as "Castra Cevana", was founded in the year 79 AD by the Romans and remained a vital outpost in Britain until well into the 4th century. Today, Chester is one of the most beautiful cities in the United Kingdom and it is not difficult to see why. A saunter through downtown features wonderfully maintained half-timbered houses and charming two-story shop arcades with wooden façades and bay windows. Chester's cathedral was a Benedictine abbey church until 1540, after being almost completely rebuilt in the 14th century. Very few remnants of the original church begun in 1092 can still be seen.

Chester cathedral (top) was built with red sandstone. The Chester Rows (above) give the city its unique flair along with the clock tower from 1897 (main picture).

CELR.AT THE EXPENCE OF RICHARD LORD GROSVENOR A·D·MDCCLXIX

THIS CLOCK TOWER WAS ERECTED
IN COMMEMORATION OF THE 60 YEAR
OF THE REIGN OF HER MAJESTY
VICTORIA QUEEN AND EMPRESS

18 97

Chester | United Kingdom 65

YORK

York Minster is the largest Gothic church north of the Alps and boasts the largest number of medieval stained-glass windows. The 163-m-long (525-ft) structure was begun in 1220 and completed in 1472. York, one of the most attractive cathedral cities in Britain, is also known for its narrow lanes and half-timbered houses.

YORKSHIRE COAST

One of Yorkshire's greatest attractions is its natural beauty, which can be enjoyed along the coast in a variety of forms: villages such as Staithes (above), and picturesque coves like Saltwick Bay (right and main photo) and Robin Hood's Bay (far right, bottom). Right, top: The view from Sutton Bank.

Hadrian's Wall is Britain's largest structure, snaking impressively through the countryside of Northern England. Parts of it have been preserved or rebuilt in typical English stone wall style.

HADRIAN'S WALL

Upon entering the port of Newcastle you will be able to see the very eastern end of Hadrian's Wall, which closely skirts the border between England and Scotland via Carlisle and ends after about 120 km (75 mi) at Bowness on Solway at the Irish Sea. Originally, the structure was built as part stone wall, part earth mound. Aside from the actual wall, which was built along an ancient military route, the complex also features military camps, milecastles (fortified structures), larger fortresses, turrets and gates. To the left is a Roman grain silo. The wall, which was about 5 m (18 ft) tall and almost 3 m (10 ft) thick, was built by Emperor Hadrian between 122 and 132, to stave off the threat of fierce Scottish tribes, especially the Picts, who continually invaded Roman territories. After the withdrawal of the Roman army in about 410, the wall quickly fell into disuse. The central portion of the wall is the best preserved.

LAKE DISTRICT

The Lake District has been a national park since 1951, but it was more than 200 years ago that the "Lake Poets", part of the Romantic movement that included the likes of Wordsworth, began extolling the beauty of this stunning landscape. Hiking, climbing, sailing, or windsurfing enthusiasts will be well served in this varied park area comprising twelve large lakes and numerous small ones such as Lake Buttermere (above). Great Langdale is one of the more beautiful lakes, and the two Langdale Pikes, the higher of which rises to 730 m (2,395 ft), can be reached on a trail that is just under 10 km (6 mi) long. A road with hairpin turns will take you to the remains of a Roman fort at the Hardknott Pass, where superb views unfold into the Eskdale Valley below.

SNOWDONIA, CONWY, HARLECH, CAERNARFON

During his campaigns in the 13th century, King Edward built nine castles in Wales within a period of nine years. Conwy Castle (main picture) was the first of them. It boasts walls up to 4.5 m (15 ft) thick and eight flanking towers.

SNOWDONIA

Densely wooded valleys, mountain lakes, expansive moors and picturesque ocean inlets all juxtaposed with a fascinating series of ragged peaks. That is Snowdonia National Park. Founded in 1951, it was the first Welsh national park and is still the largest of three (the Pembrokeshire Coast National Park was founded one year later, and the Brecon Beacons National Park in 1957). Snowdonia extends from Conwy in the north up to the peaks of Machynlleth in the south. Its highest point is Mount Snowdon at 1,085 m (3,560 ft), which is also the highest mountain in Wales. The many hills and mountains in the national park are often draped in clouds and mist. It is a paradise for ramblers and rockclimbers, and there are a number of rare plants and animals to discover in this excitingly diverse area, for example the golden eagle and the merlin. A pleasantly nostalgic way to explore the park is a trip on one of the narrow-gauge railways. At Caernarfon it is also possible to take the ferry to the island of Anglesey off the north-western coast of Wales.

CONWY, HARLECH, CAERNARFON

After conquering Wales in the year 1284, English King Edward secured his positions in the area with the construction of three strongholds on the English border. Conwy, begun in 1283 and completed in the incredibly short time of just four and a half years, is considered a masterpiece of medieval military architecture. It was built by James of St George, a leading fortifications architect who also supervised work on the castles at Harlech and Caernarfon,

Begun in 1283, Caernarfon Castle (top) was built at the mouth of the river Seiont. It was to serve not just as a fortress but also as the residence of the king and the seat of his government. Harlech Castle (bottom) was conquered in 1404 by the Welsh captain Owain Glyndwr.

both of which were started in the same year.
Together with the later castles of Aberystwith, Beaumaris and Flint they formed a chain of fortresses along the coast of North Wales. Conwy Castle was to become a monument to English rule and a starting point for the planned settlement of Wales by the English. The medieval castle has been immortalized in countless paintings by English artists.

Left: Snowdonia National Park's English name derives from the highest mountain in Wales, the 1,085-m-high (3,560-ft) Snowdon peak. In Welsh, the area is known as Eyrie (Eagle's Nest), and if we could soar above it like an eagle, we would be able to enjoy a fascinatingly rich and diverse natural panorama.

Edinburgh Castle and the bell tower of the Balmoral Hotel are the main landmarks of the Scottish capital.

Edinburgh, the capital of Scotland, features a fascinating architectural contrast between the medieval Old Town and the carefully planned, Georgian-style New Town. The fortifications of Edinburgh Castle dominate the Old Town and date back to the 11th century. St Margaret's Chapel, consecrated in 1090, is also on Castle Hill. The Royal Mile descends from Castle Rock and is formed by Lawnmarket, High, and Canongate streets. It is the main thoroughfare of the Old Town and has numerous passageways and inner courtyards, elegant mansions such as Gladstone's Land, and various religious buildings such as the late-Gothic St Giles' Cathedral. At the eastern end of the Royal Mile is the Palace of Holyroodhouse, built in 1128 as an Augustinian monastery and later used as the residence of the Scottish kings. Opposite is the modern building of the new Scottish Parliament.

From top to bottom: Dugald Stewart Monument on Carlton Hill; the Old Town; the headquarters of the Bank of Scotland, crowned with a cupola and situated on a hill between Old and New Town.

A journey through Scotland is also a journey through prehistory. The earliest evidence of hunters and gatherers in the far north dates back to about 7,000 BC. Later, when the clan system had taken hold, Scottish chiefs continued their battles to control the rugged, expansive landscape. In the Highlands alone there were roughly 180 clans. They had the land cultivated by farmers, made pacts with royal houses while simultaneously conspiring against them, and built castles and palaces as a symbol of their power. As a result of their successes, they were able to erect the impressive structures now considered typical of Scotland, all amidst this breathtaking natural environment, which is intricately and beautifully linked with the culture here.

Dunnottar Castle, for example, near the small port town of Stonehaven, enjoys a panoramic backdrop of grand rock cliffs and is so picturesque that it could be the creation of a talented set designer. Slaines Castle, on the coast north of Aberdeen, is the property of the 19th Earl of Errol and inspired Bram Stoker to pen his world-famous "Dracula" novel in 1895. Crathes Castle, situated to the east of Banchory in Aberdeen's hinterland, is famous for its beautiful gardens.

DUNOTTAR

SLAINES

CRATHES

Once heavily disputed, then forgotten: Oliver Cromwell laid siege to Dunnottar Castle for eight months in 1651/52 in order to obtain the insignias of the Scottish crown. After capitulation he found out that they had long been smuggled out of the castle.

THE HIGHLANDS

BEN NEVIS

Ben Nevis rises majestically from the Grampian Mountains to a height of 1,344 m (4,410 ft), the highest mountain in the British Isles. It is one of 284 "munros", a name in Scotland given to mountains that are more than 3,000 ft (915 m) high and whose summits stand out noticeably from others.

While the mountain's north-west slope is relatively easy for hikers to climb, the steeper north-east side, with its 460-m (1,509-ft) rock face is still a challenge even for experienced climbers.

GLENCOE

Glencoe is a beautiful and wildly romantic valley. A handful of its peaks, such as the Buachaille Etive Mór (top), rise above the 1,000 m (3,281 ft) mark.

RANNOCH MOOR

Rannoch Moor is the largest expanse of moorland in Great Britain and as such one of the last virtually untouched natural habitats in Europe.

Storm clouds gather at dusk above Ben Nevis and Loch Eil.

There is no other expanse of land that is as typical of Scotland as the sparsely inhabited Highlands, a magnificent array of mountains, valleys, lakes and coastal scenery. It is a paradise for hikers and naturalists looking to explore the local flora and fauna at their leisure.

LOCH NESS

The dark, roughly 36-km-long (22-mi) Loch Ness would be an ideal home for a monster (Nessie, in this case) – it averages 1 km (0.6 mi) wide, up to 230 m (755 ft) deep, and never gets warmer than 7°C (45°F). Nessie is said to have emerged for the first time in 556, only to be chased back into the depths by the Irish missionary St Columba with the words: "Thou shalt go no further, nor touch the man; go back with all speed!" The monster kept out of sight for some 1,000 years thereafter until, in the 16th century, it allegedly devoured three men before disappearing again until 1933. Since then, "sightings" have been reported repeatedly, even by scientists who have attempted to prove Nessie's existence. In 1976, a research team from the USA reached the conclusion that something indeed lives in Loch Ness: a roughly 15-m-long (50-ft) vertebrate that breathes with gills. Theoretically, however, some thirty to fifty specimens would need to live in the lake to have ensured the survival of the species since the first sighting.

BEINN EIGHE NATURE RESERVE

The mountains around the Torridon are one of the highlights in the Scottish Highlands. They extend to the north of Loch Shieldaig (right), which is fringed by superb woodland. A small island in Loch Shieldaig is protected thanks to its ancient stand of pine trees. On the north bank of Upper Loch Torridon you can take in 750-million-year-old sandstone mountains including the particularly impressive 985-m-high (3,232-ft) Beinn Alligin (right).

INVERPOLLY NATURE RESERVE

The remote mountain region of Inverpolly, located about 30 km (19 mi) north of Ullapool, is made up of solitary lakes and rugged rocky landscapes. The area was declared a nature reserve in the early 1960s and features badgers, stags, otters and more than 100 species of birds. The Corbett of Cul Mor (right, up one) is around 850 m (2,789 ft) high and quite popular among climbers. On the way to Ullapool you pass picturesque Loch Lurgainn (right).

DUNCANSBY STACKS

Needle-shaped rocks rise from the sea south of the promontory at Duncansby Head, near Caithness. The Stacks of Duncansby (right) were carved away by wind and water over millennia.

CLO MOR CLIFFS

The Clo Mor Cliffs (right) drop dramatically into the sea below the lighthouse at Cape Wrath, built in 1828. They are the highest cliffs on the British mainland boasting an impressive face of 281 m (922 ft).

LOCH LOMOND AND THE TROSSACHS

Scotland's first national park was opened with great ceremony on July 24, 2002, and is characterized by wooded mountains and majestic lakes such as Loch Katrine (right) and Loch Lomond, dominated by the 973-m-high (3,192-ft) Ben Lomond.
The wildly romantic Trossachs inspire nature lovers as well as poets. "Everything that we saw was loveliness and beauty in perfection", is how William Wordsworth's sister Dorothy raved about the area.

LOCH SHIEL

Superb panoramic roads make a drive through the Highlands well worth the trip. A rather windy stretch takes you from Fort William to Mallaig past roughly 72 km (45 mi) of mountains and lakes. About halfway, you come across the elongated Loch Shiel at the northern end of which is the Glenfinnan Monument. Close to the shore is a tower with the figure of a Highlander; it marks the spot where in August 1745, "Bonnie Prince Charlie" mobilized the Scottish clans against England.

BY TRAIN FROM FORT WILLIAM TO MALLAIG

A steam train makes for a lovely nostalgic trip from Mallaig to Fort William. Operating between May and October, the Jacobite Steam Train was the "Hogwarts Express" in the Harry Potter films. The journey takes you from nearby Ben Nevis (Britain's tallest mountain) via Arisag (the westernmost station in the country), Loch Morar (the deepest freshwater lake) and the Morar (the shortest river) past Loch Nevis (the deepest saltwater lake) – a journey of superlatives.

A world of imagination: "Nessie" has been a protected animal since 1934, which means, whoever succeeds in actually catching the celebrity dinosaur will have to return it to Loch Ness straightaway. Left: The ruins of Urquhart Castle on a spit of land overlooking Loch Ness.

The Hebrides archipelago is divided into the Outer "Western Isles" and the Inner Hebrides, the two being separated by the Sound of Barra. The islands stretch for more than 200 km (124 mi) and form a barrier against the rigors of the Atlantic on Scotland's west coast.

ISLES OF LEWIS, ISLE OF HARRIS

"Hand-woven Harris Tweed" are the words printed on the quality seal of the best-known export item of the "Western Isles". The trademark, which is still used today, was awarded to the Harris Tweed Association as far back as 1909. To achieve its exclusive authenticity, this luxury material must be made from 100% Scottish wool, spun and dyed in the Outer Hebrides and hand-woven there by island residents.

The complex handicraft is still practiced today on the Isles of Lewis and Harris, two islands that are connected to each other by an isthmus. Together they actually form the largest island of the Western Isles, also known as "Long Island".

Lewis and Harris differ greatly in their landscapes. While Harris is home to rocky ridges, fjords and bays, Lewis is covered in swampy moorland. From the main town of Stornoway you can head to South Harris, which captivates visitors with its magnificent sandy beaches.

ISLE OF MULL

The Isle of Mull attracts visitors with its craggy, hilly landscape and karst mountain ranges. The highest peak on Mull is Ben More at 966 m (3,169 ft). There are three car and passenger ferry routes from the Scottish mainland, the most popular being the connection from Oban. Mull's coast is more than 480 km (298 mi) long and, with a bit of luck, birdwatchers here can spot golden eagles, sea eagles and Merlin peregrines. Walks around the island lead to some spectacular sights such as this brilliant white lighthouse.

ISLE OF IONA

The Druid island off the southern tip of Mull is considered the birthplace of Christianity in Scotland. In 563, Celtic monk and missionary, St Columba, landed here and established the first monastery. Repeatedly destroyed by Vikings, St Columba Monastery was rebuilt several times. After Columba died in 597, the island became a popular pilgrimage site.

Around the year 1200, Reginald MacDonald founded a Benedictine monastery, Iona Abbey, on the site of the former abbey church.

ISLE OF STAFFA

The Hebrides Isle of Staffa, a geological wonderland of black basalt, can only be accessed by boat in clear weather from the isles of Mull or Iona. According to legend, the small isle, which measures just 200 by 600 m (656 x 1,969 ft), forms the "Scottish end" of the Northern Irish Giant's Causeway, which is said to have once connected the places where two enemy giants lived.

Fingal's Cave, named after a hero of Celtic myth, is worth seeing. It is a cave approximately 69 m (226 ft) long whose interior is reminiscent of a cathedral.

STANDING STONES OF CALLANISH

The rock monoliths of Callanish on the Isle of Lewis form what is probably the most beautiful stone circle in Scotland. Exactly forty-seven of the upright prehistoric cult megaliths (menhirs) can still be seen today, and were presumably erected by humans over various stages between the years 3000 and 1500 BC. The menhirs are made of Lewis gneiss, a type of stone typical of these islands.

The northern avenue of the complex is particularly impressive and is made up of two almost parallel rows of stones stretching roughly 82 m (90 yds) with the stones 8.2 m (9 yds) apart. In the center is a circle comprising thirteen menhirs with a large central stone in the middle that is 4.75 m (16 ft) high, weighs around five tonnes (5.5 tons) and forms the western border of a small chamber with a Neolithic communal grave. The cir-

Prehistoric evidence of an enigmatic culture: the forty-seven Standing Stones of Callanish (above and right), arranged in a circular and radial formation to create a "sun cross".

cle is surrounded by thirteen more monoliths that form a ring 11 to 13 m (36 to 43 ft) in diameter.

The megalith cult site of Callanish is certainly comparable to Stonehenge in southern England, and is considered to be the symbol of the Western Isles. The entire complex can supposedly be seen as a vast astronomical observatory.

The sky at dusk over Loch Sealg on the east coast of Lewis (left) is often a wonderful play of colors and shapes.

ISLE OF SKYE

The largest island of the Inner Hebrides, the Isle of Skye, is considered one of the wildest, most rugged and most beautiful in all of Scotland. Ranges like the Cuillin Hills at 1,009 m (3,311 ft), the Quiraings and other bizarre geological formations such as the Old Man of Storr give the island its unique character. Fog, the occasional brief shower and rainbows make the remote coastal roads an unforgettable adventure.

The green meadows with herds of cattle and flocks of sheep (top) are mostly concentrated in the south of the Isle of Skye. Dunvegan Castle (above, middle), in the north-western part of Skye, has been the ancestral seat of the MacLeod clan since the 11th century. Portree (bottom) is the island's capital.

Beinn Edra soars to a height of 611 m (2,005 ft) on Skye's Trotternish Peninsula (main picture).

The Orkney Islands, of which only
eighteen are inhabited, sit around
30 km (19 mi) off Scotland's
north-eastern coast and are best
reached from the John O'Groats
and Thurso ferry ports. Mainland,
Hoy and South Ronaldsay are
some of the larger islands in the
archipelago. Their rolling landscapes were formed by glaciers
during the last Ice Age. Despite
their location in the far north, the
Orkneys enjoy a relatively mild
climate thanks to the warm Gulf
Stream.

ISLE OF HOY

The inhabitants here are of Scottish and Scandinavian origin who
predominantly live off agriculture,
fishing and tourism. It's not just
rock climbers and ornithologists
who are fascinated by the United
Kingdom's highest headland at
347 m (1,139 ft), on the island of
Hoy. The spectacular landscape
and prehistoric monuments also
play their part in thrilling visitors.

Above: The north coast of the island of
Hoy with the "Old Man of Hoy" pinnacle
soaring 137 m/449 ft out of the sea.

MAINLAND

Mainland – the main island of the Orkney Islands – is home to a number of stunning monuments from the twilight of the Neolithic Age that document the cultural achievements of northern European civilizations between 3,000 and 2,000 BC. The most fascinating of these include the large chamber tomb of Maes Howe, which dates back to 2,500 BC and has a diameter of more than 30 m (98 ft).

The remains of the stone cross of Stenness can also be traced back to prehistoric times, and the Ring of Brodgar is also not far away. Here, stones measuring up to 4 m (15 ft) stand in a circle approximately 100 m (328 ft) in diameter. Particularly impressive is the Stone Age settlement of Skara Brae, which was exposed by accident in a storm 150 years ago and is the best-preserved Neolithic structure of its kind in Europe.

The Standing Stones of Stenness (main picture) on the Orkney Island of Mainland date back to the 3rd millennium BC and once formed a stone circle approximately 30 m (98 ft) in diameter.

Top: The roughly 5,000-year-old stone circle known as the Ring of Brodgar originally contained sixty menhirs, thirty-six of which still remain. Middle, left and right: The Broch of Gurness and Skara Brae. Bottom: Maes Howe grave mound and chamber.

DUNLUCE CASTLE, KILCHURN CASTLE, GIANT'S CAUSEWAY

Kilchurn Castle (main picture, top) and the Giant's Causeway (main picture bottom). Legend has it that, upon being challenged by his Scottish adversary, the Irish giant Finn built a path of stones leading across the Irish Sea to Scotland.

DUNLUCE CASTLE

Built in the 16th century on an imposing basalt cliff, Dunluce was home to the formidable Sorley Boy MacDonnell, a descendant of the Scottish MacDonald clan who had been intent on conquering Ireland. It was Sorley Boy's son who first made efforts at reconciliation with the English crown.

KILCHURN CASTLE

Constructed in the 15th century, Kilchurn is perched on a peninsula in Loch Awe – one of Scotland's longest lakes stretching 40 km (25 mi). It was struck by lightning in the 17th century, and the ruins have since stood forlorn in the shadow of the 1,125-m-high (3,691-ft) Ben Cruchan.

GIANT'S CAUSEWAY

Some 40,000 mostly hexagonal basalt columns rise spectacularly out of the sea near the fishing town of Ballycastle. Forming their own headland, they are estimated to be around sixty million years old and were created through crystallization when effluent lava cooled in the sea.

Its location is spectacular and its history is no less dramatic. Built on a bluff high above the sea, Dunluce Castle (left) has not been inhabited since 1639, but Sorley Boy MacDonnell once used canons from a wrecked Spanish galleon to defend his castle from English forces.

Ha'penny Bridge (main picture), built in 1816, connects the Temple Bar district to Liffey Street. The bridge was named after the road toll, which had to be paid here until 1919.

The Vikings, who were the first to settle this area, named their settlement "Dyfflin", meaning "Black Puddle". A bad omen, one might think. In actual fact, Dublin's more than 1,000 years of history have largely been shaped by external forces, primarily the English, whose first "colony" was Ireland. Dublin eventually became a role model of Anglo-Irish administration and yet, at heart, it was never really British at all. Gaelic traditions, music, poetry, storytelling, and playful banter were nurtured throughout the occupation until the battle for Irish independence began with the Easter Uprising in Dublin in 1916.

In the 1990s, Dublin experienced a dramatic boom and the Irish economy grew more quickly than any other in the European Union. This freed up some finances to refurbish some of the city's more charming districts and renovate some of the beautiful 18th-century Georgian architecture. Distinctly modern urban lifestyles and attitudes are particularly noticeable in the Temple Bar district (left, bottom), with its upscale galleries, lively bars and fancy restaurants. Some of the main sights include St Patrick's Cathedral, built in the "Early English" style (left, top), and Trinity College (above) with the Old Library. Of course, any tour of the city should include a visit to the local pub where you can imagine yourself in the setting of James Joyce's great Dublin novel, *Ulysses*. Davy Byrne's pub in Duke Street is an option.

DONEGAL

FANAD

The Fanad Peninsula offers visitors a variety of scenery and features a coastline with beautiful sandy beaches, wooded areas and truly amazing rock formations. The lighthouse high up on Fanad Head (main picture) is spectacular.

In the nearby Carmelite Friary at Rathmullan, an event took place in 1607 that was to be a turning point in Irish history: The counts O'Neill and O'Donnel, hugely outnumbered by the English Army, fled the scene, thus clearing the way for Northern Ireland to be settled by Scottish Protestants.

NORTH COAST

The north coast of Donegal is a sparsely populated, lonely stretch of land. From top to bottom: Five Finger Beach; 16th-century Doe Castle, surrounded by the sea on three sides; and the Atlantic surf washing against the jagged coast.

WEST COAST

The cliffs of Slieve League fall a dramatic 601 m (1,972 ft) into the sea and are among Europe's highest. Oddly, Donegal's hinterland is as infertile as the west coast is spectacular.

GLENVEAGH

At some point in the 19th century, a speculator named John George Adair bought this piece of land and drove off the peasants who lived there. Breeding sheep, he had figured out, was more profitable than rental income. In the 20th century, Henry P McIlhenny, an American of Irish descent, bought and donated the land to the state. Today it is a national park once again open to the public.

CONNEMARA

Connemara is still one of the wildest and most barren regions in Ireland. It is bordered by the Atlantic in the west, allowing the people to earn a modest income from fishing. A number of lakes dot the remote, sparsely settled land.

CONNEMARA NATIONAL PARK

Connemara, in the western part of County Galway, is a mountainous region with lakes and moors that possesses an almost mythical beauty. Peat bogs stretch between two mountain ranges, the Twelve Bens and Maam Turks, and are surrounded on three sides by a delicately indented coastline dotted by countless little islands. For the purposes of nature conservation, a region of approximately 20 sq km (8 sq mi) on the north-western slopes of the Twelve Bens was made into Connemara National Park, which is open all year round and can be explored on two signposted tracks starting from the visitors center.

The inhabitants of Connemara have traditionally been quite poor, but the relaxing effect of the sparsely settled region has proven a boon to both locals and city dwellers. After the famines of the 1840s, when the potato blight deprived almost everyone of their staple food, many gave up the battle to subsist on the paltry soil here and emigrated to the United States.

ON THE WEST COAST

Fresh Atlantic air, a magnificent location above the mouth of the river Owenglin, and the nearby Twelve Bens Mountains all make the city of Clifden the most popular place on the west coast of Connemara. Even Celtic culture was able to thrive here for many years as no invaders were interested in the infertile soil.

Only Oliver Cromwell finally came in the 17th century, although not for economic reasons. He forced his opponents to the western part of Connemara and on to the nearby island of Inishbofin (right).

CLIFDEN HINTER-LAND

Moors, barren mountains and lakes dominate the scenery as soon as you head inland in Connemara. Except for peat fuel and sheep's wool, the land, strewn with granite boulders, does not yield much else. However, Connemara's landscape delivers a wide variety of hues: from scarlet and brown heather at Killary Harbour to the deep green of lush ferns at Derryclare Lough (right) and the gray of the craggy cliffs near Maam Cross.

ON THE SOUTHERN COAST

Connemara's southern coast is extremely craggy and rugged, a damp stony desert with endless lakes that converges almost seamlessly with the sea, which is itself dotted with little islands (right: Lettergesh Beach). Padraig Pearse, an author and one of the martyrs of the Republican uprising in 1916, chose the remote region for his summer residence in the wine-growing town of Rosmuck. Dog's Bay and Gurteen Beach, two other western beaches near Roundstone, are known for their clear water and white sand.

KYLEMORE ABBEY

After crossing the raised bogs where turf cutters still pursue their traditional trade as they have for centuries, the well-tended park of Kylemore Abbey (right) is a welcome change of scenery.

Around the mid-19th century, a businessman had this dream castle built for his young wife in neo-Gothic style. Today, a residence with thirty-three bedrooms is no longer of any use to most private individuals, so Kylemore Abbey has become home to Benedictine nuns and a boarding school for girls. Some of its rooms, such as the library and dining hall, are still open to visitors.

The restoration of the Victorian Walled Garden with its lovely greenhouses was carried out in more recent times. Flowers and herbs thrive there, a fact that the original builder hoped would please his young wife.

ARAN ISLANDS

The three inhabited Aran Islands became the epitome of devotional, rustic life on the Irish Atlantic coast. Playwright John Millington Synge spent many summers here in the 1890s while supporting the revival of Celtic culture and describing life on the islands.

Geologically, they are a continuation of the Burren Limestone Plateau, appearing to comprise only limestone slabs and turf. The largest island, Inishmore, is a sloping limestone plain where drystone walls protect the fields and meadows against storms.

The stone forts on these islands are typical of prehistoric fortress complexes. The rocky, only sparsely developed island of Inishmaan as well as the smallest island, Inisheer (right), both boast remains from early times.

The Connemara National Park includes the northern peaks of the Twelve Bens (left). The highest of the twelve is the Binn Bhán at 730 m (2,395 ft) while the others are only slightly smaller. The lower regions were previously settled, and some ruins testify to this even today.

THE BURREN

An English officer who arrived in the karst landscape of County Clare with Cromwell's army was not impressed by what he encountered there. He found "no water to drown a man, no tree to hang him, and no soil to bury him".

The limestone plateau that occupies much of the area spreads over 250 sq km (96 sq mi) and is known as the Burren (from the Irish "Boireann", meaning "stony land"). At first glance it is indeed a bleak and desolate place, but in spring, an astonishing number of flowers including Alpine, Mediterranean and Arctic varieties sprout from the rock crevices.

CLIFFS OF MOHER

The stunning cliffs of Moher are Europe's highest coastal escarpment and extend for 8 km (5 mi) along the spectacular shoreline. Between Liscannor and Doolin the cliffs reach dizzying heights of more than 200 m (656 ft) and provide impressive panoramic views. Looking down from the vertiginous cliffs to the churning surf and gnarled rock formations you get a good idea of the immense forces at work in the Atlantic. Hikers can enjoy a beautiful footpath here that follows the craggy coast for 35 km (22 mi). The southern end of Moher, near Hag's Head, is an ideal place to take in this extraordinary nature spectacle.

Poulnabrone Dolmen, a stone tomb shaped like a table, is one of the most remarkable remains of early human settlement to be found on the Burren limestone plateau. More than sixty megalithic tombs and some 500 stone circles from the Stone and Iron Ages also provide evidence of ancient human activity.

CLONMACNOISE

The unique monastery settlement of Clonmacnoise (main picture) is situated in a bend of the river Shannon, in County Offaly. Its isolated location long protected it from most attacks, but in 1552, pillaging English soldiers put an end to 1,000 years of cultural development. In the Middle Ages, the monastery was a center for religion and learning and was renowned throughout Europe. The complex is home to two round towers as well as the remains of the cathedral and eight smaller churches from various eras. A highlight is Ireland's most extensive collection of Celtic high crosses, the most precious of which date back to the first millennium AD. They provide protection against wind and weathering at the visitors' center, which also presents the town's history.

ROCK OF CASHEL

An imposing limestone cliff with the ruins of a fortress complex towers over the vast plain of County Tipperary. Its strategic location has always meant the Rock of Cashel was of enormous importance. According to legend, the cliffs are said to have fallen from the devil's mouth when he flew over and saw Saint Patrick. From the 5th century, the fort (Irish: "Caiseal") served as the residence of the kings of Munster, whose rule extended across large parts of southern Ireland.

Toward the end of the 11th century, the complex was handed over to the church and in 1647, it was plundered by the troops of English military leader, Oliver Cromwell. Some 100 years later it was completely surrendered. Next to the church is Cormac's Chapel, a gem of Romanesque architecture that features a very nicely preserved round tower that measures 28 m (92 ft). The cathedral was erected later when the chapel ultimately proved to be too small for the droves of worshippers. The Hall of the Vicars Choral, which is home to the St Patrick's Cross, was built for lay brothers in the 15th century.

ARDMORE

In the pretty resort town of Ardmore, which has a vast sandy beach and is located on a headland between Ardmore Bay and Youghal Bay, everything revolves around Saint Declan, who founded a monastery in the early 5th century looking out over the bay.

A well named after the saint, which was previously used by pilgrims to refresh themselves, has its source next to three old stone crosses on a hill at the edge of the city. Today's pilgrims walk along the 90-km (56-mi) St Declan's Way, which connects Ardmore with the Rock of Cashel sanctuary. There are a 30-m-high (98-ft) round tower and a cathedral from the 12th century (above) still on the site of saint's former monastery. The magnificent Romanesque elements include scenes from the Old Testament such as Adam and Eve, the Judgment of Solomon, and the adoration of the kings. They have been preserved on the western façade but the church itself no longer has a roof.

KING JOHN'S CASTLE

With a population of 60,000, Limerick was originally a Viking settlement – like most Irish port cities – that is now the third-largest city in Ireland. The positive developments of recent years mean the town on the river Shannon has a friendlier appearance than a generation ago, but it was only with great difficulty that Limerick was able to shake off its reputation as a rough industrial town.

The inner city is divided into the districts of English Town, Irish Town and Newtown Pery. The English Town area, located north of the confluence of the Abbey and the Shannon rivers, is home to St Mary's Cathedral (also known as Limerick Cathedral) as well as King John's Castle with its mighty ramparts. In 1210, King John of England even traveled here to consecrate the castle, which was considered inpenetrable at the time: a pentagonal fortress complex with an imposing main building, three round towers and a twin-towered gate building. The Gaelic inhabitants had to live outside the forts in Irish Town, which caused distrust between the ethnic groups.

DINGLE, BEARA, IVERAGH, KILLARNEY

Idyllic coastlines, picturesque villages, enchanting lake districts, steep cliffs, islands cloaked in myth and legend, remnants of ancient civilizations, and towns that are as historically exciting as they are vibrant – that is what awaits you in Munster, Ireland's largest province.

DINGLE

The Dingle Peninsula is the northern-most of five spits of land in County Kerry that point westward like fingers. With its gorgeous mountains, romantic rocky coast, and magnificent beaches it is one of Ireland's most beautiful and most popular regions. The mountains on either side of the Connor Pass, which at 456 m (1,496 ft) is the high-est pass in Ireland, are a paradise for ramblers, while surfers will find ex-cellent if cold conditions on the 5-km (3-mi) Surfer Beach near Inch on the peninsula's south coast.

Like everywhere in the west of Ireland, Dingle boasts relics of early Christen-dom. Especially impressive are the "beehive cells" of the early Irish her-mit monks. In the early 6th century, Kerry's patron saint, St Brandon, alle-gedly prayed atop Mount Brandon (953 m/3,127 ft) before starting on his legendary journey to America in a cur-ragh, a traditional sailing boat, with fourteen other monks. Mount Brandon is Ireland's second-highest mountain after Carrauntoohil, which checks in at 1,041 m (3,416 ft).

BEARA

Beara was the ancestral home of the O'Sullivans, the lords of Dunboy Castle near Castletownbere. When English troops took the castle in 1601, 1,000 clan members began a march across Ireland to the remote county of Leitrim; only 35 of them made it. Subsequent waves of emi-gration further reduced the popu-lation and today Beara is still a sparsely populated area.

In a bay near Castletownbere, the ruins of the Victorian Puxley Man-sion are a reminder of the former copper mines of Beara. The home of a hated family of mine owners, it was burned down in the 1920 by the Irish Republican Army.

Right, top: The narrow road around the rocky Beara Peninsula offers superb views over more than 140 km (87 mi). Below that is a view of beautiful Ballydonegan Bay near Allihies.

IVERAGH

The drive around the Ring of Kerry takes you 170 km (106 mi) along the Iveragh Peninsula and is a high-light of any trip to Ireland. The ever-changing views of mountains and bays are simply breathtaking. A popular starting point for the tour of the Ring is Kenmare, a pictur-esque town with pastel-colored houses at the end of Kenmare Bay. Founded in 1775, Kenmare was known for its silk production.

Puffin Island (right) just off the west coast near the Bay of St Finan, is a popular nesting place for puf-fins, gannets and boobies.

Right, bottom: In a valley about 4 km (2.5 mi) from the south coast of Iveragh is the 2,000-year-old ring fort of Staigue. It once served as the residence of the kings of Munster and is today one of the best-preserved monuments of its kind in all of Ireland.

The Dingle Peninsula enchants with its wildly romantic coastal scenery (left). In the background is Mount Brandon shrouded in clouds. Behind it on the left, are the Three Sisters cliffs facing the opposite coast.

KILLARNEY

Ice Age glaciers formed the Killarney region, a mountainous lakeland area comprising more than 8,000 hectares (19,768 acres) near the town of the same name. Parts of the region have been made into a national park where the roads are free of cars. Any visit to the national park should include a trip by horse-drawn coach through the Gap of Dunloe, a mountain pass in the

On a swath of land near Lough Leane stands the late 15th-century Ross Castle (top).
Southwest of the town of Killarney is a region with three attractive lakes (middle, bottom and right).

shadows of Purple Mountain, which owes its name to the heather that flowers here in late summer. More demanding is the tour to the top of Carrauntoohil, Ireland's highest peak at 1,041 m (3,416 ft).
The oak and yew trees that grow in the park are fairly rare in Ireland, since most of the woods were cut down centuries ago. The strawberry tree is part of the unusual flora of the region, a shrub with red, edible fruits that normally only grows in the Mediterranean.

Tree masts were rammed as much as 30 m (98 ft) deep into the peaty ground to form the foundations of Amsterdam's Old Town. The result was not only seventy islands on stilts, but also the romantic ambience of a town on the water. At the height of the "Golden 17th Century", construction began on the Three-Canal-Belt (left) whose half-moon shape includes the Keizersgracht canal (main picture). Four hundred bridges now crisscross the historic center alone, and the water level is kept constant with the help of a system of locks and pumps. Even commercial loads are still transported on the city's canals.

Hundreds of houseboats lie in anchor on the quays of Amsterdam's 160 waterways as well. They have become an iconic element of city life, just like the bicycles and the flower stalls selling "tulips from Amsterdam".

KINDERDIJK

The landscape of the Kinderdijk-Elshout is characterized by reservoirs, dykes, pumping stations, administrative buildings and the beautifully preserved wooden windmills. In the early 17th century, the Belgian Simon Stevin refined the technology for draining the polders. By erecting a neat row of windmills at Kinderdijk, he was able to create an ingenious system in which the water was "milled" away. It took place in two stages. First, water was transported from a lower canal to one that was higher up. Then it was moved to a system of locks that would remove it.

Today, such windmills still stand tall along the canals between Kinderdijk and Alblasserdam farther south. This cultural landscape so typical of Holland is the largest and best-preserved collection of historic windmills in the country. And they are not just there for show. A majority of these windmills have been in constant use since the 18th century. Just one of them was transformed into a museum that is now open to visitors.

KEUKENHOF

Visitors to the Bollenstreek, or "bulb region" situated between Haarlem and Leiden, can enjoy a drive through a veritable sea of flowers. The fields of around 8,000 nurseries specializing exclusively in the wholesale trade of flowers are on display here. The Tulip Route, as it is also known, takes you to the most important operations in the area. One such mecca for flower lovers is the famous Keukenhof, founded by a cooperative of growers in 1949.

GRAND PLACE

The Grand Place, or great market square, in the Belgian capital is a modest-sized square by European standards at 110 m (345 ft) by 68 m (220 ft), but it is surrounded by glorious rows of guild houses and a beautiful town hall that make it one of the most attractive of its kind on the entire continent. In the 15th century, when the powerful and prosperous guilds in Brussels replaced traditional aristocratic rule of the city, they created this square with its exquisite patrician houses as a monument to their newly found wealth.

Narrow guild houses with ornately structured façades surround the Grand Place (top). Equally impressive are the Gothic Town Hall (bottom right), the Maison du Roi (bottom left) and the Italianate Maison des Ducs de Brabant (bottom middle).

BRUGES

Bruges Town Hall was built in the year 1376, making it one of the oldest town halls in Flanders.

In the Middle Ages, the prosperous trade in textiles between England and the European continent went primarily via Bruges. Merchants from seventeen countries owned factories there. Thanks to generous patrons, Jan van Eyck and Hans Memling then transformed Bruges into a center of art and culture. Bruges reached its zenith in the 15th century when the dukes of Burgundy, active supporters of late-Gothic court culture, took up residence within its walls. International trade, however, soon began to decline when the river Zweyn silted up, thus blocking access to the sea.

The town, oval in its planning, is accessed by numerous canals and long streets with rows of gabled houses. These patrician mansions, the counting houses of the merchant princes, and the magnificent town hall (above center, the Large Council Chamber) – where the counts of Flanders "liberated" the people – tell of the former prestige of the city. Its proudest icon is the belfry of the Cloth Hall (above left) while the Grote Markt (above right) represents the center of the Old Town.

Ghent, the capital of the Belgian province of East Flanders, is located at the confluence of the rivers Schelde and Leie.

GHENT

A center of the textile industry since the Middle Ages, Ghent has managed to remain loyal to this tradition even in modern times. The second most important industry in the city is the cultivation of fruit, vegetables and flowers. The city's most famous sights are nestled in the well-preserved historic heart of the city, between the Grafenburg and the 14th-century St Bavo's Cathedral, which is slightly elevated and visible from afar. Its greatest religious treasure is the famous "Ghent Altar" by the brothers Hubert und Jan van Eyck (15th century). The 95-m-high (312-ft) bell tower opposite the church was a symbol of the rising bourgeoisie in the 14th century. Also worth a visit are the Cloth Hall, the Large Meat Hall, the Grafenburg and the Town Hall.

The Belfry of Ghent (above) was built between 1313 and 1380. The so-called Dragon of Ghent has adorned the tip of the bell tower since 1388. On the ground floor, the charters of the privileges of Ghent's citizens have been kept in a secret chamber with multiple locks, the "secreet", since 1402.

ANTWERP

The lifeblood of Antwerp, Belgium's second-largest city, is its bustling port. An array of automotive and chemical companies are based there, and as one of the busiest ports in the world it has cultivated an atmosphere of openness to the world for centuries – a fact that has contributed significantly to the rise of Antwerp as a world center for diamonds.

Antwerp boasts a number of historic monuments and an exceptionally vibrant cultural life. Most of its sights are in the city center, which forms a semi-circle on the right bank of the Schelde. The most remarkable sight in Antwerp is probably the Steen, a former castle complex whose oldest parts date back to the 9th century. Today it houses the National Maritime Museum, which features a fascinating Flemish warship from the 15th century.

The castle's viewing platform offers superb views across the Schelde – more than 500 m (1,650 ft) wide at this point – of the bridges, the old quay, and the countless derricks scattered across the horizon down at the port.

The French capital is steeped in history, and yet always ahead of the times. It is breathtaking in size, and yet seductive in its charm. One of few genuine world cities, Paris boasts a bewildering array of historic buildings and cultural landmarks.

Especially rich in history are the areas along the banks of the Seine, between Pont de Sully and Pont d'Iéna, beginning with the Île St Louis where the statue of Paris's patron saint stands, Ste Geneviève. Farther west, on the Île de la Cité, is the heart of Catholic Paris, with its Gothic Notre Dame Cathedral and Ste Chapelle, a filigree masterwork of High Gothic style.

Continuing along, opposite the Concièrgerie you come to one of the world's most important art museums, the Louvre. Farther down the Seine you arrive at the Musée d'Orsay, the Grand and Petit Palais, and the National Assembly. At the end of this stretch you reach the Eiffel Tower, a revolutionary steel structure completed in 1889 for the Exposition Universelle.

The Seine excursion boats, or "bateaux mouches," go right past the cathedral Notre Dame de Paris on the Île de la Cité in the Seine.

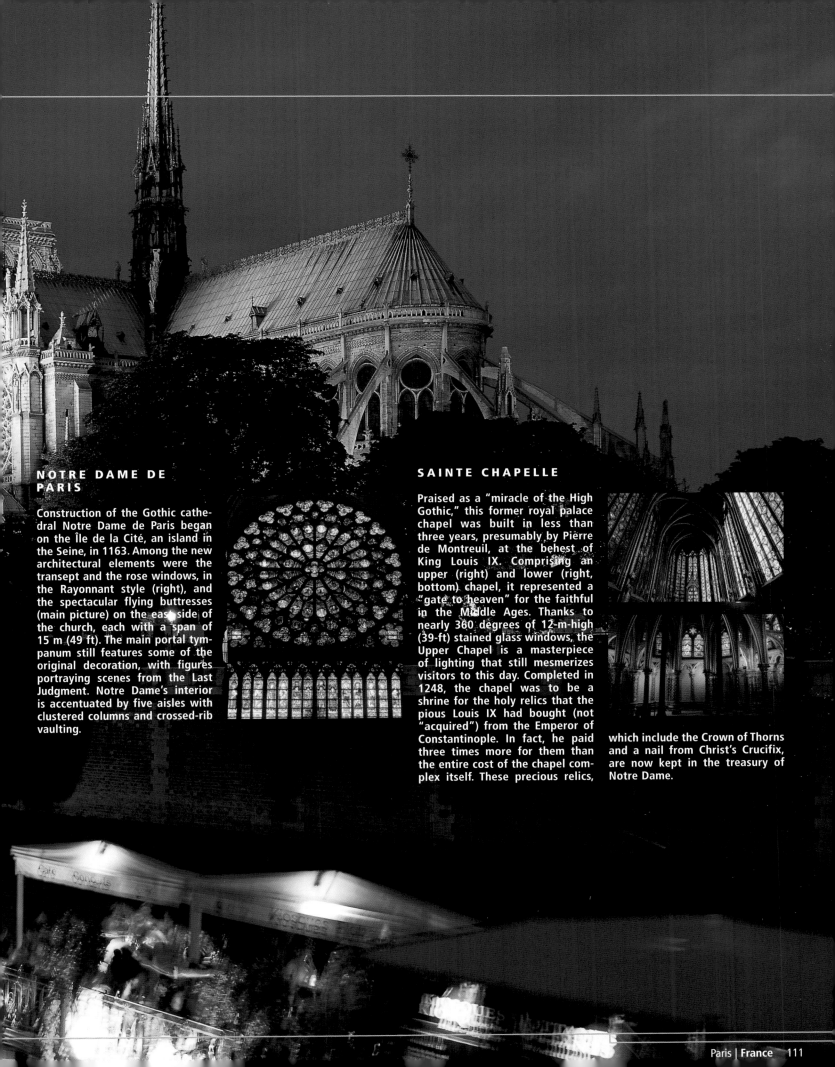

NOTRE DAME DE PARIS

Construction of the Gothic cathedral Notre Dame de Paris began on the Île de la Cité, an island in the Seine, in 1163. Among the new architectural elements were the transept and the rose windows, in the Rayonnant style (right), and the spectacular flying buttresses (main picture) on the east side of the church, each with a span of 15 m (49 ft). The main portal tympanum still features some of the original decoration, with figures portraying scenes from the Last Judgment. Notre Dame's interior is accentuated by five aisles with clustered columns and crossed-rib vaulting.

SAINTE CHAPELLE

Praised as a "miracle of the High Gothic," this former royal palace chapel was built in less than three years, presumably by Pierre de Montreuil, at the behest of King Louis IX. Comprising an upper (right) and lower (right, bottom) chapel, it represented a "gate to heaven" for the faithful in the Middle Ages. Thanks to nearly 360 degrees of 12-m-high (39-ft) stained glass windows, the Upper Chapel is a masterpiece of lighting that still mesmerizes visitors to this day. Completed in 1248, the chapel was to be a shrine for the holy relics that the pious Louis IX had bought (not "acquired") from the Emperor of Constantinople. In fact, he paid three times more for them than the entire cost of the chapel complex itself. These precious relics, which include the Crown of Thorns and a nail from Christ's Crucifix, are now kept in the treasury of Notre Dame.

The Louvre has been rebuilt several times over the centuries. The most recent addition, completed in 1989, was the glass and metal pyramid in front of the building (main picture). The structure was designed by Ieoh Ming Pei to allow more light into the museum below.

OPÉRA NATIONAL – PALAIS GARNIER

Opened in 1875, the national opera house reflects the opulence of the Second Empire. Thirteen years previous, in 1862, a vote had been taken to select among 171 tendors for the building's design. The unanimous winner was a hitherto unknown architect, Charles Garnier. However, construction on the project was delayed when the ground water rose unexpectedly. In order to maintain the water, a giant

The full splendor of Garnier's opera house only becomes apparent once you are inside. Marc Chagall did the auditorium's ceiling fresco.

underground concrete basin was built, the ceiling of which provided support for the entire opera house. This "lake" below the opera served as inspiration for Gaston Leroux's novel, Phantom of the Opera (1910), a piece that has since been very successfully adapted as a musical by Andrew Lloyd Webber.

LOUVRE, JARDIN DES TUILERIES

The Louvre was originally to be "a museum for the people" that required no admission fee for visitors. That was the decree of the revolutionary government when the museum was opened in 1793 – the year Louis XVI and his wife Marie Antoinette were executed by the guillotine. From the 14th century until 1682, when Louis XIV moved his court to Versailles, the Louvre was actually the Paris residence of the kings of France. After that, the former town palace was transformed into one of the world's most important art museums. On the occasion of its 200th anniversary, the Louvre was remodeled as the "Grand Louvre," the largest museum in the world (the exhibition space was doubled to roughly 60,000 sq m/645,600 sq ft).

At the same time, the long-neglected Tuileries also received a facelift. During their redesign, architects Wirtz, Cribier and Benech preserved the long perspectives that royal landscape gardener Le Nôtre had originally created in the 17th century.

After the French Revolution, the Louvre's valuable collections were opened to the general public. Today, some 300,000 exhibits are on display there, including (above, from left) Michelangelo's *The Dying Slave*, Leonardo da Vinci's *Mona Lisa*, and the Greek sculpture *Venus de Milo*, discovered on the Cycladic island of Melos in 1820.

The Louvre's glass pyramid, flanked by the Denon and Richelieu wings, as seen from the Sully Wing. To the left of the pyramid stands an equestrian statue of Napoleon (left).

PLACE DE LA CONCORDE

Conceived as a "royal square" in 1755 by Jacques-Ange Gabriel during the reign of Louis XV, it was here in 1794 that the "Reign of Terror" unleashed its full wrath during the French Revolution – over 1,300 people, among them Louis XVI, were put to the guillotine. One year later the square was given its more reconciliatory name, Place de la Concorde. The roughly 3,200-year-old obelisk from Luxor has stood at its center since 1836.

The two bronze fountains on Place de la Concorde were designed by German architect Jacob Ignaz Hittorf (1792–1867).

CHAMPS-ÉLYSÉES, ARC DE TRIOMPHE

The Champs-Élysées is Paris' most famous avenue. It begins at Place de la Concorde and ends at Place Charles de Gaulle, the latter of which is home to the 50-m-high (164-ft) Arc de Triomphe (1836), built to commemorate Napoleon's victorious army. Unlike the gates from antiquity upon which it was modeled, Arc de Triomphe architect Jean-François Chalgrin dispensed with the arrangement of columns that was customary at the time and instead constructed a single, 29-m-high (95-ft) opening in the arch.

Napoleon's triumphal arch is the focal point of the Avenue des Champs-Élysées.

Alexandre Gustave Eiffel got the idea for the Eiffel Tower from his colleagues, Maurice Koechlin and Emile Nougier. Architect Stephen Sauvestre divided the tower into three sections and gave it rounded arches, creating transparency. An enthusiastic Eiffel directed and executed the project.

MUSÉE D'ORSAY

In many ways, the building opposite the Jardin des Tuileries that houses the Museé d'Orsay is itself the first work of art to be admired by visitors. A daringly engineered structure made of iron and glass, it features magnificent façades and is a textbook example of fin-de-siècle (turn-of-the-century) architecture. Originally a train station built for the Exhibition Universelle in 1900, trains departed here for south-western France up until 1939. Not until forty-seven years later, on December 9, 1986, did it become the museum that it is today. Complementing the collections in the Louvre, it houses masterpieces of French art from the years 1848 to 1914.

EIFFEL TOWER

Built in 1889 for the Paris Exhibition Universelle, the Eiffel Tower was a pioneering achievement in its day. In just over two years, 3,000 Gustave Eiffel Company metal workers, under the supervision of architect Stephen Sauvestre, assembled the tower, which is made of approximately 20,000 prefabricated parts and about 2.5 million rivets.

It was originally supposed to remain standing for only 20 years, but its usefulness as a radio tower ensured its longevity. The fact that the steel structure is still standing also speaks for the quality of the flexible "puddled" steel that was used in its construction.

The Eiffel Tower, visible from great distances and beautifully illuminated at night, was initially rejected by the populace. Today, it is impossible to imagine Paris without it.

Eiffel (1832–1923), a descendant of German emigrants from the Eifel region, had an excellent nose for business. Working with his Paris office, where he employed only first-class architects and engineers, Eiffel was not only responsible for the world-famous tower in Paris that is named after him, but was also active in many other projects both in France and abroad, some as far afield as Africa and South America. They build viaducts, train stations, engine and trade fair halls, and the scaffolding system for another equally world-famous piece: the Statue of Liberty in New York. Eiffel projects were oriented toward new "graphic styles" and were therefore always in step with the aesthetics of the time.

The Musée d'Orsay cannot hide its former incarnation as a train station (left). Between 1980 and 1986, the building was transformed into a museum that specializes in French art. One of its exhibits is the historical painting *The Romans of the Decadence* (far left) by Thomas Couture (1815–79).

HÔTEL DES INVALIDES

As can be surmised from the name, Louis XIV built the Hôtel des Invalides for the victims of his many wars. Today it houses one of the world's largest military museums. In 1767, a dome was added as a royal vault, but it is Napoleon who now lies buried there instead of the Sun King.

The shiny golden cupola of the dome of Les Invalides rises above Napoleon's sarcophagus of red porphyry.

PALAIS BOURBON

The Palais Bourbon near the Pont de la Concorde is the seat of the National Assembly. The building, erected around 1730 for one of the daughters of Louis XIV, was given a neoclassical portico and an array of sculptures during its many remodels. In 1827, it was bought by the Chamber of Deputies. The library housed there holds about 350,000 volumes, the most important of which is the original protocol of the trial of Joan of Arc.

Michel de l'Hôpital, a 16th-century lawyer and statesman, stands guard in front of the National Assembly.

The Palace of Versailles outside of Paris is the archetype of an absolutist sovereign's residence and became a model for many European royal palaces. Main picture: Wrought-iron fencing separates the Place d'Armes from the palace.

FONTAINEBLEAU

In the 12th century, King Louis VII commissioned a small hunting lodge in the forest of Fontainebleau, about 60 km (37 mi) south of Paris. After being abandoned for a while, François I had it rebuilt in 1528. Now only a single turret from the original building remains standing.

For the interior design work he hired Italian artists including Rosso Fiorentino and Francesco Primaticcio, both of whom were well known for their adaptations of the mannerist style known as the "School of Fontainebleau." The palace was subsequently remodeled on a number of occasions, in particular during the reigns of Henry IV and Napoleon.

Today Fontainebleau houses some outstanding baroque, rococo and neoclassical works of art from Italy and France. The palace was eventually extended to contain five courtyards, all with differing designs. Among its most impressive rooms are the horseshoe-shaped staircase and the luxurious ballroom. The palace gardens are also well worth seeing.

VERSAILLES

In 1661, King Louis XIV began the expansion of his father Louis XIII's hunting lodge, a location that would soon serve him as his permanent seat of government. The two leading architects, Louis Le Vau and later Jules Hardouin-Mansart, created a palace complex comprising roughly 700 rooms and vast manicured gardens that is a work of art in and of itself with plants, fountains and sculptures as well as the auxiliary garden palaces Petit and Grand Trianon.

For 100 years, Versailles was the political heart of France. At times,

This portrait by Hyacinthe Rigaud (today in the Louvre) was intended to help further glorify this absolutist monarch.

as many as 5,000 people lived at the palace, including a considerable number of French aristocrats, and up to 14,000 soldiers resided in the outbuildings and in the actual town of Versailles.

Of the many magnificent staterooms at the palace, the Hall of Mirrors has historically been seen as the most important. The room, which bewilders visitors with its size, is so named for the seventeen giant mirrors that reflect the light from the windows opposite. It is here that the German emperor was crowned in 1871 and the Treaty of Versailles was signed in 1919.

The Hall of Mirrors at the Palace of Versailles (left) measures 73 by 11 m (240 by 36 ft) and is one in a sequence of rooms created in 1678 that extends along the entire garden façade. It is a masterpiece of the baroque decorative arts. The Sun King held his morning and evening audience in his bedchamber (middle) and the palace had its own opera house (right) and theater.

In 1645, landscape architect André Le Nôtre – creator of the park at Versailles – designed the Grand Parterre at the Palace of Fontainebleau, a terraced garden with low-lying plants intended primarily for representational purposes (left).

The museums at Versailles (left, the Musée des Carosses with its historic coaches) help to recreate a grandiose past. An important conceptual component of the parks are the water gardens – canals and fountains adorned with sculptures (right). Particularly spectacular is the Apollo Basin, from which the god rises in his sun chariot pulled by horses (middle).

Reims represents the starting point for the Christianization of Gallia (Latin for Gaul), and it remained a bulwark of the Catholic Church for centuries, as is symbolized by the abbey church of St Rémi (main picture).

REIMS

Reims is in the heart of the Champagne region and enjoys a glorious history. In around 500, Clovis was anointed first King of the Franks here by St Remigius. The archbishop's bones are interred in the 11th-century St Rémi Abbey Church, where an early-Gothic choir adjoins the narrow nave and the windows date from the 12th century.

Notre Dame Cathedral, the coronation church of the French kings,

The high-Gothic cathedral of Reims has a richly decorated western façade as well as beautiful stained-glass windows by Marc Chagall.

was erected starting in 1211 on the site of an earlier church that had burned down. The building is adorned with expressive stone sculptures and the lovingly restored stained-glass windows (including some by Chagall) are vibrant masterpieces of light and color.

The archbishop's Palais du Tau, built around 1500, served as a stopping post for the French kings. Its interior features superb tapestries.

AMIENS

Situated about 115 km (71 mi) north of Paris, Amiens is both a university town and a bishop's see. The cathedral, Notre Dame d'Amiens, is one of the great churches of the French High Gothic, and its dimensions are awe-inspiring. Covering a total area of 7,700 sq m (82,852 sq ft), it is the largest church in all of France, and became the model for the famous cathedral in Cologne, Germany.

Bishop Evrard de Fouilloy laid the foundation stone for the church in 1220 and within about fifty years, by the end of the 13th century, Robert de Luzarches' plans had been nearly completed. Construction here began not with the choir but with the west towers. The cathedral consists of a three-aisled nave rising to an astonishing height of 43 m (139 ft). The west front is divided into three portals and crowned by two wide towers. It also features a large, artfully designed rose window. The portals are decorated with scenes from the Old and New Testaments, a highpoint of medieval sculpture.

About a dozen archbishops, cardinals and other church dignitaries are buried in Notre Dame d'Amiens (left).

CHARTRES

Notre Dame de Chartres is the cathedral par excellence of the High Gothic. Unlike many other cathedrals, it boasts an array of fully preserved original furnishings. The triple-aisled basilica with transept and five-aisled choir is considered one of the first purely Gothic structures and was the model for the cathedrals in both Reims and Amiens. Construction here began in the early 12th century, and the church was consecrated in 1260. Below the choir is the

The two contrasting spires of Notre Dame de Chartres (top) date from the 12th and the 15th centuries. The emphasis on vertical lines is characteristic. Middle and bottom: The church's nave and the ambulatory.

Crypt of St Fulbert (1024) – with a length of 108 m (354 ft) it is the largest Romanesque crypt in France.
New construction technologies were employed at Chartres, for example the use of flying buttresses. This permitted the walls to be interrupted by large window surfaces. This led to the use of stained-glass windows in the 12th and 13th centuries, which provide a unique light inside the building.

On a rocky island out in the English Channel, in an exclusive spot about 1 km (1,100 yds) off the Normandy coast, is the former Benedictine Abbey of Mont-Saint-Michel, the most famous landmark in the region (main picture).

CHALKSTONE CLIFFS OF NORMANDY

It is not exactly delicate, this country-side stretching along the English Channel in the north-west of France. But the wind-battered coast and verdant green hinterland have their own undeniable magic that it is impossible to escape.

The Atlantic surf, the rugged shoreline, the gleaming white chalkstone cliffs and the long sandy beaches scattered in hundreds of bays along the spectacular Normandy coast present a nature full of brute force and primordial beauty. Strewn throughout the area are sleepy fishing villages and lively port towns as well as elegant seaside spas and pleasant holiday re-

sorts. The zenith of the Normandy chalkstone cliff landscape can be found at Étretat. This tiny fishing village was "discovered" by artists in the 19th century who thought it was particularly picturesque. Situated in a quaint cove, it is romantically framed by alabaster-white cliffs with bizarre rock formations that stretch along the steep coastline.

MONT-SAINT-MICHEL

The story of Mont-Saint-Michel began in the 8th century with the Vision of St Aubert: the Archangel Michael appeared before the bishop, and in return the bishop had a small prayer hall built for pilgrims. In 1022, a new structure that incorporated the original walls was built atop the earlier church of Notre-Dame-sous-Terre. The crypt and choir, possibly the first choir ambulatory without radial chapels, were built first. After its collapse, the church was rebuilt in the late-Gothic style. In the 11th century, under Abbot Randulf of Beaumont, work continued on the crossing piers and transept, and the nave was completed at the beginning of the

12th century, under Abbot Roger I. The cross-ribbed vaults of the side aisles and central nave walls have been preserved only on the south side. The west front, with its twin towers, was completed in 1184, but burned down in 1776. People eventually settled at the foot of

the abbey and some houses from the 14th century are still standing. Due to driving sands and strong currents, Mont-Saint-Michel was difficult to reach even at low tide – it was besieged but never conquered.

The coast between Le Havre and Le Tréport is known as the Alabaster Coast – Côte d'Albâtre – after its white chalk cliffs. In some parts, they reach more than 100 m (328 ft) in height. The eroded arch west of Étretat (left) is particularly famous; it resembles an elephant's trunk plunging into the water.

BRITTANY

Brittany was home to a civilization even before the Common Era that puzzles scientists to this day. Who were the people of this megalithic culture? Did the menhirs, large stones erected between 5,000 and 2,000 BC, function as solar or lunar calendars? Or were they symbols of fertility, cult sites or markers for processional routes? We can't even begin to answer these questions.

The veil of mystery only begins to lift as of the year 500 BC. Around that time, the Celts had arrived and settled in Brittany, a region they appropriately called "Armor": land at the sea. Although they eventually converted to Christi-anity, many of their pre-Christian customs and legends have prevailed, as has the Breton language. Certain character traits of the Celts also live on: Bretons are quite imaginative people, and are known to be strongheaded and proud.

Brittany, which covers roughly 27,200 sq km (10,499 sq mi) of northwestern France, is dominated by fishing and agriculture – just about every single sea bass or monkfish ("loup de mer") that lands on European plates comes from the Breton coast. Other areas of strength here include the export of early vegetables as well as the processing of meat and milk. In addition, with 1,200 km (746 mi) of coastline, it ranks as one of the country's most popular tourist regions after the Côte d'Azur. The windswept shores, the craggy rock formations, the lush green meadows and the powerful Atlantic surf are all highlights.

Oddly, the region first achieved international fame through Asterix and Obelix. The best-known Celts since King Arthur, these cartoon characters have delighted readers around the world since 1959, when the first story by René Goscinny and Albert Uderzo was published. Unfortunately for would-be seekers, the villages they visited were only imaginary.

POINTE DE SAINT-MATHIEU

About 20 km (12 mi) west of Brest, a unique architectural complex stands atop a promontory that rises 30 m (98 ft) from the ocean (main picture): a 36-m (118-ft) lighthouse, a rectangular signaling tower, the nearby village church of Saint Mathieu, and the ruins of the former Benedictine abbey church of Notre Dame de Grâce, parts of which date back to the 12th century (west front) while most of the church goes back to the 13th to 16th centuries. The lighthouse was built in 1835, partly using the stones from the ruined church. It guides ships and sailors along the Côte des Abers, one of the most dangerous strecthes of the Breton coast.

ST. MALO

This old Corsair town, which was restored to its original state after World War II, has a lot to see including the Old Town and promenade along the fortifications.

CÔTE DE GRANIT ROSE

Off the coast from the fishing port of Paimpol lies the Île-de-Bréhat, a bird reserve. The stony shorelines and the surrounding eighty-six islands consist of red granite, which gave its name to the entire coast: Côte de Granit Rose.

POINTE DU RAZ

Pointe du Raz, near Cape Sizun, is a narrow spit of land jutting out into the Atlantic. It is almost 80 m (262 ft) high and the view across the cliffs is breathtaking.

LOIRE VALLEY

A unique collection of historic monuments is concentrated along the roughly 200-km (124-mi) stretch of the Loire Valley between Sully-sur-Loire in the east and Chalonnes in the west, a short way downstream from Angers. France's longest river meanders through sensational countryside toward the Atlantic, traversing the historic regions of the Orléanais, Blésois, Touraine and Anjou.

The establishment of towns along the Loire Valley began between 371 and 397 with St Martin, Bishop of Tours and patron saint of the Franks. After his death, his tomb in Tours became an important pilgrimage site. In 848, Charles the Bald was crowned in Orléans, and in the 10th and 11th centuries the river valley became the preferred place of residence for the Capetians. There are several important Romanesque landmarks on the Loire, among them the abbey churches of St Benoît-sur-Loire with 11th-century narthex and crypt, Germigny-des-Prés (with a mosaic from the 12th century), frescoes in Liget and Tavant, and Notre-Dame de Cunault. Fontevraud Abbey is one of Europe's largest monasteries and the burial place of the Plantagenets.

The coronation of Henry Plantagenet as King of England in 1154 created a massive empire whose centers of power were at Angers and Chinon. It was there, in 1429, during the Hundred Years' War, that Joan of Arc met the still uncrowned Charles VII and set off to liberate the town of Orléans, which was under siege by the English. Many beautiful châteaux were rebuilt or remodeled under Francis I, including the magnificent Château Azay-le-Rideau (1527) on the Indre; Chambord, the model for all Renaissance châteaux on the Loire; Blois and Amboise; and the bridge château of Chenonceaux. Villandry and Saumur are also worth seeing and there are numerous vineyards scattered throughout the region.

BLOIS

A mighty bridge leads across the Loire into the old town of Blois, which is dominated by an imposing château. In 1498, under Louis XII, Blois became the royal residence of the House of Valois, and for a few years it enjoyed status as the capital of France. The château was enlarged on several occasions, which is why the individual tracts are fashioned in different styles. Catherine de Medici, who died here, is remembered by her Oratory.

AMBOISE

Château Amboise, atop a promontory overlooking the Loire, was commissioned in 1490, by Charles VIII who hired Italian artists and landscape gardeners to build the magnificent palace on the foundations of an older castle. Francis I based his glamorous court there. An avid patron of the arts, the king invited Leonardo da Vinci to spend his last years in Clos Lucé, a mansion connected to the château via tunnel. He is allegedly buried in the château chapel.

CHENONCEAUX

Château Chenonceaux is unique thanks to the location of its extraordinary two-story gallery, which straddles the charming Cher. Built by Philibert Delorme, this important Renaissance structure was commissioned by Catherine de Medici, but the château itself had already been completed in 1521. Its isolated donjon is a relic of an earlier building, the keep, which was a characteristic element of French castles.

CHAMBORD

Chambord (main picture and above) is the largest of the Loire châteaux. Francis I commissioned this extravagant structure in1619, as a hunting lodge, with stout towers and chimneys. It has more than 400 rooms and can accommodate up to 10,000 guests during festivities and hunts. Conceived as a symbol of the king's absolutist powers, the château was actually deserted most of the time. Even later its usefulness was inversely proportional to its size. Particularly noteworthy among the furnishings are four stoves with Meissen porcelain tiles and a double-helix staircase that is said to have been designed by Leonardo da Vinci.

VILLANDRY

The magnificent Renaissance gardens are the main attraction at Château Villandry, completed in 1536 and situated 15 km (9 mi) west of Tours. Laid out in large squares, the 7-hectare (17-acre) complex is subdivided into water, music, pleasure, vegetable and herb gardens. Even the different vegetables are grouped such that their colors create geometric patterns. The plants are irrigated by an elaborate underground watering system.

AZAY-LE-RIDEAU

This château on the Indre, built in 1524, boasts harmonious proportions and a romantic location on the water – which originally served as a moat. But it did not bring good fortune to its sponsor, Gilles Berthelot, then the mayor of Tours. King Francis I was very particular when his subjects displayed their wealth too openly. Shortly after its completion, the king accused Berthelot of disloyalty and summarily confiscated his château.

CHINON

Chinon, at the confluence of the Vienne and the Loire, is dominated by a mighty castle whose origins date back to the 10th century. Henry II, King of England, enlarged the complex and made it into his residence. Only the castle's ruins remain, but it is well known as the location where Joan of Arc met with Charles VII in 1429 with the intention of persuading him to entrust her with an army to drive the English out of France.

SAUMUR

Château Saumur became world-famous as an illustration on a calendar page in the Duke du Berry's book of hours, the Très Riches Heures. Despite later enlargements, the defensive structure with four towers standing on a rocky promontory has been more or less preserved its original 14th-century state. Today, in addition to the Musée des Arts Décoratifs, the palace houses the Musée du Cheval, which documents the history of equestrianism.

FONTENAY, SAINT-SAVIN-SUR-GARTEMPE, VÉZELAY, FONTEVRAUD

With murals dating from the 11th and 12th centuries, Saint Savin sur Gartempe, known as the "Sistine Chapel of Romanesque Era", possesses the largest collection of Romanesque paintings in France (main picture: Noah's Ark).

FONTENAY

The Order of Cistercians was a closed society that rejected the reforms of the Benedictines and strove toward a more literal observance of the Rules of Saint Benedict of Nursia. The Cistercians built their first monastery in the swamps of Cîteaux in 1098, and other monasteries soon followed, all of them tucked away in rural isolation. The Order rejected any show of affluence.

The Abbey of Fontenay, consecrated by Pope Eugene III in 1147 and located some 50 km (31 mi) north-west of Dijon, was partially replaced by new buildings in the 18th century, but the ideal layout of a Cistercian monastery can still be clearly recognized: high walls surrounding the simple, harmonious complex, church and monastery forming a very closed, largely unadorned block, and around the dual-purpose structure are several service buildings that are freely arranged among parks and wooded areas. A smithy and a mill dating back to the 12th century remain in a preserved state on the grounds.

SAINT-SAVIN-SUR-GARTEMPE

The Abbey Church of Saint Savin has been miraculously spared from the destruction and pillaging that other such buildings have suffered over the centuries. Having fallen into disrepair following the French Revolution, writer Prosper Mérimée, who had become the official inspector of historic monuments in France in 1831, rediscovered the church in 1836 some 35 km (22 mi) east of Poitiers and placed it immediately under a protection order.

Thanks to modern technology employed during restoration work in the 1970s, the cycles of expressive

The frescoes in the abbey church of Saint Savin were meant to explain the contents of the Bible in popular images to the faithful, who were mostly illiterate.

murals that had been created in the 11th and early 12th centuries were saved. The paintings adorn the vaults of the central nave, covering an area of more than 400 sq m (4,304 sq ft) and representing a complete Old Testament cycle from Genesis to Exodus. The murals in the gallery and narthex depict the Life of Christ and the Apocalypse of St John. The images of saints in the crypt are executed in a simpler style. Aside from these inestimably precious murals, the abbey church also houses valuable altars from the Romanesque era.

The abbey church of Fontenay conforms to strict Cistercian ideals. Instead of benches, its interior features a bare clay floor. The choir's tombstones display the names of noblemen from Burgundy (far left) At left are the Romanesque cloisters.

VÉZELAY

On a hill above the old town of Véze-lay, about 100 km (62 mi) west of Dijon, the Basilica Sainte Madeleine (above) stands surrounded by mighty fortifications. The largest monastery church in France and a highlight of the French Romanesque, Sainte Madeleine was built between the 11th and 13th centuries and constitutes the crowning glory of the city's hill.

FONTEVRAUD

The Abbey of Fontevraud near Saumur was founded as a mixed monastery in 1101. Once the wealthiest and most powerful monastery in France, it also owes its importance to a connection with the royal house of Plantagenet, who made this their burial place.

The abbey church features strict, simple Romanesque forms. The decorations of the capitals on the clustered pillars are masterpieces (above).

The astronomical clock on Strasbourg Cathedral (main picture) is a miracle of precision and depicts the apostles passing in front of Christ.

STRASBOURG

The icon of Strasbourg is its stunning cathedral, one of the most important sacred buildings of the European Middle Ages. Begun in about 1015, it was originally Romanesque in style, but as construction work spanned several centuries, the cathedral also features elements of the Gothic.

The west front, praised for its sheer proportions and ornate portal sculptures, is an especially important element of the structure. It was a way for the citizens to create a monument for themselves after having taken on the financing of mammoth edifice in 1286. Further highlights of the cathedral are the magnificent stained-glass windows and its astronomical clock.

The cathedral square is lined with half-timbered houses, some of which are up to five stories high, including House Kammerzell and Palais Rohan, built around 1740 in Louis XV style. The historic cityscape also includes the picturesque tanners' district, La Petite France, from the 16th/17th centuries, the Ponts Couverts (a formerly covered bridge), and the Vauban Weir.

COLMAR

Colmar, the capital of the Département Haut-Rhin, combines all of the delights of the region. The river Lauch flows through the Old Town, which boasts some very picturesque and romantic sights such as the St Martin Collegiate Church, the tanners' district, and "Little Venice." Art lovers typically head straight for the renowned Unterlinden Museum. At the heart of its collection of medieval art is Matthias Grünewald's Isenheim Altar (above), created between 1512 and 1516. The highlight of the nearby Dominican Church is Martin Schongauer's grand *Virgin at the Rosebush* (1473).

RIQUEWIHR

The older inhabitants of Riquewihr often refer to their town as the "pearl of the vineyard." And rightly so: No other wine village has preserved its 16th-century appearance as well as Riquewihr. Mighty gate towers, long rows of stately Renaissance homes, and no fewer than five museums bear witness to its centuries of prosperity. Not even the line of kitschy souvenir shops along Rue de Gaulle detract from the village's charm.

The four defiant towers of the Ponts Couverts (left) are the last of originally eighty towers placed along the walls of the old imperial town of Strasbourg. The bridges linking them were covered until the 18th century, hence the name "covered bridges".

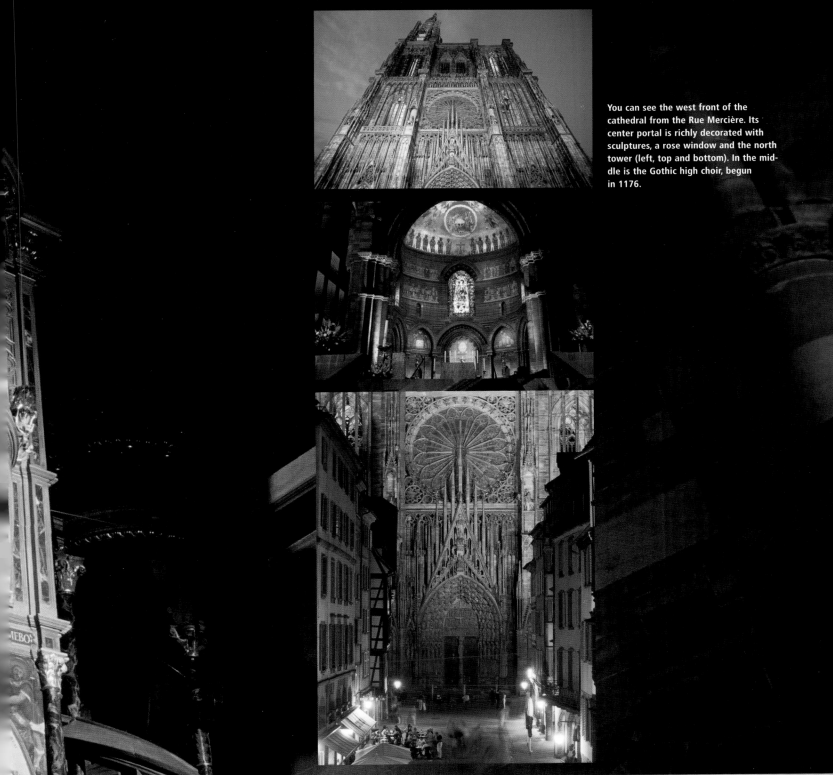

You can see the west front of the cathedral from the Rue Mercière. Its center portal is richly decorated with sculptures, a rose window and the north tower (left, top and bottom). In the middle is the Gothic high choir, begun in 1176.

MONT BLANC

No peak in the Alps is higher than "White Mountain" at 4,810 m (15,782 ft), and this fact alone draws a considerable number of visitors every year. The most common ascent is from the west along the route from Nid d'Aigle. Jacques Balmat and Michel Paccard, however, the two climbers who first scaled the mountain in August 1786, chose the route via the Grand Plateau that is only rarely used today. The venture, which basically inspired the rise of Alpinism, was initiated by Geneva scientist Horace-Bénédict de Saussure, who himself reached the summit one year later. Not much later, in 1808, Marie Paradis from Chamonix became the first woman to climb the mountain.

From the Aiguille du Midi cable car, the route continues over a steep snowy ridge to the Cosmiques Refuge at 3,613 m (11,854 ft) (main picture). The final assault on the summit (left) usually starts from there on the following day or the day after that. Left, bottom: The Mont Blanc Massif refelected in Lac Blanc in the Aiguilles Noires.

The largest gorge in the Alps lies at the extreme south-west of the chain, in the Provençal foothills, where one suddenly feels much closer to the sea than to the mountains. The Grand Canyon du Verdon is around 25 km (16 mi) long and up to 900 m (2,953 ft) deep in places. Its walls are completely vertical in some spots and are renowned for rockclimbing. Canoeists enjoy the river's twists and turns as well. The Route Panoramique affords beautiful views as you drive around the spectacular canyon.

The "Sentier Martel", established by the French Touring Club, is an excellent footpath for hikers down in the canyon. It leads from Chalet de la Maline to Point Sublime and takes six hours of meandering through towering rock formations.

West of Castellane, the modest Verdon flows between imposing rock faces that in some places are no more than 6 m (20 ft) apart at river level (above and main picture).

Cannes (main picture) is a popular stomping ground among the rich and famous, and one of the most glamorous towns on the Côte d'Azur. Luxury yachts line the port like pearls on a string.

SAINT-TROPEZ

Dense pine, oak and chestnut forests push their way down to the coastline between Fréjus and Hyères, two hills that drop off steeply toward the sea and leave no room for construction and development along the Corniche des Maures. The coastal road is all the more attractive thanks to this, winding along the wooded hills often half way up the incline and frequently offering superb views across the sea. In the numerous coves and bays, small former fishing villages huddle together having lost little of their original charm.

The motto in Saint-Tropez is to see and to be seen. The exclusive village first became famous through the film "And God Created Woman," which was shot here in 1956 by director Roger Vadim and featured his wife at the time, Brigitte Bardot. The idea of a decadent life by the sea first lured the youth of the world before the throngs of high-end tourists came rushing in. On her 40th anniversary, "BB" celebrated her retirement from cinema on the beach of Pampelonne just a couple miles from Saint-Tropez.

NICE

This secret capital of the Côte d'Azur is a town full of contrasts. While the grand boulevards cling to memories of the Belle Époque, life in parts of Nice's Old Town resembles the scenes in a village in Italy.

The Greeks founded what they referred to as Nikaia, the "victorious town", in the 5th century BC, while the Romans preferred a location higher up in the hills for their settlement, Cemenelum, present-day Cimiez. The trademark icon of Nice is the Promenade des Anglais, built in the 1830s along the waterfront by wealthy English folks who

Top: The legendary Hotel Négresco adorns the eight-lane, 5-km (3-mi) seaside promenade in Nice.
Bottom: One of the most beautiful squares in the city, Cours Saleya.

had already recognized the benefits of Nice as a desirable place to retire in the mid-19th century.

The most impressive edifices from that period are the famous Hotel Négresco and the Palais Masséna. The Old Town features narrow, winding alleyways and houses with a distinctly Italian feel. The main square, Cours Saleya, has an attractive farmers' market. From the Castle Hill you can enjoy amazingly beautiful views of the Old Town and the Mediterranean.

Jet-setters discovered the dreamy fishing village of Saint-Tropez (left) in the early 1950s. The town is said to have been named after a Roman soldier who had died a martyr's death as a Christian under Nero.

CANNES

The Celts and Romans had already established settlements around the Golfe de la Napoule in their times, but the bay did not become a popular destination until the 19th century, with the arrival of the British. Initially, they built beautiful villas for themselves before the upscale hotels followed. The Boulevard La Croisette was built around the entire bay.

Le Suquet, the Old Town, covers Mont Chevalier, a tiny hill that rises above the old port and whose summit is crowned by a watchtower dating back to the 11th century. Next to it, the Musée de la Castre displays relics from antiquity. The Gothic Notre Dame de

The luxury Carlton Hotel on the Croisette in Cannes.

l'Espérance dates from the year 1648. Magnificent views of the entire bay of Cannes unfold from the viewing platform behind the church, and on the edge of the Old Town is a giant hall that houses the Forville Market.

Cannes is of course also a town of festivals: the month of May is firmly set aside for the Film Festival, when the Golden Palm is awarded for the best film; in June, the international advertising industry meets in Cannes to select the best cinema and TV advertising spots; and in the fall, TV bosses from around the world gather there to buy and sell their programs. The venue for these activities is the Palais du Festival, at the western end of the Croisette.

The Abbaye de Sénanque (main picture) was founded by Cistercians in 1148, and had its heyday in the early 13th century before being destroyed in 1544. In 1854, seventy-two monks chanced a new beginning: Lavender fields now frame the abbey complex with its church and cloisters.

LUBÉRON

East of Avignon, halfway between the Alps and the Mediterranean, is the expansive limestone plateau of the Lubéron, a rocky landscape with lonely oak groves, small mountain villages and stone houses that has done well to preserve its impressive natural beauty. The mountains reach 1,125 m (3,691 ft) and contain some largely uninhabited stretches of land with more than 1,000 different species of plants. The "Parc Naturel Régional du Lubéron" was founded in 1977 to protect this unique environment.

The present-day isolation of many parts of the Lubéron is, however, deceptive – the limestone ridge, which was formed in the Tertiary period, has actually always been settled. The villages huddled in the hollows and valleys sprung up in the Middle Ages. Houses here have thick walls and churches served as both places of worship and refuge. The inhabitants of the Lubéron mostly depended on meager agriculture. When the harvests were no longer sufficient, the villages on the north side were abandoned.

AIX-EN-PROVENCE

In 122 BC, the Romans founded the hot springs colony of Aquae Sextiae Saluviorum on the ruins of the Celtic-Liguric settlement of Entremont. It later enjoyed the status of capital of Provence for centuries. During the Middle Ages, Aix first became an important center for the arts and learning after the 12th century.

The Old Town extends from the Cours Mirabeau, an avenue with

Developed as early as 1651, the Cours Mirabeau (top: Atlas on a house façade) forms the southern edge of the Old Town.

sycamore trees and beautiful city mansions from the 18th century, to the St Sauveur Cathedral, which has a baptistery dating back to Merovingian days. Other sights worth seeing are the 17th-century town hall, the Musée des Tapisseries and Paul Cézanne's studio. The favorite motif of the city's most famous son was Mont St Victoire to the east of Aix-en-Provence, which is worth a detour.

Flowering lavender fields are the trademark of Provence. Here, the proverbial "light of the south" is combined with beguiling scents and a riot of colors.

PONT DU GARD, ARLES, ORANGE, NÎMES

Arles was founded by the Romans due to its strategic position on the Rhône (main picture). The city also has a place in art history as the home of Vincent van Gogh, who painted some of his most famous works here.

PONT DU GARD

This famous bridge aqueduct was built between AD 40 and 60, during the reigns of the emperors Claudius and Nero, in order to supply water to the fast-growing ancient town of Nemausus, present-day Nîmes. The bridge, which spans the Gard Valley, was considered a daring feat of engineering at the time and is still a very impressive sight even in the days of glass skyscrapers.

The bottom level has a road between its six arches, which vary in width from 15 to 24 m (49 to 79 ft). The middle level has a total of eleven arches. The thirty-five arches on the top level are about 5 m (16 ft) wide and support the actual water duct, which transports roughly 40,000 cu m (1,412,587 cu ft) to Nîmes every day during high demand. The uppermost level of the bridge is about 275 m (900 ft).

The aqueduct increasingly fell into disrepair after the 4th century, and during the Middle Ages the central level was tapered so it could be used for traffic of various kinds. The structure was finally restored in the 18th century.

ARLES

Among the oldest Roman structures in Arles are the subterranean corridors of the Cryptoporticus, below the Roman Forum. More than 100 m (328 ft) long and about 70 m (230 ft) wide, the vast tunnels were likely used to store grain.

Two amphitheaters from the 1st and 2nd centuries also date back to the Romans. One of them measures

The Arena in Arles (top) is a relic of Roman days; the mighty St Trophime Cathedral (center; above: the Place de Forum) a jewel of the romanesque style.

135 m (443 ft) wide and 100 m (328 ft) long, the largest remaining open-air stage from antiquity. Its vast arena is now used for bullfights. The thermae on the right bank of the Rhône date from the late-Roman period and are part of an approximately 200-m-long (656-ft) palace complex.

The necropolis of Alyscamps and its well-preserved sarcophagi provide insight into burial customs of pre- and early-Christian days. Meanwhile, the nave at St Trophime Cathedral dates from the 11th century and is one of France's most remarkable Romanesque buildings.

The Roman aqueduct over the river Gardon (left) is a masterpiece of Roman engineering. It is part of a roughly 50-km (31-mi) pipeline that runs from the Fontaines d'Eure springs to Nîmes. The limestone blocks were placed without mortar – pressure and shape hold them together.

ORANGE

Orange enjoys a history of more than 2,000 years going back to the Romans who originally founded the town of Arausio on the site of a conquered Celtic settlement in the Rhône Valley. It is not only home to one of the best-preserved Roman amphitheaters, but it is also the largest from antiquity with a stage backdrop that measures 103 m (330 ft) by 37 m (150 ft). The theater accommodated up to 10,000 spectators to watch shows in front of the beautifully adorned wall.

Also worth seeing is the Arc de Triomphe, completed in about AD 25. It is the most completely preserved Roman archway in the region of Gallia and once marked the entrance to the town on the Via Agrippa.

NÎMES

Nîmes, a town of temples, thermae and theaters, was founded in the year AD 16 by Emperor Augustus. The most impressive Roman structure here is the amphitheater with its oval arena and rising rows of stone seats that accommodate to 25,000 spectators. The Maison Carrée, or "square house" (above) – also from the time of Augustus – features Corinthian columns and an impressive decorative freeze. It is one of the best-preserved Roman temples in Europe. The Jardin de la Fontaine has a large number of hot springs, temples and a theater.

Camargue horses (main picture) have a compact build, slightly angular heads and a dense mane. The coats on these half-wild horses are not white until their fifth year.

AVIGNON

Catholic Church history was made in the 14th century in this southern French town on the Rhône: Between 1309 and 1376, the Roman Curia found refuge here from the political turmoil in Rome and went into "Babylonian exile." In 1348, Pope Clement VI bought the sovereignty of Avignon from Joan of Naples and it became the center of Christianity. Seven popes and later two antipopes resided here in the roughly 100-year period that eventually led to the Western Schism.

The papal residence consists of an Old and a New Palace. On the north side is the 12th-century Roman cathedral Notre Dame des Doms. Also part of the bishops' district is the Petit Palais, built in 1317, which was intended to compensate the archbishop for the demolition of his original palace.

From the 14th century, Avignon was surrounded by an imposing town wall that was strengthened with fortified towers such as the Tour des Chiens and the Tour du Châtelet. The latter controlled access to the world-famous Pont d'Avignon.

MARSEILLE

France's second-largest city and the most important port in the country, Marseille boasts more than 2,500 years of history. Its importance as a major gateway for incursions into North Africa is also mirrored in the composition of its population.

The town of Massalia was originally founded by Greeks from Asia Minor on the hill where Notre Dame de la Garde stands today. Initially Rome's allies, it was not until 49 BC that Caesar finally conquered the Greek republic. The port town experienced its first major period of prosperity in the 12th century when armies of crusaders brought lucrative business to the city for their trips from Marseille to Jerusalem. In the centuries

Notre Dame de la Garde watches over the port of Marseille.

that followed it was the most important port in the Mediterranean.

Today, the heart of Marseille still beats in the old harbor. It is from there that La Canebière, the city's main boulevard, starts its way through the entire city. It was once the symbol of a vibrant city with a penchant for extravagance. The entrance to the port is flanked on the north side by Fort St Jean and on the south side by Fort St Nicolas.

The basilica Notre Dame de la Garde is Marseille's most enduring landmark and is visible from quite a distance. The square in front of it, the Plateau de la Croix, affords the best views of the port and city. Another excellent vista point across the water to Marseille is from the summit of the Château d'If rock.

Also worth seeing are the St Victor Basilica, Notre Dame de la Garde, Château d'If on a rocky island offshore from the port, and the Citadel.

View of Avignon, capital of the Département Vaucluse, from the opposite bank of the Rhône. Only four original arches remain of the much-celebrated Pont St Bénézet bridge (left). The medieval city is surrounded by 4.5 km (3 mi) of heavy fortifications.

CAMARGUE

The estuary between the two main distributaries of the Rhône comprises 140,000 hectares of swamps, meadows and grazing land as well as dunes and salt marshes – it is one of Europe's largest wetlands. Agricultural use, mostly for the cultivation of rice, is concentrated in the northern part of the Camargue; in the south-eastern portion salt is harvested in shallow lagoons. The south, however, is a nature paradise unique in Europe, with half-wild horses, bulls, and aquatic birds and waders.

The grassy meadows of the estuary are a home to the Camargue horses (top) as well as to many waterfowl and waders: about 10,000 pairs of flamingos (bottom) breed here.

More than 350 species of migratory bird stop at the "Parc Ornithologique du Pont-de-Grau" in the south-west of the Camargue. The main distinctive feature of the black Camargue bulls are their lyre-shaped horns. The white horses of the Camargue were even depicted in the ancient cave paintings of Solutré. When trained to take saddle and tack, they are untiring companions and can be of great service for herding livestock. A number of operators also offer guided excursions on horseback even for inexperienced riders that lead into the swamps, out to the beaches and to see the bulls. They allow you to see some of the normally less accessible parts of the Camargue to be enjoyed.

CARCASSONNE

Even before the Romans, Iberians had settled on the hill above the river Aude along the old trading route linking the Mediterranean and the Atlantic. In 418, the Gallo-Roman town of Carcasso fell to the Visigoths, who built the inner town fortifications in 485. In 725, the Moors conquered the town, followed by the Franks in 759. In 1229, Carcassonne fell to the French crown.

The impressive Romanesque St Nazaire Basilica was built from 1096 to 1150, during the course of the town's expansion in the Middle Ages. It was remodeled in the Gothic style in the 13th century, and the magnificent stained glass windows date from the 14th to 16th centuries. Around 1125, Château Comtal was integrated into the inner town wall complex. Construction of the outer wall and its fortified towers began at the end of the 13th century. An imposing gate, the Porte Narbonnaise, was added later, and the Pont d'Avignon is from the 12th century. The fortifications fell into a state of disrepair after about 1660 but they were reconstructed in 1844. The project was not completed until 1960.

The Great Hall of the Bulls (main picture) in Lascaux Cave features the partial portrayal of a bull among a herd of horses. The impressive prehistoric pictures impart a surprisingly realistic sense of movement.

LASCAUX

The Vézère is a tributary of the Dordogne in the heart of the Périgord Noir, a picturesque landscape whose name refers to the dark leaves of the "evergreen" oaks. The area is known for its unparalleled concentration of prehistoric cave paintings along a roughly 40-km (25-mi) stretch of the Vézère Valley. They provide us with insight into the "dawn of civilization", the humans of the Paleozoic and the Neozoic.

The most significant remains and caves are Le Moustier, La Made-

The Lascaux Cave (above) is near the Montignac am Vézère River in the valley of the same name.

leine, Lascaux and Cro-Magnon, where in 1868, five skeletons from the late Paleozoic Age were found that later became synonymous with one type of Homo sapiens. The cave paintings in the Lascaux Cave were discovered by accident on September 12, 1940, by four youths – Marcel Ravidat, Jacques Marsal, Georges Agnel and Simon Coencas – who were on an outing in the hills above the village of Montignac. There they uncovered an archaeological sensation: proof that as early as 30,000 years ago, hunters and gatherers who had settled southern France during the Ice Age had produced the first works of art in Europe. The pieces document the basic concepts of man during the Stone Age, a religion centered on animals that could be hunted for their meat, skins and fur. Since 1963, the cave has been closed for conservation reasons, but reproductions of the paintings can now be visited in another cave nearby, at Lascaux II.

CASTELNAU-BRETENOUX

The Dordogne Valley forms a deep cleft between the Limousin and the Quercy regions. The area around the gentle Dordogne River was once settled by the Petrocorians, a Gallic tribe and the reason the region is still known as the "Périgord" today.

This harmonious tourist region features gentle alluvial meadows, numerous grottoes, and even caves, some of which boast giant stalactites while others play host to impressive prehistoric paintings.

In addition to the lovely landscape scenery, the Château de Castelnau-Bretenoux is definitely worth seeing. The castle, dating back to the 13th century, attained its present size during the course of the Hundred Years' War when the somewhat irregular triangle with its three round towers and three concentric rings of walls was built. The château had space for 1,500 servants and 100 horses. Today, the magnificent panoramic views from the old fortification walls will take your breath away.

Visible from great distances, protected by massive fortifications, and famous for its mighty towers, the giant Château de Castelnau-Bretenoux (left) sits perched above the confluence of the rivers Dordogne and Cère.

ROCAMADOUR

Until the Reformation, the pilgrimage to celebrate Saint Amadour – an obscure saint whose existence is not even certain – was among the most famous in Christendom. The miraculous "Black Madonna" has been around since the 13th century as well; today she is venerated in the Chapelle Notre Dame. A rich treasure of frescoes can be admired at the Chapelle Saint Michel. To experience the extent of the entire complex, visitors should climb the 233 steps of the Via Sancta, visiting the Francis Poulenc Museum of Sacred Art en route.

Rocamadour extends along the walls of a roughly 150-m-high (492-ft) promontory that towers above the river Alzou.

SAINT-CIRQ-LAPOPIE

This village owes its double name to Saint Cyrus, the village's patron saint, and to the aristocratic La Popie family, who ruled over castle and village in the Middle Ages. The once powerful fortress was then demolished in 1580 by Henry of Navarre. Magnificent views unfold from the ruins at the highest point on the rock. The sturdy village church was built as a fortified structure in the 16th century and the narrow alleyways of the small town are lined by Gothic half-timbered houses that are leaning with age.

Saint Cirq Lapopie with its castle and fortified church crowns a roughly 80-m-high (262-ft) rock above the river Lot.

Saint-Émilion, with its mighty bell tower rising above the monolithic church (main picture), is the leading wine village in the Bordelais region. The town even has its own appellation.

BORDEAUX

Although it is about 50 km (31 miles) from the Atlantic coast, Bordeaux's position on the river Garonne has made it an important port since Roman times. One of its most important exports is the wine for which the town and the surrounding region are famous. Bordeaux preserved its medieval character until the early 18th century when, during the Enlighten-

BIARRITZ

It was here that France's wealthiest class gathered during the

SAINT-ÉMILION

This small town, which was originally formed around a monastery, is nestled amid the vineyards of the St-Émilion appellation, a region of top-quality wines. Its very special sight is the monolithic church (9th–12th centuries), whose somewhat unremarkable façade faces the pretty market square. The collegiate church dates back to the 12th century and has a Romanesque nave. Visitors should not miss the well-preserved cloisters.

The charming little town is dominated by the donjon of the Château du Roy, a relic of the royal castle. This is where the "Jurade" Confrérerie meets to judge the new wines – every year members festively declare the start of the vine harvest from the keep's platform.

ment, the prevailing intellectual climate inspired a remodel of the town into a neoclassical ensemble. First, Jacques Gabriel designed the Place de la Bourse in 1730. Then, between 1743 and 1757, the Marquis of Tourny, Louis-Urbain Aubert, took over the community. He replaced the medieval city gates with neoclassical buildings including the Place Gambetta, the Place d'Aquitaine, the Place de Bourgogne and the Place Tourny, and laid out new streets as well as gardens and parks. The façades along the quays of the Garonne were also built during that time. Many new public buildings were erected as well. Between 1810 and 1822, the first stone bridge across the Garonne was built. The old port on the left bank has been preserved in its original form.

Belle Époque. In the 1850s, Empress Eugénie chose the town as her favorite spa, and the rest of high society followed suit. Many of the hotels, such as the Hôtel du Palais, still exude the aura of that period.

Two popular destinations for strolls along the seaside include: to the north of downtown, the 44-m (144-ft) lighthouse from the year 1834, and farther south, the Rocher de la Vierge, a rock connected to land by a bridge and crowned with a statue of the Madonna. The Art Deco Musée de la Mer, which doubles as an aquarium, is also on the seashore.

Opposite the Hôtel du Palais you can see some evidence of Russian influence from Biarritz's heyday: the multi-turreted Orthodox Saint Alexander Nevsky Church.

ARCACHON

The Arcachon Basin forms a vast bay covering about 200 sq km (77 sq mi) on a coastline that is otherwise pretty straight. Part of it is protected by a nature reserve. The section of the coast from the bay to the elegant seaside resort of Biarritz is known as the Côte d'Argent, which merges into the Spanish-French Côte Basque. Aside from excellent swimming and watersport options, the main attraction here is the fascinating landscape, in particular the Dune de Pilat (far right), Europe's largest and highest sand formation. The dune measures nearly 3 km (2 mi) long, 500 m (1,640 ft) wide, and varies in height between 105 and 120 m (345 and 393 ft).

CORSICA

With the white limestone near Bonifacio (main picture), red granite rock in the Calanche and green wilderness of the Castagniccia, it is not surprising that the Greeks once called Corsica "Kalliste", meaning "the beautiful". The island not only features wide beaches and small swimming coves along a strikingly beautiful coastline, but it also has mountains and green forests that have somehow retained their unspoiled state despite the continued encroachment of civilization. Napoleon, Corsica's most famous native son, was born in Ajaccio in 1769, but he left his island home only ten years later, in 1779. After his military successes he assumed power in France and, in 1804, had himself crowned Emperor. After the "great Corsican" failed in his Russian Campaign of 1812 and the Battle of Nations at Leipzig in 1813, he was exiled to Elba. He escaped and returned to power a year later, but lost at Waterloo in 1815. He eventually died in exile on the island of St Helena.

CORTE

The citadel rises high above the town in Corte, home to the interesting Musée de la Corse. Ville Haute, Corte's upper town, has charming narrow alleyways and ancient buildings covering the eastern slope of the mountain. Corte also boasts the only university on the island, which gives the village a very special ambience. During the struggle for Corsican independence, coastal Corte was the site of many a dramatic event

GOLFO DI PORTO

Since 2006, the official term has been "Gulf of Porto: Calanche of Piana, Gulf of Girolata, Scandola Reservation". This nature reserve, part of a larger regional park on Corsica, is an ideal nesting and breeding area for many species of waterfowl such as seagulls, cormorants and the now rare white-tailed eagle. Large sections of the

BONIFACIO

The most southerly town on the island of Corsica is perched precariously on a narrow rock that has been hollowed out from below by the waves over the centuries. The bluff is surrounded by water

CAPU PERTUSATO

Along the cliffs of the "Promenade des Falaises" near Bonifacio, a coastal path leads southward for 5 km (3 mi) from the Chapelle St Roch to the Pertusato promontory. Ramblers will be rewarded by a relaxing swimming beach, a lighthouse and a beautiful view of the chalkstone cliffs. The way back is particularly impressive in the late afternoon, when the light of the setting sun illuminates the old town on the craggy coast.

on three sides. Down in the bay of Bonifacio is the district of La Marine with the small harbor. Ville Haute, as the Old Town itself is called, features narrow alleyways and tower-like buildings that bear witness to earlier sieges. Many homes still have wells and cisterns along with food storage rooms. Steep wooden stairs that could be quickly pulled up in moments of danger lead to the first story of the houses.

because the island's interior was considered a stronghold of fierce Corsican nationalists. Pasquale Paoli, the "General of the Nation", made Corte the capital of the island from 1755 to 1769. Corte is also the main starting point for excursions into the surrounding mountains. At least one day should be set aside for a visit to the magnificent Restonica Valley, which extends to the south-west town.

rocky La Girolata peninsula are covered with natural woodland where it is still possible to see vast expanses of macchia pine, which is typical of the Mediterranean. Dense eucalyptus groves also fringe the sandy beaches. The coves and grottoes on the rugged rocky coastline possess a variety of underwater fauna and flora, including some rare algae species. The area has been wonderfully preserved.

CABO FINISTERRE

The four provinces of northern Spain include Galicia, Asturias, Cantabria and the Basque Country. It was here, in small duchies in these remote hinterlands, that Christians were able to hold out against the Moors of North Africa in the early Middle Ages.
Fishing was and still is a mainstay in the area and although the weather is unpredictable, the climate is relatively mild due to the

Gulf Stream. Agriculture is also important and many small farms still operate in the green, wet valleys while steep cliffs, sandy beaches and fjord-like inlets characterize the coast.
Cabo Finisterre (main picture and lighthouse left) is the westernmost point in Spain and, for the people of the Middle Ages, was once considered the edge of the Earth. Unless it is holiday season, verdant Galicia presents itself as a tranquil landscape with a rugged coastline and long fjords cutting into the bays. People here still live off fishing and the small farms and fields are often worked using traditional methods. Over centuries of relative isolation, these provinces also have distinct languages including Gallego, Asturian, Cantabrian and Basque.

VIGO

Even in Roman times, Vigo was already an important harbor on their route between the Mediterranean and Britannia. Today it is a major transshipment hub for international commerce as well as a tuna and sardine fishery. In recent years it has also become an important sports marina.

With a natural harbor basin, Vigo boasts a lively Old Town around the former fishing district of Berbés, with charming, narrow alleyways, small bars and picturesque little plazas.

Similarly attractive are the small islands off the coast that feature superb beaches and the Parque Nacional de las Islas Atlánticas. Oyster farmers have set up their bateas, or platforms, in the middle of Vigo Bay (above).

LA CORUÑA

This vibrant port city on the wild Atlantic coast is also the capital of Galicia. The houses in the port (above) feature glazed balconies and façades that have been worn by the frequent rain and damp weather, but they exude the scent of the ocean. Medieval town walls surround the Old Town here. The many churches and palaces dating from the 18th century are also worth seeing.

PONTEVEDRA

Only a short distance from Vigo, at the end of a fjord-like inlet that extends deep into the green, hilly landscape, is the town of Ponteverde. The many churches, city palaces and burghers' mansions in the romantic Old Town are characterized by Gothic, Renaissance and baroque styles. The Plaza de la Herrería, with a 16th-century fountain of the same name (above), is the historic heart of Pontevedra.

The paintings in the Altamira Cave (main picture) were not discovered until the 19th century, but they are an important testimony to Paleolithic culture in Europe. They display quite keen skills of observation and surprising artistic mastery.

SANTANDER

The Costa Verde (right, near Santander), or "green coast", is considered by many to be the most attractive coastal landscape in northern Spain. High mountains, stunning sandy bays, and rustic fishing villages on the beautiful estuaries combine with romantic towns to give this region a very special charm. The mountainous and wooded region of the Parque Natural de Somiedo is a popular destination for hikers.

In Santander, make sure to visit the La Magdalena Peninsula with a palace built in the English style as a summer residence for King Alfonso XIII in the early 20th century. North-west of the city are some superb beaches.

ALTAMIRA

The Altamira Cave, located in the hills above Santillana del Mar, was rediscovered in 1879. At first, the paintings that were found here were believed to be fakes – it was hard to believe that Stone Age humans would have possessed such advanced artistic skills. Only further research and the discovery of additional caves whose paintings were easier to date finally proved beyond doubt that they were genuine.

Especially famous is the ceiling painting in one of the auxiliary caves. On a surface area of 18 m (60 ft) by 9 m (30 ft) it depicts a herd of bison. Brown, yellowish and red ochre paints were used, as

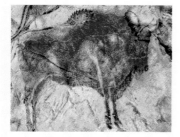

A herd of bison is depicted as life-size animals in the cave of Altamira.

well as black manganese oxide and charcoal. The shape of the natural rock was even incorporated into the images, which gives the animals an almost three-dimensional effect. The entire work inspired a nickname as well: the "Sistine Chapel of the Stone Age". Thanks to recent examinations it has now been possible to prove that the drawings date from the Old Stone Age, the Paleolithic, a time around 16,000 years ago. Today they are considered the most important remains of prehistoric art in the world.

For reasons of conservation, the original cave is more or less closed to the general public – very few visitors are allowed in and there is a waiting list – but a faithful replica has been reconstructed in a museum.

BASQUE COAST

The Costa Vasca, the coast of the Basque Country, stretches from Castro Urdiales (right) to San Sebastián (whose Basque name is Donostia) on the Bay of Biscay. Picturesque inlets, dramatic cliffs and beautiful beaches do much to attract visitors.

SAN SEBASTIAN

The capital of the Basque Country sits in the picturesque Bahía La Concha, the "Conch Bay" (right). It has one of the most attractive city beaches on the Iberian Peninsula. In the Old Town (Parte Vieja), elegant buildings reveal the glamour of the Belle Époque, when San Sebastián was the seaside resort of nobility. The lively bars are still a big draw here, and San Sebastián is the capital of tapas, known as "pintxos" in Basque. Virtually all of the signage is in two languages, for the Basques are proud of their culture. They have a long history, their own traditions, and a totally distinct language – and the city has long been a stronghold of Basque separatists.

The Guggenheim Museum, Frank O. Gehry's architectural gem in Bilbao, is one of the main attractions in the region, offering frequently changing exhibitions of paintings, video installations and sculptures by famous artists such as Roy Lichtenstein, Robert Rauschenberg, Jeff Koons, Jackson Pollock, Anselm Kiefer and Andy Warhol.

BILBAO

Bilbao has become a world city for art and architecture thanks to a unique program of urban renewal in which famous architects were asked to develop a new look for the city. The most beautiful old buildings are in the Old Town's Siete Calles (below) where seven streets feature 19th-century neoclassical buildings with bay windows and wrought-iron balconies. Among the most important new contributions are the Puente del Campo Volantin pedestrian bridge (above); the Museum of Navigation (right) and the futuristic airport, both designed by Santiago Calatrava; and Sir Norman Foster's metro stations. Bilbao's main attraction, however, is the Guggenheim Museum (main picture) by star architect Frank O. Gehry. Enthroned on the banks of the river Nervion, the imposing metal roof of this structure, made from limestone, titanium and glass and costing over 100 million US dollars, is known by locals as the "metallic flower".

Over the centuries countless pilgrims have trudged along the Way of St James from the foothills of the Pyrenees to the tomb of their beloved saint in Santiago de Compostela. The important role played by this path in the cultural exchange between peoples can be seen in the outstanding buildings that have been erected along its route. The Way itself consists of a network of several paths spread along the entire northern coast of Spain. Historically, royal protection and support from wealthy monasteries ensured safe passage through the Basque country, Cantabria and Asturias all the way to Santiago. Divided into two main routes, the Way also serves as a cultural connection between the somewhat isolated reaches of the Iberian Peninsula and the rest of Europe.

LEÓN

An important station on the Way of St James is León, once the capital of the mighty kingdom of the same name. In the middle of the Old Town is the famous cathedral (main picture) built in the 13th and 14th centuries. Among its special attractions are the ornate portals and rose windows, which are richly adorned with detailed sculptures (above).

BURGOS

The cathedral of Burgos was built in the between 1221 and 1539 from white limestone that looks like marble. The star in the dome above the tomb of the General Pedro Hernández de Velasco was designed in the shape of an eight-pointed star (above).

ASTORGA

The Via de la Plata pilgrimage route from Seville to Gijón joins up with the Camino Francés in Astorga. Highlights in the center of this small town are the cathedral dating from the 8th century (above) and the adjacent bishops' palace, designed by Antoni Gaudí, which today houses the Museo de los Caminos.

In the heart of the Old Town of León is the Santa María de Regla Cathedral (main picture), built in the 13th and 14th centuries.

LEÓN

PUENTE LA REINA

The Puente la Reina bridge (left), in the village of the same name, dates back to the 11th century and is a junction for a number of pilgrimage routes. The paths originating in Roncesvalles and Somport come together as one in the Camino Francés – pilgrims on their way to Santiago de Compostela have to cross the bridge.

PONFERRADA

Ponferrada is the last sizable town before the final destination of Santiago de Compostela. The Roman citadel was transformed into the Castillo de los Templarios (left) as early as the 12th century. An important center for the Order of the Knights Templar, it was also a refuge for pilgrims on the Way of St James.

The cathedral of Santiago de Compostela was consecrated in the year 1211 and later enlarged with chapels, a cupola and cloisters. The masterstroke and final element was the late-baroque façade. The magnificent entrance hall, Pórtico de la Gloria, dates from the Romanesque period.

Legend has it that in the 8th century pious Christians rescued the bones of the apostle St James the Greater from the Saracens in St Catharine's Monastery on Mount Sinai and brought them to Galicia. The relics were buried in a church that was built especially for that purpose. It was around the church that the town of Santiago (derived from Sanctus Jacobus) de Compostela then developed. In Spain, James became the patron saint of the Christians in their struggle against the Moors, and victory in the Battle of Clavijo in 844 was credited to his divine intervention. The news spread quickly through Europe and Santiago soon became the most important pilgrimage destination after Rome and Jerusalem. Today, thousands of pilgrims come here in July for James's Day to venerate their saint. The cathedral above the Apostle's grave dates from the 11th and 12th centuries and is Romanesque in style, but it was enlarged and remodeled several times until the 18th century. Behind the portal of the façade is the masterpiece "Pórtico de la Gloria," a narthex by Master Mateo with a Romanesque group of sculptures completed in 1188.

Pilgrims' mass is celebrated several times each day in the cathedral. The Capilla Mayor was set up above the supposed tomb of the saint. It is a splendid main altar that features a silver-plated sculpture of St James. One of the church treasures is the altar with the crucified figure of Christ.

The Pyrenees form a natural border between Spain and France. Only in the east has the small principality of Andorra managed to squeeze itself between the two countries. In the Parque Nacional d'Aigües Tortes, the peak of the Estany d'Amitges (main picture) rises to 2,380 m (7,809 ft).

NATIONAL PARKS IN THE PYRENEES

Like the Alps, the Pyrenees emerged some 50 to 100 million years ago as so-called fold mountains. Peaks in the range reach heights of more than 3,000 m (9,843 ft). On the Spanish side, two large expanses are now national parks that serve to protect the landscape, animals and plantlife: the Parque Nacional de Ordesa y Monte Perdido, and the Parque Nacional d'Aigües Tortes farther to the west with countless lakes and rich flora and fauna at the foot of rugged mountains. The name of the latter means "contorted waters" and refers to the streams that wind their way through the deep gorges and valleys.

The heart of the Parque Nacional de Ordesa y Monte Perdido in the upper valley of the river Arazas is a gorge whose walls are roughly 1,000 m (3,281 ft) high. In the spring, snowmelt rushes down the mountains from peaks that are still covered by glaciers. The footpaths of the Circo de Soaso are best explored between May and September.

SALARDÚ

Because of its strategically important location at the confluence of the Garona and the Unhóla rivers, the Aran Valley town of Salardú (1,265 m/4,150 ft) was fortified back in the Middle Ages. At the time, the upper village was dominated by a castle. The Sant Andreu Church dates from the 12th and 13th centuries; the bell tower was not added until the 15th century. The interior (above) is adorned with frescoes from the 16th century that depict scenes from the life of Christ and images of numerous saints. It also houses a Romanesque sculpture of Christ of Salardú dating from the end of the 12th century.

VALL DE BOÍ

Between the 11th and 12th centuries, every village in the Catalan Boí Valley on the edge of the Pyrenees was given a church of its own. These Romanesque structures are of an outstanding artistic quality, especially considering their rural surroundings.
They were probably built on the initiative of the priest St Raymond of Barbastro, who wished to assert his claim to spiritual jurisdiction. The village of Taüll is home to Santa María and Sant Climent, the most important churches in the region (above, a fresco detail).

The Valle de Ordesa (far left) runs through the heart of a national park of the same name. Here, the Cinca Waterfalls (center) cascade over fabulous rock formations. The Cañon de Añiscló (left) is a deep gorge tucked into the rugged limestone rocks of the Pyrenees.

MONASTERIO DE SAN JUAN DE LA PEÑA

The famous monastery of Saint John of the Rock can be reached either from Santa Cruz de la Serós on a narrow bumpy road leading roughly 8 km (5 mi) through oak and beech forests, or from Jaca via the Oroel Pass at 1,080 m (3,543 ft). At the summit of Monte Pano is the 17th-century "upper monastery", which was plundered when Napoleon invaded and of which only the baroque façade remains. Entering there, visitors step into a complex whose most important component is the "lower monastery", which is more than 1,000 years old. This was a unique structure in the Romantic period, hewn from a giant

The cloisters of the San Juan de la Peña Monastery, which is also famous thanks to the legend of the Holy Grail, were built under a rock overhang.

natural cave in the rocks. According to legend, the Holy Grail was even kept here at some stage.

The complex of buildings comprises two churches. The older one contains the tomb of Jimena, wife of legendary nobleman El Cid. The other one holds the tombs of the kings, including the mortal remains of the first monarchs of Aragon. A room that was originally a dormitory for Benedictine monks can also be visited.

The magnificent cloisters are a unique site, positioned between the rocks and the abyss like a guardrail. The capitals depict scenes from the Old and New Testaments in a series of chronological sequences.

For most visitors, a visit to the Costa Brava means relaxation on golden beaches with clear waters, picturesque fishing villages, small towns and excursions into the mountainous hinterland. With its mild climate and low precipitation, this coast was an early discovered for tourists. The small village of Cadaqués is here, tucked into a charming bay and once frequented by artists such as René Magritte, Pablo Picasso and Henri Matisse, and where Salvador Dalí lived. Girona, further inland, is the largest town on the Costa Brava. One of the most attractive villages is Tossa de Mar, where Marc Chagall lived for a while. Some of his paintings are exhibited in the Museu Municipal in the old town.

Above the bay of Tossa de Mar is the Old Town of Vila Vella guarded by the round towers of the still intact fortifications (main picture).

TOSSA DE MAR

The name of this small village goes back to the ancient Roman town of Turissa, whose ruins can be visited in an excavated site. Tossa, considered one of the flagship resorts of the Costa Brava, which extends northward from here, has largely managed to pre-serve the charm of its more than 1,000 years of history.

The only way to reach this charming town is on a winding coastal road. Along the way it is worth stopping at one of the many viewpoints (left). Below: The beach in Tossa de Mar.

FIGUERES

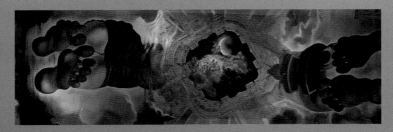

The most important attraction in Figueres is by far the Dalí Museum (above, a Dalí fresco inside the museum). In fact, after the Prado in Madrid it is the most visited museum in the country.

The surrealist painter Salvador Dalí was born near Figueres in 1904. He lived there for many years and also died in Figueres in 1989. Right: A detail of the museum's exterior.

CADAQUÉS

This fishing village is off the beaten track for most tourists, and was hardly known at all until famous artists such as Salvador Dalí visited or even settled here. Dalí's former house is down at Port Lligat. From then on, the Surrealists and other like-minded artists flocked to the isolated and beautifully situated village. Today, Cadaqués is still an attractive small town with picturesque white buildings. Like in an open-air museum, you can still come across pieces by the artists who once frequented the enclave.

GIRONA

Girona straddles both banks of the Onyar, a river that is easy to cross on one of the dozen or so bridges. On the right bank of the river there are significant remains of the original town walls. On the left bank of the river is the very lively, so-called New Town,

which actually dates back to the 19th century.
Girona Cathedral (above, seen through the bridge balustrades) harmoniously combines different architectural styles, making it one of the most beautiful churches in all of Spain.

BARRI GÒTIC, LA RAMBLA, PLAÇA DEL REI, LA BOQUERIA

Barcelona, bustling metropolis with 1.7 million inhabitants, is the capital of Catalonia and for some the true capital of Spain. A Mediterranean city, it has a romantic Old Town as well as a New Town with wide boulevards that invite strollers and shoppers.
The city has a lively history: Hannibal's father is said to have originally founded it, and it eventually became an important stronghold for the Romans. During the Middle Ages it was in the hands of the caliph of Córdoba before becoming the residence of the kings of Aragón. Today, Barcelona is a city of culture, industry and trade. The Barri Gòtic, the Gothic Old Town, invites you to wander the alleyways; la Rambla leads down to the port where a monument to Columbus has been erected. On the medieval Plaça del Rei is the palace of Catalan and Castilian kings. The nostalgic La Boqueria market presents an overwhelming selection of goods.

PALAU DE LA MÚSICA

The Palau de la Música Catalana (Palace of Catalan Music) is the most important concert hall in Barcelona. Designed by Domènech i Montaner in 1908 for the "Orfeo Catalá" chorus, the steel frame of this Art Nouveau building is clad in shiny, colorful materials, including ceramics and stained glass. Some famous artists of the Catalan Art Nouveau style joined in the design of the interior as well, making the harmonious combination of light and space a particularly impressive element. Also noticeable are the lavish flowers and climbers ornamenting the ceiling, walls and columns of the hall along with dragons' heads and other sculptures.

The Art Nouveau style is embodied in a special way by the Sagrada Familia (main picture), which features spindly turrets and organic shapes inspired by nature. Left from top: The Plaça del Rei; La Boqueria; a street artist on la Rambla.

In the very heart of the Barri Gòtic is Barcelona's cathedral, which dates from the 14th century. Following a very long tradition, geese are the guardians of the prayer in its cloisters.

SAGRADA FAMILIA, PALAU GÜELL, PARQUE GÜELL, CASA MILÀ, CASA BATLLÓ, CASA VICENS, COLONIA GÜELL

Architect Antoni Gaudí i Cornet is considered an outstanding representative of Modernism, or Catalan Art Nouveau. He created some of his most magnificent buildings in Barcelona such as the Sagrada Familia (main picture), a church that was originally designed in the neo-Catalan style in 1882, and which has still not been completed. For Eusebi Güell, a generous patron of the arts, Gaudí designed an idiosyncratic city mansion, the Palau Güell, which was completed in 1889 after four years of construction. Typical for the artist, ornamentation and organic forms dominate here.

The Parque Güell was conceived as a small garden city. Although the park was created according to detailed plans from 1900 to 1914, it seems to have grown naturally. The Casa Milà (left), built between 1905 and 1911, is a multi-story apartment block whose bizarre design makes it hard to distinguish architecture and sculpture. The Casa Batlló (right) is a magnificent city mansion with a roof designed by Gaudí to represent a large dragon and adorned with mosaic chimneys. For the interior design of the Casa Vicens, Gaudí adapted some ideas from Mudéjar architecture. Of the Colonia Güell Church, he was only able to complete the crypt, but a drawing by the master exists that gives you an idea of how the structure was supposed to have looked in its final form.

Plaza Mayor de Salamanca (main picture) is a square surrounded by arcades laid out in the baroque style according to plans by Alberto Churriguera. All buildings have four stories and balustrades.

SEGOVIA

The medieval Old Town of Segovia straddles a mountain ridge and boasts a rich architectural heritage that includes more than twenty Romanesque churches. In order to channel fresh water from the Río Frío to Segovia over a distance of 18 km (11 mi), the Romans built an impressive aqueduct with a total length of 730 m (750 yds). The bridge, erected in the 2nd century AD, rests on 118 arches and was built from specially designed granite blocks that do not require the use of mortar. The complex was last renovated in the late 15th century.

The city's many Romanesque churches are remarkable for their characteristic ambulatories, which served as meeting places for guilds and fraternities. Work on Segovia's late-Gothic cathedral was begun in 1525 on the site of an earlier structure that had been destroyed by fire.

In 1474, Isabella of Castile's coronation took place in the Alcázar fort, which stands high above the town on a rock and received its present Gothic look in the 13th century.

SALAMANCA

Salamanca was conquered by the Romans in the 3rd century BC and destroyed later on several occasions by the Moors. It achieved great importance after 1085, when it was reconquered by King Alfonso VI of Spain. The university, founded in 1218 by Alfonso IX, was regarded as one of the four most important universities in the West along with Oxford, Paris and Bologna. Its façade is a masterpiece of the plateresque Renaissance style.

Plaza Mayor (top) is the heart of Salamanca and is dominated by the baroque façade of the town hall. Center and above: New and Old Cathedrals harmonize despite their different architectural styles.

Salamanca is also rich in Romanesque and Gothic buildings. The 12th-century Old Cathedral is one of few preserved churches showing Romanesque-Byzantine influences. The church was eventually incorporated into the complex of the New Cathedral, which was begun in 1513 and features late-Gothic, plateresque and baroque elements.

Two buildings tower over Segovia's Old Town (left): the Gothic cathedral in the center of town and the Alcázar (from the Arabic for fort) on the western fringes.

ÁVILA

Ávila is perhaps the most attractive example of a medieval town in all of Spain. Ávila's Gothic cathedral rises like a bastion above the battlements of the nearly flawlessly preserved town fortifications. Construction of the town walls was started as early as about 1090, but it was not until the 12th century that they received their present appearance, which reflects a rather simple rectangular plan. The "ciborro" is the mightiest of its towers, and serves at the same time as the church's apse.

Ávila's town walls feature nine gates and eighty-eight towers (top). The interior of the church is spectacularly high (center). Bottom: The interior of San Vicente, one of the most beautiful churches in the town.

The church, which is incorporated into the fortifications like a bulwark, is one of the oldest cathedrals in Spain. Its interior houses masterly sculptures. There are also some remarkable medieval churches outside the town walls, the most interesting of which is probably the 12th-century San Vicente with its historically significant collection of Romanesque sculptures.

EL ESCORIAL

In 1561, eager to express his hunger for power and bolstered by his successes in the war against France, Philip II commissioned the construction of a vast palace in Escorial, some 60 km (37 mi) northwest of Madrid. The original architect was Juan Bautista de Toledo; after his death, Juan de Herrera took over in 1567, supervising construction until near completion in 1584. The rectangular complex (above) covers a vast area of more than seven acres and provides space for sixteen courtyards. It is equipped with nine towers.

The composition of the buildings was inspired by the Temple of Jerusalem, and thanks to its perfect symmetry it remained for a long time the prototype for many other extravagant palaces across Europe. The magnificently furnished royal mausoleum houses the remains of all Spanish monarchs since Philip II. In addition to the countless private and staterooms of the royal family, the comprehensive library (main picture) is an impressive feat that contains many priceless volumes.

MADRID

The capital of Spain is not only the geographic heart of the Iberian peninsula, but it was at one point also the center of an empire in which "the sun never set." Over centuries, dynasties such as the Habsburgs and the Bourbons each left their own mark on the city. Accordingly, the cityscape is wildly diverse even in the center. Since the end of the Franco dictatorship in 1975, Madrid has undergone a rapid change and developed from a sleepy administrative town into a pulsating world city.

As the capital, Madrid has been a big draw for artists and merchants since the 16th century. Velazquez and Goya were invited as painters to the Spanish royal court, during which time they created some of their famous masterpieces. A com-

prehensive collection of paintings from them and other artists can now be admired in the Museo del Prado, one of the most famous classical collections in the world. It comprises more than 9,000 works of art including Goya's 1814 piece *The shooting of the rebels on May*

3, 1808 (above), 5,000 illustrations and 700 sculptures. The capital naturally has a wealth of other world-renowned museums as well. In terms of its architecture, Madrid features a great variety of styles ranging from the Renaissance in the "Madrid de los Austrias" district (for example, the Monasterio de las Calzas Reales, right) to the baroque and neoclassicism in the Palacio Real (top) and a range of Art Deco and postmodernist edi-

fices around town. The impressive main square of the city – and the model for many other Spanish squares – is the 17th-century Plaza Mayor (top left with the equestrian statue of Philip III). San Francisco el Grande (left bottom) is a domed church built in 1770 on the site of an earlier Franciscan monastery and holds important paintings by Goya, Velázquez and others.

Documentation shows that a church was built as early as the 9th century where today the Nuestra Señora de la Almudena Cathedral (top right) stands. Incidently, the cathedral was not consecrated until 1993, after more than 100 years of construction.

TOLEDO

The Middle Ages still seem to be alive wherever you go in this city on the Tagus, and its location is superb. Toledo's Old Town straddles a rock surrounded on three sides by the river far below in a deep gorge (main picture). A first panoramic view from the opposite bank of the river gives you some insight into Toledo's architectural gems. The cathedral, the Alcázar (from the Arabic for fort), and a number of medieval structures form a wonderful architectural ensemble, and narrow alleyways typify the Old Town, which is surrounded by a wall with towers.

Toledo is a veritable treasure chest of Spanish architectural jewels. The town's icon is the Cathedral, built from the 13th to the 15th centuries on the site of a former Visigoth church and an old Moorish mosque. While its exterior displays the typical features of pure French Early Gothic, the building's interior, which is a stately 110 m (350 ft) in length, is a textbook example of Spanish Late Gothic. The three portals on the main façade are richly adorned with reliefs and sculptures. The Capilla Mayor shows a multitude of biblical scenes in which

the life-size figures are carved from larch pine and then painted or gilded. At the highest point in the town is the Alcázar. The façade of this almost square building dates mostly from the 16th century. The way up to the fortress starts from the Plaza de Zocodover and the centrally located triangular square is the true heart of the city.
Other attractions in Toledo include the Franciscan San Juan de los Reyes Monastery (15th-17th centuries) and the Casa El Greco; the painter lived in Toledo for nearly forty years.

ARANJUEZ

This town, which was laid out according to a strictly geometric plan, is famous for its gardens – and not just since the Concierto de Aranjuez by Rodriguez. The largest park is the Jardín del Príncipe in the north-east, which was created from plans by French landscape gardeners in 1763. The Casa del Labrador is a small palace in the garden that is worth seeing. In another building, the Casa de Marinos, six royal boats are on display. The royal palace (left), to the south of the gardens, was rebuilt after two fires in the 17th century. Its main façade combines style elements from the Renaissance and the baroque.

The Casa Lonja Archive (main picture) houses documents that provide an insight into the relationship between Spain and its former colonies. Of the mosque that once stood here, only the La Giralda Minaret (inset below) has been preserved – now the steeple of the city's cathedral. It is one of the most important religous buildings in the world.

Moorish invaders from North Africa built the Great Mosque after their initial conquest of Seville in 712, but it was ultimately destroyed during the Reconquest in the year 1248. Only the Giralda minaret survived, indeed a masterpiece of Almohade architecture from the late 12th century, but it was converted into the steeple of the new cathedral, the largest Gothic structure of its kind in the world. Its chapels house important paintings by Murillo, Velazquez and Zurbarán.

The mighty Alcázar (from the Arabic for fortress) obviously also goes back to Moorish times and features detailed ornamentation in its beautiful court-yards. In the 13th century, the palace became the seat of the king and in subsequent centuries it was enlarged in the Mudéjar style (a name given to Muslims who stayed but did not convert to Christianity). Its beautiful gardens are an example.

Casa Lonja (1598) was once the main market for goods from the colonies. In 1785, it was converted into the Archivo General de las Indias, where documents about the history of Latin American exploration are kept.

The Alcázar (left), begun in 1364 on the remains of another Moorish fortress, is one of the best-preserved examples of the Mudéjar style, which combines elements of Islamic architecture with Gothic influences. The cathedral's organ and the sarcophagus of Columbus are impressive pieces (below).

MEZQUITA

Córdoba was an important center of politics and culture even in Roman times, as is evidenced by the Puente Romana bridge across the river Guadalquivir (above). With its sixteen arches, it was once part of the Via Augusta, a road stretching from Cádiz to the Pyrenees. One of Córdoba's most important sons was the Roman philosopher Seneca. In the year 929, the Caliphate of Córdoba also rose as the shining star of Al-Andalus and thus competed for fame with Baghdad, also a major world city. As in many cities at the time, Jewish, Arabic and Christian cultures lived peacefully together here while science and philosophy flourished.

In the Old Town, around the Mezquita, some of this spirit can still be experienced today. At its height, Córdoba was a powerful city of one million inhabitants with great influence within the Caliphate. It is now a provincial capital with a population of only about 300,000, but Córdoba is still a magical city in white. In particular, the Old Town with its narrow alleyways, whitewashed houses and flowery courtyards is truly idyllic. In the center stands the Mezquita, the mighty fortress that was once a mosque and is now a cathedral.

The vast former prayer hall (main picture) of the Great Mosque has 856 ornate columns and creates an wonderful ambience. Nineteen naves and thirty-six transepts, splendid Moorish adornments and mysterious light between the columns make any visit to the Mezquita an unforgettable one.

JUDERÍA

Immediately next to the Mezquita is the Judería, the former Jewish quarter with its narrow alleyways and flower bedecked balconies (above). One of the most attractive of these is the Calleja de las Flores (Lane of Flowers).

Also worth a visit are the former synagogue and the bullfighting museum, which happens to be one of the most interesting of its kind in Spain. The Alcázar de los Reyes Cristianos, the royal palace built as a fortress in the 14th century, has beautiful gardens. The Museo Arqueológico Provincial, housed in a stunning Renaissance building, displays Roman, Visigoth and Moorish relics. Not far away, in the quarter around the Christian churches, stands the inviting Palacio de Viana, a manor house with twelve courtyards and magnificent gardens.

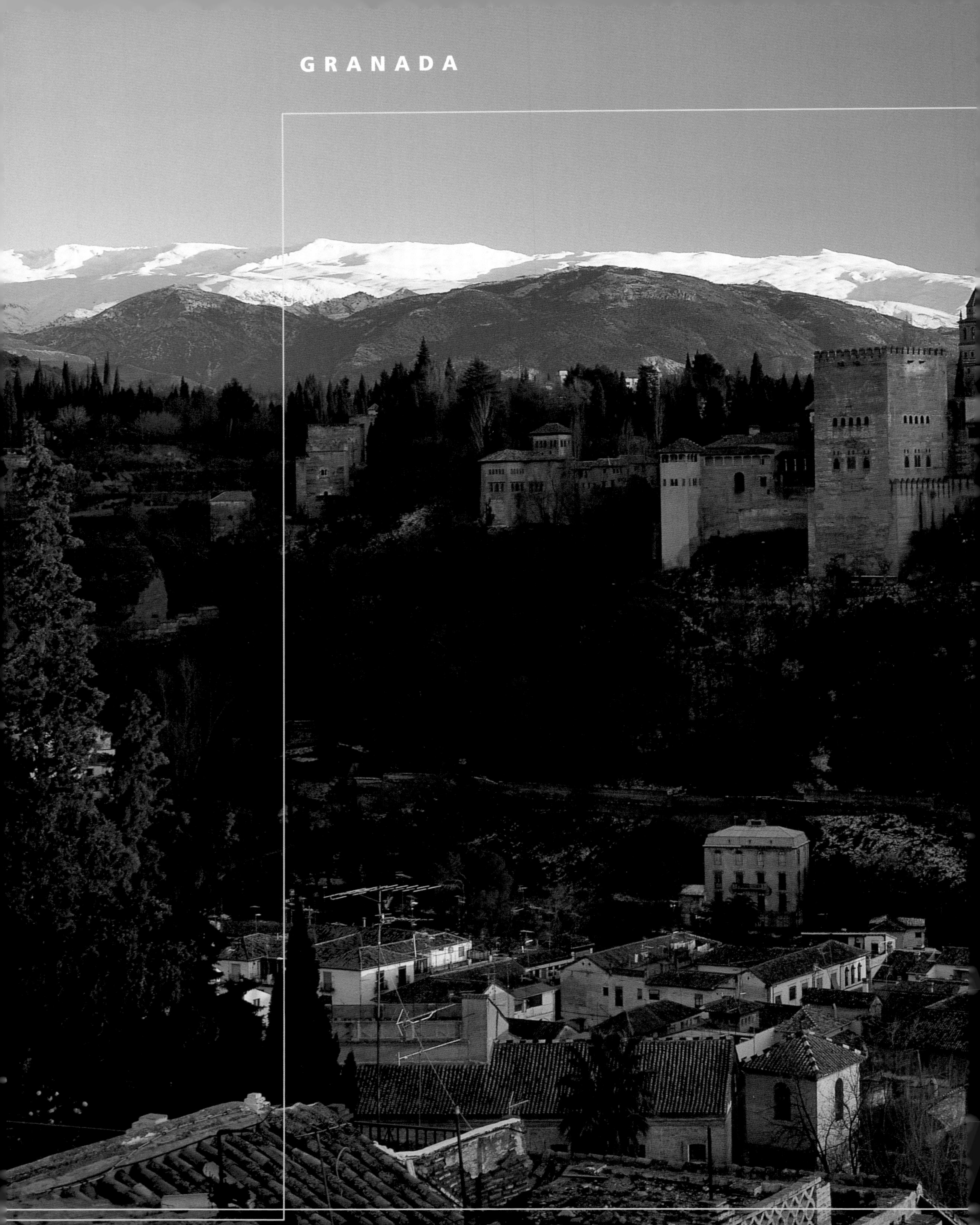
GRANADA

ALHAMBRA

The south of Spain remained under Moorish rule even after the so-called Caliphate of Córdoba had ended in 1031. In 1238, for example, Granada became an independent Islamic kingdom, and its rulers built the magnificent complex of the Alhambra. In 1492, the town was the last Moorish possession to be "reconquered" by Christian Spanish rulers.

Probably the most famous part of the Alhambra is the Patio de los Leónes, the Court of the Lions (far left). In the middle of the patio, surrounded by richly decorated arcades (far left), is a fountain supported by twelve lion sculptures the likes of which are extremely rare in Islamic art outside of the Iberian Peninsula. They endow the ensemble with a very special character.

After the 16th century, the fortress palace of Alhambra grew more and more dilapidated until a large part was lavishly restored in the 19th century.

The cathedral, which was built after the end of Moorish rule, contains the graves of the Spanish kings. In the Alhambra district stands the uncompleted palace of Charles V, which was begun in 1526, with total disregard for the existing Moorish structure.

JEREZ DE LA FRONTERA, CÁDIZ, GIBRALTAR, COTO DE DOÑANA

JEREZ DE LA FRONTERA

the advanced culture of Islam; Jerez is renowned as the origin of sherry, as the British called it (left, Pedro Domecq Bodega); and for horse lovers, Jerez thoroughbreds have an excellent reputation as the icons of the Royal Riding School (bottom).

For some, the name of this town conjures up the year 711, when Moorish General Tarik beat the Visigoths. Others think of sherry, the most important local product, and for others horses come to mind. Indeed, all of these views would be accurate: the Moorish armies opened medieval Spain to

CÁDIZ

Cádiz, founded by the Phoenicians as an important trading port west of the Strait of Gibraltar, is one of Europe's oldest towns. The golden dome of the New Cathedral towers above the Old Town (above). Among its church treasures is the largest and most precious processional monstrance in the world.

COTO DE DOÑANA

Since 1969, the marshy estuary of the Guadalquivir River has been protected in the Coto de Doñana National Park. Many rare animals including golden eagles, flamingos, cranes, herons, storks, lynxes (above) and wild horses live in this pristine national park, the largest in Spain.

GIBRALTAR

This British enclave, covering only about 6 sq km (2 sq mi) but still inhabited by some 30,000 people, controls the strait that passed between Europe and Africa (above). Its name derives from "Djebel al-Tarik", the "Mountain of Tarik", named after the Moorish conqueror who arrived in 711.

The ocellated lizard (main picture) also enjoys life in the marshes of the Coto de Doñana National Park. Europe's largest lizard, it normally grows to between 50 and 70 cm (20–28 in) in length.

Steep cliffs are typical of the Cap de Formentor in the north-east of Mallorca. Wind and water have created a spectacular coastline here.

MALLORCA

"If you like Paradise," wrote Gertrude Stein, "Mallorca is paradise." Every year, this Mediterranean island is visited by millions of tourists, and yet it still has some quiet bays and breathtaking landscapes. Mallorca is an island like an entire continent, with wilderness and surprisingly high mountains in the north, vast almond plantations and cornfields in the interior, and miles and miles of beaches and coves in the south. A holiday paradise with an area of 3,640 sq km (1,405 sq mi) and surrounded by turquoise seas, its capital Palma (right center with the La Seu Cathedral towering high above the port) is the most

prosperous town in Spain by gross national product. And those who wish to escape the bustle of the coastal resorts between Andratx and Arenal, and discover the beauty of nature and meet the people in the small villages, will only have to go a short way inland. The mountain village Vall-

demossa (right bottom), for example, boasts a charterhouse whose monks' cells were converted into small apartments in the 19th century. In 1838/39, Frédéric Chopin and George Sand lived there, a fact that has attracted music lovers from around the world ever since. Near the Port de Vallde-

mossa is the majestic Son Marroig (far left top), former summer residence of the Austrian Archduke Ludwig Salvator on the "Costa Brava Mallorquina." An excursion to Cap de Formentor, the northernmost point of this spectactular island, is indeed breathtaking (above and main picture).

MENORCA

IBIZA

Covering an area of 716 sq km (276 sq mi), Menorca is only about one-fifth the size of Mallorca. And it is this fact to which it owes its name, Menorca (the "smaller one"). "La Isla verde y azul", or "the island of blue and green", is divided into two regions named after the prevailing north and south winds: the Tramuntana in the north and the Migjorn in the south. The border between these two regions, which are very different geologically, runs along the road from Maó (above), the island's capital, to Ciutadella (top right). Around sixty per cent of the roughly 87,000 people on Menorca live in these two towns. It is the

least densely inhabited island in the archipelago with less than ten per cent of the total Balearic population.
The Cala Macarelleta (below) is one of Menorca's paradisical bays. Many visitors come by boat and drop anchor in the bay, which can only be reached via footpath.

Ibiza and Formentera form the western end of the Balearic Islands, which together form an autonomous region (and province) of Spain. High above the steep coast at Cap Jueu on the south-western tip of the island, you can see the uninhabited islands of Vedranell and Es Vedrá from the "Torre del Pirata".
Eivissa, the official Catalan name for Ibiza (above) is the island's main town, administrative center and also a bishops' see. Though it is most famous for having the most lively party scene and night-clubs in the Mediterranean, Ibiza also has an imposing fortress in the upper town.

GRAN CANARIA

Gran Canaria is an island of contrasts. The poet Miguel de Unamuno called its wildly rugged central mountain range, with V-shaped valleys ("barrancos") converging like rays on the island's edge, the "tempestad petrificada," or the "petrified thunderstorm". The Tamadaba Nature Park on the west coast of the island is a superb adventure.
The main picture shows the "Dedo de Dios," the "finger of God" – tall needles that have withstood the waves of the Atlantic for millennia. The subtropical north with its lush vegetation is contrasted by the desert landscape of Maspalomas (bottom) in the south.

Columns on the rocky coast at Los Gigantes on Tenerife with the summit of Pico de Teide in the background. It is covered in snow until mid-spring.

TENERIFE

The landscapes of Tenerife are as varied as its climate zones, and range from verdant green in the north to rugged mountains and desert-like expanses in the south. Life in the coastal towns is modern European. San Cristóbal de La Laguna is a lively university town and the cultural capital of the island. In the more isolated mountain villages, people still lead more traditional lives.

Thanks to its species-rich vegetation, many visitors regard Tenerife as the most beautiful of the Canary Islands. The Teide National Park, for example, is not only home to Spain's highest mountain, Pico del Teide (left) at 3,718 m (12,199 ft), but also to a fascinating volcanic landscape with a vast variety of flora and fauna.

LANZAROTE

Like Aphrodite, the Greek goddess of love, the Canary Islands were born out of the sea, shaped by the power of the Atlantic Ocean and the eruptive force of magma in the Earth's core. Volcanic plumes rose 1,500 to 3,000 m (4,922 to 9,843 ft) or even higher, through the African tectonic plate, which then drifted eastward.

This natural spectacle is most conspicuous on Lanzarote which, along with Fuerteventura, is one of the oldest islands in the Canaries, estimated to have developed some sixteen to twenty million years ago. More than 300 volcanoes and craters mark the surface of Lanzarote.

In the middle of Lanzarote, roughly between Uga and San Bartolomé, is La Geria (left), the largest wine-growing area in the Canaries. In a necessary but painstaking process, the Lanzaroteños work the local black lava landscape in which each vine is placed behind a small semicircular wall in order to shelter it from the constant strong winds off the coast. From a distance it looks like a multitude of small, green oases in the middle of a black desert. Quite a sight.

More than one-fifth of the surface area of Lanzarote (main picture) is covered by a layer of hardened lava and ash. And yet plants continue to find rock fissures to grow in.

LA GOMERA

Of the seven major Canaries, La Gomera possesses the greatest climatic diversity within the smallest area. The terraced fields of the farmers dominate in the rainy north, while hotels and beaches characterize the south. The Garajonay National Park (above) covers 4,000 hectares (9,884 acres), roughly one-tenth of the entire island, and includes all six of the island's communes. On the slopes

of the Alto de Garajonay you will find the dense but last remains of southern Europe's virgin subtropical forest, including the only laurel forest on earth from what used to be referred to as the Tertiary. Surrounded by the ocean, forests of that geological era, which is more than 65 million years ago, managed to survive the deteriorating climatic conditions during the Ice Age. Many of the animal and plant species occurring in this area are native.
The mists in Garajonay National Park often creep to the laurel forest floor, creating a sort of horizontal rain. This primeval ecosystem allows us to contemplate how the forests may have looked like when the islands were still part of the European landmass.

LA PALMA

La Palma, the green island ("Isla Verde"), is also known as "Isla Bonita", "the beautiful island". Mountains with alpine diversity, deep gorges, a mild climate, evergreen vegetation and low-key tourism give this, the most northwesterly of the Canary Islands its charm. Above: Historic houses on the Avenida Marítima in the harbor of Santa Cruz de la Palma, the island's capital.

EL HIERRO

In antiquity, the smallest of the islands was known as the westernmost point of the Old World, and the prime meridian was defined in 1634 as running through a promontory on its west coast (replaced by the Greenwich prime meridian in 1884). The middle of the island features a high plateau with around 1,500 ash cones, dominated by the 1,501-m-high (4,025-ft) Malpaso. Above: El Golfo Bay.

TORRE DE BELEM

The richly adorned tower of Belém (main picture) was built in 1521 on the orders of Manuel I as a watchtower to protect the Tagus estuary, the location where Portuguese sailors once embarked on their journeys of exploration. With its many balconies and battlements, Belém is an impressive example of Manueline architecture and also one of Lisbon's most famous landmarks.

The massive multi-story building, which in later periods served as both a weapons arsenal and a state prison, displays Moorish, Gothic and Moroccan influences. Its grand presence was meant to welcome home the captain and crew of richly loaded ships and at the same time, because of its similarity with a ship's bow, persuade potential enemies that the armada had left the harbor for a counterattack.

Over centuries, the Tagus silted up so much that the tower today no longer stands at the estuary but on the riverbank. There are superb views from the highest platform at 35 m (115 ft).

ALFAMA, BAIRRO ALTO, BAIXA

A sea of houses climbs from the wide estuary of the river Tagus up the steep hills of the "white city". Lisbon, the capital of Portugal, has a superb location that attracts visitors from around the world who, like the locals, travel aboard the city's "eléctricos", rickety old trains that squeak their way through town. Particularly worth seeing is the Alfama, Lisbon's oldest and most picturesque neighborhood, a labyrinthine Old Town on Castle Hill, which is crowned by the ruins of the Castelo de São Jorge. Between the castle ruins and the medieval Sé Cathedral are two of many miradouros, attractive viewing platforms that Lisbon is famous for and from which you can enjoy spectacular views across the city. Author Fernando Pessoa, a native of Lisbon, said of his city there exists "no flowers that can match the endlessly varied colors of Lisbon in the sunlight.".

Lisbon is divided into an upper town (the bairro alto) – the entertainment quarter with its lively pubs, traditional restaurants and fado bars – and a lower town (the baixa), which was rebuilt after the devastating earthquake of 1755 according to the city's original plans and is today the banking and shopping district.

The best view of the baixa can be enjoyed from the Elevador de Santa Justa, a cast-iron lift between lower and upper town that was built in 1901 (left).

186   **Portugal** | Lisbon

HIERONYMITE MONASTERY

Emanuel I the Fortunate, king of Portugal from 1495 to 1521, was an avid supporter of the country's maritime explorations, in particular those of Vasco da Gama and Pedro Cabral, credited with the discovery of the sea route to India and Brazil, respectively. Indeed, during his reign, the arts and sciences flourished. To honor Vasco da Gama, in 1502, he commissioned the enormous Hieronymite Monas-tery on the site where the Infante (Prince) Henry the Navigator had earlier built a chapel. The plan for the overall complex dates back to Master Boytac and the column-less transept is a late work by João de Castilho. An impressive testi-mony of contemporary statuary is the sculpted decoration in the church's south and west portals. The spectacular church itself (left), a hall church with late-Gothic and early-Renaissance styles, measures 92 m (300 ft) in length and 25 m (85 ft) in width.

Many important figures from his-tory were buried in the Hierony-mite Monastery. It holds, for exam-ple, the tomb of Vasco da Gama (below, the sarcophagus), whose discovery of the sea route to India secured the finance for furnishing the monastery.

COIMBRA, ÓBIDOS, FÁTIMA, TOMAR, ALCOBAÇA

The University of Coimbra, perched atop Alcácova hill, is the oldest in Portugal and one of the oldest in the world. It was founded in 1290, and initially alternated its location between Coimbra and Lisbon. It finally took up residence here in the Coimbra royal palace in 1537.

COIMBRA

The city on the steep banks of the Rio Mondego (main picture) is one of the oldest university cities in Europe (13th century) and was actually the only one in Portugal until 1910. The city center is home to the fortress-like Old Cathedral

(Sé Velha), Portugal's largest Romanesque structure dating back to the 12th century. On the hill behind the church is the Old University, which is also the former royal palace. The showpiece here is the world-famous Joanina Library (1716–1728), Portugal's most beautiful baroque building (left), which is color-coded for each area of specialization. Not far from the library is the Museu Machado de Castro, located in the former bishop's palace. Towering opposite that is the Sé Nova (New Cathedral), a former Jesuit church built around 1600.

A short walk through the city's winding alleyways will take visitors to the Mosteiro de Santa Cruz, a former Augustinian monastery where the Parque de Santa Cruz offers a lovely place to relax. It is also home to the Quinta de Lagrimas, where the love story between Spanish crown prince Pedro and his lover, Ines, came to its tragic end.
The life of the city is shaped by some 20,000 students who often still wear the traditional "capa", a long black cloak and not just for special occasions like the "Queima das Fitas".

ÓBIDOS   **FÁTIMA**   ∞ **TOMAR**   **ALCOBAÇA**

Óbidos is a really a must-see for anyone who makes their way to Portugal. This picturesque village owes its appeal to charming alleyways with their beautiful white houses decorated with flowers (above), and the well-preserved city wall, which surrounds the town and is up to 15 m (49 ft) high in some places.

Fátima has been an important pilgrim site in the Catholic world since 1917, when the Virgin Mary is said to have appeared a total of six times to three shepherd children. On the last occasion, 70,000 people witnessed the "Milagre do Sol", when the sky allegedly darkened and the sun rotated and turned blood-red.

The Convento de Cristo, Portugal's largest monastery complex in Tomar, was used by the Knights Templar as a fortress starting in the 12th century. The minster of Santa María do Olival is said to have been modeled on the Church of the Holy Sepulcher in Jerusalem. No other monastery in Europe has seven cloisters like Tomar.

The Santa María Monastery was founded in Alcobaça, located in the Alcoa and Baça river valleys, as a reward for the victory over the Moors in Santarém. The minster (17th/18th century) is Portugal's largest religious building, and is home to the ornate sarcophagus of King Pedro I and his lover, Ines de Castro (above).

ALTO DOURO

Grape vines have been cultivated in the Alto Douro region for roughly 2,000 years now. As a result of this tradition, an extraordinarily beautiful natural and cultural landscape has emerged whose most famous product is port wine.
The basis of port consists of twenty-one grape varieties that are grown on the rocky slopes of the upper Douro river. Since these wines did not travel well across the Atlantic, British merchants added brandy or marc during the fermentation process and this is how, eventually, in the 17th century, port wine was invented.
Vines have grown in the upper Douro since Roman days. Not only the landscape with its steep, terraced slopes, but also the streets and villages with their churches and quintas, or wineries, have been defined by this 2,000-year-old tradition. The full-bodied, robust red wines of the Alto Douro region are still matured in oak barrels.

PORTO

This port city on the Rio Douro estuary on the Atlantic has much to offer its visitors. Five bridges link Porto with Vila Nova de Gaia, its sister city on the opposite banks and home to most of the port wine cellars. The Ponte de Dom Luís I railway bridge was designed in the offices of Gustave Eiffel (main picture, with the town hall on the hill above the Avenida dos Aliados in the background).
The streets and houses of Porto's Old Town cling tightly to the steep granite rocks beneath it. In the heart of the town, at the bottom end of the Avenida dos Aliados, is the Praça Liberdade with the Torre dos Clerigos, the highest church steeple in Portugal at 75 m (246 ft). At the top of the hill is the town hall with its 70-m (230-ft) bell tower.
At the São Bento station, the giant azulejo murals are especially worth seeing. The name of these brightly hand-painted and glazed floor and wall tiles, which decorate all types of buildings in Porto including the Capela das Almas (below), is probably derived from the Arabic word "al-zulayi", meaning small polished stone, or possibly from the word "azul", meaning blue.
On the way to the Ponte de Dom Luis I you come to the cathedral with its superb silver altarpiece. From there you can descend into the Bairro da Sé quarter, Porto's oldest district.
The Praça da Ribeiro and the Praça Infante Dom Henriques are the center of the Ribeira district, rich and poor clash harshly – the stock exchange sits among narrow dingy alleyways.

ALGARVE

The south of Portugal is a paradise destination for many holidaymakers with its superb white sand beaches, crystal clear water, and charming little coves (main picture). The fascinating sandstone formations at the Praia de Dona Ana beach (top) and the rocky cliffs on the Ponta da Piedade about 2 km (1.3 mi) south of there are typical of the Algarve.

The town of Lagos was once a major staging point for Portuguese explorers setting sail for the New World, and since the days of Henry the Navigator (1394–1460) it has been a center of shipbuilding. The darker side in its history involved the transshipment of captured African slaves. The first recorded auctions in fact took place here on the Praça da República in 1443.

Sagres was once the location of Henry the Navigator's legendary nautical school, remembered by a giant stone compass with a diameter of 43 m (141 ft), on the rocky Ponta de Sagres, not far from the Fortaleza de Sagres. Cabo de São Vicente (above) is almost visible from Sagres jutting out to sea with its 24-m-high (79-ft) lighthouse. It is Europe's south-westernmost point. The cliffs, which are up to 60 m (197 ft) high, were still thought of as the "end of the world" in the days of Christopher Columbus.

ÉVORA, MONSARAZ

The Corinthian columns of a temple dedicated to Diana (above) still stand at the heart of the Roman settlement of Évora. In addition to that, the preserved remains of an aqueduct and a castellum also remind us of the town's former significance in Roman commerce on the Iberian Peninsula. The town also has some Moorish influence from hundreds of years of rule that ended in 1165.

The mighty cathedral here (right) was started in 1186, and with its two colossal steeples the Romanesque-Gothic structure looks like a fortress. In the 14th century, some impressive cloisters modeled after those at the Alcobaça monastery were added.

The royal palace, built in its present form under Emmanuel I, is arguably the most beautiful building in Évora. The Jesuit University is now home to a Collegium and a valuable collection of ancient manuscripts. Other important buildings in the town are the São Brás Chapel, the Church of St John the Evangelist, built in the Mudéjar style and the St Francis Church. The medieval village of Monsaraz (below) is just 50 km (31 mi) east of Évora and is worth an excursion.

FUNCHAL, CÂMARA DE LOBOS, PONTA DO PARGO, LAURISILVA

Green banana plantations, bright flowers in the gardens, lovely parks, and giant exotic trees and dense laurel woods along the paths – Madeira simply radiates fertility. This island far out in the Atlantic invites its visitors to stroll along charming channels, visit Portuguese memorial sites, take a refreshing dip in the ever-cool waters of the ocean and enjoy the vibrant city of Funchal (main picture), the capital of Madeira with grand avenues ranked on both sides by fragrant Jacaranda trees. The heart of Funchal is the Sé Cathedral, the interior of which was dedicated in 1514, and features an astonishing, finely carved wooden ceiling with ivory marquetry.

In stark contrast to the cathedral stands the Zona Velha, the former fishing district. Low houses fringe the narrow alleyways, while elegant restaurants welcome visitors in the former harbor dives. From the Zona Velha, a cable car takes you up the Monte to the Nossa Senhora pilgrimage church, a popular annual pilgrimage site.

In the old and slightly run-down fishing village of Câmara de Lobos, people are proud of their wharf, where ships are still built according to traditional models. The Nossa Senhora da Conceição Chapel is said to have been donated by the Portuguese explorer of the Madeiras, João Gonçalves Zarco in 1419. West of Câmara, the steep cliffs of Cabo Girão rise 580 m (1,903 ft) almost vertically from the sea, offering magnificent views. The coast is so steep here that tunnels were required.

A strong wind usually blows around the lighthouse at the Ponta do Pargo, but the view of the cliffs on the west coast is breathtaking. When it gets too chilly, an original English tea-house invites visitors to warm up with pastries and small snacks.

Originally, Madeira was covered by dense forest, but logging has decimated much of it. Luckily, however, the Laurisilva laurel tree

(insets) still survives in some large tracts of primary forest. Found at altitudes 600 to 1,300 m (1,969 and 4,265 ft), these forests – like those in the Garajonay National Park on the Canary Island of La Gomera – are leftovers of the once vast laurel woods found in the Mediterranean region. And they are central to the island's water supply: the leaves of the laurels "collect" moisture from the clouds, which is then captured by undergrowth and eventually stored in the soil.

THE AZORES

The wild and primitive Azores archipelago emerged from the ocean depths long ago due to mighty uplifting forces in the earth's core. The chain is located roughly 1,500 km (932 mi) west of Portugal's capital, Lisbon, and just 3,600 km (2,237 mi) east of North America.

Nine inhabited islands and a few uninhabited ones are scattered over 650 km (404 mi) – from west to east, Flores, Corvo, Faial, Pico, São Jorge, Graciosa, Terceira, São Miguel and Santa Maria – and attract an increasing number of nature lovers and hikers as well as sailors and watersports enthusiasts. Similar to Madeira, the Azores were able to retain their status as an autonomous region of Portugal in the wake of the "Carnation Revolution".

SÃO MIGUEL

The eastern cluster of the Azores is home to the largest and most densely populated island of the archipelago, São Miguel. Ponta Delgada is the island's main port. The Vista do Rei lookout at 550 m (1,805 ft) provides a breathtaking view over the crater lake of Sete Cidades (above) which, according to legend, was filled by the tears of two lovers.

TERCEIRA

Angra do Heroísmo (below), the capital of Terceira island, is set in the shadow of a volcanic crater. It has been an important port since as early as the 15th century, making it the oldest city in the Azores with a town charter from 1534 and an Old Town dating back to the 16th–18th centuries. A surprising number of houses from the early days are still standing.

Particularly worthwhile in your wanderings is the cathedral, completed in 1618 in Angra do Heroísmo. With its three naves it is the largest religious building in the Azores.

Terceira is also known for its unique form of bullfighting in which experienced men hold the bull by a long rope, while it runs through the streets.

The Azores are the result of massive volcanic activity, and numerous formations such as the Lagoa do Fogo on São Miguel demonstrate the impressive forces at work here. The islands are the tips of giant submerged mountains.

Signs promote whale watching excursions on Pico Island. And what could be more memorable than spotting a giant fluke smoothly emerging from the sea, seeing a sperm whale (main picture) for the first time, or observing one of these great ocean creatures breach?

FAIAL

Faial, which was uninhabited at the time, was first settled around 1460. Large numbers of Flemings soon arrived in search of valuable mineral ores. Ultimately, the beautiful landscape and excellent agricultural conditions were all they needed to settle permanently, and the small village of Flamengos in the hinterland of Horta still bears witness to these adventurers.

Construction of the port of Horta begun in 1876. Today, up to 2,000 yachts visit here during the summer months. An excursion out to

Top: In good weather, the Port of Horta on Faial (top) offers great views of Pico on the neighboring island of the same name.
Bottom: Lush fields of hydrangea.

Faial's westernmost point, the barren volcanic landscape of Capelinhos, takes us to the location of the most recent volcanic eruption on the Azores. The first tremors were felt on the small island, which was still offshore from Faial at the time, in September 1957. Ever more eruptions followed, at times accompanied by clouds of volcanic ash. By October of the following year, more than 2 sq km (200 hectares) of new volcanic land had appeared and Capelinhos had become connected with Faial. The former lighthouse, of which today only the tip is visible in the sand and ash, impressively marks the course that the coastline had taken before the eruptions.

PICO

The second-largest island in the Azores chain lies roughly 250 km (155 mi) west of São Miguel. Pico is often called "Ilha Montanha", the Mountain Island, because the mighty volcanic cone of Pico dominates the landscape. At an altitude of 2,351 m (7,714 ft), the volcano is not only Portugal's highest mountain but also the highest peak in the Atlantic ridge. It was formed 250,000 years ago.

The inhabitants of Pico have learned to live with their fire mountain, which is fertile and frightening at the same time. The rich volcanic soil is excellent for the cultivation of grapevines. Hiking to the top of Pico, which takes four to six hours and should be undertaken with a local guide if possible, is rather arduous, but it makes for a spectacular experience.

For a long time, whaling was the most important source of income for the Azores, but since whaling was banned in the 1980s, some former whalers have started offering their services as well as their safe and maneuverable boats to whale watchers.

The Portuguese have been growing grapes on the Azorean island of Pico (left) ever since the first settlement in the 15th century. They built dry-stone walls in order to protect the vines and grapes from the fierce winds and the seaspray it carries.

SÃO JORGE

Arriving at São Jorge you will notice the elongated shape of the island. Measuring 56 km (35 mi) in length and between 6 and 8 km (4 and 5 mi) in width, this mountainous island in the middle of the Azores is ideal for hiking. On its north side, the cliffs drop dramatically down to the ocean. Among the island's peculiarities are the so-called "fajas", or spits of land, that were formed by shifting plates often caused by minor earthquakes. In total there are forty-six such fajas. They were settled and cultivated as early as the mid-15th century.

Velas, on the south-western coast of São Jorge, has some 2,000 inhabitants and is the island's economic center.

Several agricultural cooperatives produce the delicious Queijo de São Jorge, an aromatic hard cheese made from cow milk. The unique types of grasses growing in the meadows combined with the damp and permanently salty Atlantic air endow this cheese with a very special flavor.

Most of the villages, including Velas, the island's tranquil capital, are on the gentle southern coast. Stress is more or less an unknown concept here. A short walk takes you past shops, cafés and attractive burgher homes that bear witness to the prosperity of the island due to its primary export: oranges. Ferries, freighters and – after a large expansion project – even small container ships often dock in the port.

KURFÜRSTENDAMM

"Great Berlin, the open city – it should not be just a German city," wrote Mexican author Carlos Fuentes, before adding, "It is our city, a city of the whole world." And in fact, Berlin stands at the heart of the world like virtually no other city. History was, and still is, made in this city on the river Spree, and the past and the present connect with whatever the next future may be. As the capital and seat of government, home to muses and museums, and as a multicultural center, Berlin is a city like no other. Or more precisely: "a city of the whole world."

The capital of the German Empire should have a grand boulevard modeled after the Champs-Elysées in Paris. That was the decision by Chancellor Otto von Bismarck upon his return from the French capital after the Franco-Prussian War. And so the former corduroy road to the hunting palace in Grunewald forest was transformed into a 3.5-km (2-mi) long, 53-m (174-ft) wide avenue where only those who could afford it lived. Today, the shops here compete with the up-and-coming Mitte (center) district, but as a shopping street, Kurfürstendamm (above) is still number one in Berlin.

Two warriors guard the forecourt of Charlottenburg Palace with its equestrian statue of the Great Elector Friedrich Wilhelm (main picture).

SCHLOSS CHARLOTTENBURG

In the heart of the Charlottenburg district and originally conceived as a summer residence for Electress Sophie Charlotte, this grandiose edifice was built in several stages between 1695 and 1746. The domed tower rises almost 50 m (164 ft) above the palace forecourt with its equestrian statue of the Great Elector. After World War II, the historic rooms in the central building – the oldest part of the complex, which also comprises extensive palace gardens – were rebuilt in their original splendor.

KAISER WILHELM MEMORIAL CHURCH

"Everything passes" was the main theme of the sermon in the Kaiser Wilhelm Memorial Church on November 22, 1943. It was the last Sunday before Advent, commemorating the dead. Bombs soon after reduced the church to the now famous ruin (above, through the sculpture "Berlin" in Tauentzien Street). The damaged west steeple, reduced from 113 to 63 m (371 to 207 ft), was then given the nickname "hollow tooth" by locals. Despite their irreverence, however, Berliners did not allow the destroyed church to be demolished and in 1961, Egon Eiermann built a monument church over the ruins.

BERLIN

BRANDENBURG GATE

Carl Gotthard Langhans began construction of the iconic Brandenburg Gate in 1788 as the triumphal end to the grand boulevard Unter den Linden. Completed in 1791, this severe sandstone structure is 26 m (85 ft) high and 65 m (215 ft) wide, a stout edifice indeed. Twelve Doric columns divide the double portico into five passages, with the center reserved for the king's coach and the narrower passages used by the infantry.

The relief on top of the attica, the Quadriga, depicts the entry of the gods of peace into the city while the reliefs in the passage feature the labors of Hercules. The gods Mars and Minerva stand guard in the side halls.

THE REICHSTAG

The Reichstag building, designed by Paul Wallot and opened in 1894, was meant to symbolize the vastness and power of the German Empire. After being badly damaged in World War II, it was restored as a conference venue after 1961. From 1995 to 1999, a modern, more environmentally-friendly parliamentary building was created behind the historic façade of the old Reichstag building according to plans by Sir Norman Foster. The glass dome, which is open to the public, quickly became a new landmark for the capital.

POTSDAMER PLATZ

For years, visitors from around the world were awed by Europe's largest urban building site as the internationally acclaimed architects altered the skyline of Berlin. The likes of Renzo Piano, Richard Rogers, Arata Isozaki, Hans Kollhoff, Helmut Jahn and Giorgio Grassi created a 21st-century city that is both admired and criticized. Construction began in October 1994; in 1996, Daniel Barenboim conducted dancing cranes for the topping-out ceremony; and in 1998, ten new streets and seventeen buildings became operational.

HOLOCAUST MEMORIAL

Near Brandenburg Gate is an ensemble of 2,711 dark concrete blocks in uneven, narrow rows of varying heights. According to its creator, Peter Eisenman, the memorial is meant to disorient visitors while inspiring reflection. The space below contains important facts about the Holocaust and in the "Raum der Familien" (Room of Families) are some exposés about the lives of European Jews before the Holocaust. In the "Raum der Namen" (Room of Names), the names and short biographies of missing Jews are read aloud.

GENDARMENMARKT

The Gendarmenmarkt, named after the "gens d'armes," a regiment of cuirassiers, is one of Berlin's most attractive plazas. It is surrounded by the Schauspielhaus (national theater), Deutscher and Französischer Dom (German and French cathedrals) and the Schiller Monument. In the 18th century, Frederick II had built a comedy theater on the square and commissioned Carl von Gontard to add the mighty domes to the churches, which had been erected nearly eighty years earlier. The Schiller statue before the theater was done by Reinhold Begas.

MUSEUMSINSEL

Museum Island, between the Spree and Kupfergraben, covers an area of less than 1 sq km (247 acres) but contains five outstanding museums that together representing more than 5,000 years of human history – a concentration of art and artefacts that is unique in the world. On the island are: the Altes Museum (Old Museum, right), one of the first museums in Germany built in 1828; Neues Museum (New Museum, 1855); Alte Nationalgalerie (Old National Gallery, 1876); Bodemuseum, opened in 1904; and the spectacular Pergamonmuseum (1930).

BERLINER DOM, ALEXANDERPLATZ

Berlin Cathedral, the burial church of the Hohenzollern family (far right), was built between 1893 and 1905 on the orders of Emperor Wilhelm II. The vaults hold ninety-four tombs and sarcophagi of the ruling dynasty that span four centuries. Alexanderplatz developed as an ox market in front of the Oderberg Gate around 1700. In 1805, it was renamed to honor the Russian Czar Alexander I. Not much remains of its original structures, but worth seeing are the World Time Clock and the Fountain of Friendship between Peoples (both 1969).

The Brandenburg Gate (left) was based on the propylaea of the Acropolis in Athens. The Quadriga (far left) was created in 1789 to 1791, to a design by Johann Gottfried Schadow.

SYLT

Sylt, known for its see-and-be-seen ambience, is the northernmost island in Germany. At the northern tip of the island is the tiny community of List, the northernmost place in the republic. Sylt splitt off from the mainland some 8,000 years ago when the seas began rising. In 1927, the two were linked again by the Hindenburgdamm.

Since then, up to 650,000 holiday-makers a year cross the dam to the 39-km-long (24-mi) island which, at its widest point is just over 1 km (0.6 mi) wide. While the west coast is lashed by the wind and the waves of the North Sea, the eastern Wadden Sea coast is much quieter and calmer. It is also home to Wadden Sea National Park, famous for its diversity of flora and fauna as well as its tidal mud flats.

FÖHR

Christian VIII, King of Denmark and Norway, had already discovered the beneficial effects of the fresh air, beautiful scenery and the almost 15 km (9 mi) of sandy beaches in the south of the island of Föhr back in the middle of the 19th century. The center of the nearly circular island, 82 sq km (32 sq mi) in size, is the North Sea resort of Wyk.

The west and south of Föhr was formed by a moraine – a glacial relic from the Ice Age. It is higher and drier than the marshlands of the north and east, which only gradually grew with increased land reclamation.

AMRUM

South-west of Föhr lies the quiet island of Amrum, about 20 sq km (8 sq mi) in size and featuring dunes up to 30 m (98 ft) high. Amrum also has a sandy beach that is up to 2 m (1.3 mi) wide and 15 km (9 mi) long – the famous Kniepsand beach. The small island has a population of roughly 2,200 people living in five villages, of which the Friesian village of Nebel is the best known and most popular. To get an good view of the island with its dunes, forests and marshlands, it is best to climb the 66-m-tall (217-ft) lighthouse between Nebel and Wittdün. From there you can see the entire island and sometimes as far as neighboring Föhr.

HELGOLAND

You have to catch a boat if you want to visit Helgoland, with its famous buntsandstein (red sandstone) formations and breeding grounds for guillemots and kittiwakes. Germany's only solid rock, high-seas island was actually in British hands for many years before becoming German in 1890, when it was swapped for the island of Zanzibar. During World War II, Helgoland was a military base, and as such was frequently bombed. After the war, the island was used as a bombing range by the British but by 1952 it was given back to Germany and by the mid-1950s, the first inhabitants had begun returning to the island, rebuilding their lives, and welcoming the first visitors, who came to enjoy the fresh air and duty-free shopping. Daytrippers still arrive in large numbers.

An estimated 10,000 lighthouses still exist around the world, and some of the most attractive ones can be found on the German North Sea coast. This one stands on the Ellenbogen Peninsula, the northernmost tip of the island of Sylt.

National Park provides more than 3,000 different animal and plant species with an ideal environment. Schleswig-Holstein was the first German state to place the northern stretches of the Wadden Sea under protection, declaring it a national park in 1985, and then a biosphere reserve in 1990. The Wadden Sea National Park is divided into three protection zones. The first zone includes the seal colonies, where humans are either not allowed at all, or only allowed on designated paths. Part of the second zone is the whale protection area. The third zone is open to fishing, tourism and even oil drilling.

The Wadden Sea is a perfect ecosystem that is rich in nutrients. Many animal and plant species have even adapted to living in the salt marshes, the best-known among being is the lugworm.

The Wadden Sea is an annual stopover for more than two million migratory birds as well as a summer retreat for about 100,000 breeding shelducks, eider ducks, seagulls and swallows. In addition, the tidal area is a breeding ground for herring, sole and plaice as well as a habitat for gray seals, harbor seals and harbor porpoises.

In an area covering more than 4,000 sq km (1,544 sq mi), from the Danish border to the estuary of the river Elbe, Wadden Sea

LÜBECK, WISMAR, SCHWERIN, ROSTOCK, STRALSUND

LÜBECK

Lübeck's most famous icon is the Holstentor, built in 1478 and one of only two remaining city gates (the other one is the Burgtor). Part of the mighty fortifications, this Gothic gate is so heavy that shortly after construction the subsoil began to sink. Since then, the southern tower has had a slight lean. Today it houses a permanent exhibition on the Hanseatic League.

Visitors to Lübeck's Old Town will enjoy a journey back in time to the Middle Ages through a maze of alleyways from Holstentor to Burgtor and the cathedral district. Behind the old merchants' homes and warehouses, narrow passages run through secluded courtyards. Aside from the splendid Marienkirche (Saint Mary's church), there are five other historic churches that are worth visiting as well as the St Anne's Monastery Art Museum and one of the oldest hospitals in northern Europe. From St Petri, fascinating views unfold over the sea of magnificent structures including the town hall, the various churches and the two surviving town gates.

Salt, an essential element in preserving foodstuffs was known as "white gold" by Hanseatic merchants who dominated the trading routes between Lübeck and the port cities of Mecklenburg West Pomerania along the Baltic Sea coast.

WISMAR

Wismar is a town that resembles an open-air museum of the Hanseatic League. Many of its churches, burghers' mansions and the market square (right) date back to this period, as do the harbor basin and the "Grube," an artificial waterway to the Schwerin lake. All have survived virtually unchanged and it was here that the bulky cogs entered and left the port. The remains of one such ship were found off the island of Poel in 1999 – the "Wissemara" in the port is a faithful reconstruction at 31 m (100 ft). After the Hanseatic League came the Swedes who ruled Wismar for 250 years. Some buildings such as the baroque arsenal of 1701, or the "Baumhaus"are from that period. The tall steeples of the parish churches of St Mary and St Nicholas demonstrate that the town was oriented toward the sea. They served as orientation markers for ships.

SCHWERIN

After the fall of the Berlin Wall, the state of Mecklenburg-West Pomerania needed to designate a new capital for itself. As a result, the small town of Schwerin was chosen despite Rostock's greater size. But if you visit this smallest of the German state capitals, you will easily understand why the choice went the way it did.

Schwerin was and still is a ducal residence and with a picturesque location amid charming lakes, a largely restored Old Town, and a fairy-tale palace on the Schlossinsel island, it resembles an extravagant film set.

In 1990, Schwerin Palace (right, in the background) became the seat of regional government – the "residency" continues, albeit in less glamorous style than during the days of the dukes of Mecklenburg-Schwerin. It is also a cultural center with a state theater, an art gallery in the regional museum, and an open-air summer festival on the grounds.

"Concordia Domis Foris Pax" – "Harmony inside, Peace outside," is the motto on the portal of Lübeck's Holstentor since 1863 (far left). Lübeck's beautiful Old Town (left) is surrounded by water and features the brick architecture typical of northern Germany. In the background is St Mary's Church.

ROSTOCK

Rostock has an obsession with seven. The "Rostocker Kennewohrn", or the seven symbols of Rostock, is a poem from 1596 that extolls the seven icons that define the cityscape, each of those in turn having seven telltale features. Among them are the originally medieval town hall with seven spires, for example.

Indeed, Rostock is a fine example of a flourishing medieval town. After Danish King Valdemar destroyed it in 1161, this former Slav castle village was given its town charters in 1218. Soon after, in 1229, it became the main principality in the Mecklenburg Duchy of Rostock and by the 14th century had become the most powerful member of the Hanseatic League after Lübeck. The remains of the city wall with its three gates, the tall Gothic St Mary's Church, and a row of old warehouses bear witness to its former importance. After heavy damage during World War II, much of the city has thankfully been lovingly restored.

STRALSUND

Millions of rectangular roof tiles make up the distinctive face of Stralsund (left the Old Market with town hall and St Nicholas Church). It is one of the most attractive examples of northern German Brick Gothic.

The town on the Strelasund is situated between the Baltic Sea and the Greifswalder Bodden, opposite Germany's most popular holiday island, Rügen. Since 1936, the Rügendamm has connected the mainland with both Rügen and Dänholm, once known as Strela, the name given to the island's main town founded in 1234.

In the time of the Hanseatic League, Stralsund became one of the mightiest cities in the Baltic Sea, with splendid buildings such as the St Nicholas Church and the town hall with its elaborately ornamented gable all dating from that period. During the Thirty Years' War, Stralsund was able to defend itself against General Wallenstein by allying itself with Sweden. It is from this period that the baroque Commandantenhus stems.

RÜGEN

Rügen, Germany's largest island, has an area of 976 sq k (377 sq mi), and actually comprises five islands that have grown together over the course of centuries. Jasmund, isolated between sea and shallower coastal waters is only reachable via two spits of land and was the first of the five.

The forested northern half of Rügen is home to the Jasmund National Park established in 1990. At only 30 sq km (12 sq mi) it is Germany's smallest. The highlight here are the chalk cliffs (top left). Cape Arkona juts far into the Baltic Sea and is one of the sunniest places in Germany. Its exposed location on Rügen's northernmost tip make it important for shipping. When visibility is low or navigation errors occur, ships are in danger of running aground there. No wonder then, that Cape Arkona is home to the oldest lighthouse on the Baltic Sea (above). Built by Schinkel in 1826, the 21-m (69-ft) tower was operated until 1905. Beside the neoclassical old tower is its successor, which is still in use. More than 100 years old, it isn't exactly a new feature here either.

Apart from lively holiday resorts, Rügen also boasts many hidden gems where romantics can find a bit of seclusion, for example by the Gager Marina, on the hilly Thiessow Peninsula in the southeast of the island (above).

The Sellin pier on Rügen was destroyed by ice drift in 1941, and finally rebuilt in 1998, in the style of the Art Nouveau original. From the 30-m-high (100-ft) cliffs on which the Baltic Sea resort of Sellin is located you can get lovely views of the beach and the pier.

FISCHLAND-DARSS-ZINGST

Fischland, Darss and Zingst were once three separate islands that grew together over time and were finally linked by dykes in the 19th century. "Fischland is the most beautiful place in the world," said the female protagonist, Gesine Cresspahl, in Uwe Johnson's book, *Jahrestage*. But it is small, and the water laps conspicuously up on both sides of this narrow piece of land that is home to the Baltic Sea resort towns of Ahrenshoop (left) and Wustrow. The Darss peninsula forms the central part of the present-day Fischland-Darss-Zingst chain, an island wilderness that served as a pirate's bolt hole until the end of the 14th century. The Zingst peninsula and the Baltic Sea resort of the same name form its easterly continuation. Parts of Darss and Zingst belong to the Vorpommersche Boddenlandschaft National Park (West Pomerania Lagoon Area National Park) that was set up shortly after German reunification. Large parts of it are covered by water that is only knee-deep ("bodden" means shallow lagoon). For many species of animals, especially cranes, this is a unique habitat. Every year, up to 60,000 of the proud birds stop over at the national park, the "kingdom of cranes".

HIDDENSEE

"Dat söte Länneken," is how this small island is lovingly described in Low German, and a "sweet little land" it is indeed. Hiddensee and its four villages, Grieben, Kloster, Neuendorf and Vitte, is a miniature world of its own without cars, spa resorts or even a pier. Just under 1,100 people live here in what some would consider self-imposed isolation. Many outsiders like it here as well, however, and visit the island to find peace and tranquility, as Gerhard Hauptmann once did. In 1930, he purchased "House Seedorn" in Kloster and came every summer until 1943. A memorial remembers the Nobel Prize winner. West of Rügen is Hiddensee, a flat island in the Vorpommersche Boddenlandschaft Park, that has virtually no forest, but features salt marshes, reed belts and heathland. The sea buckthorn also grows here, which is used to make Hiddensee specialties such as jam, juice and liqueur.

In the age of satellite navigation, lighthouses have become increasingly obselete, but as historical landmarks many of them still serve dual functions as both icon and maritime orientation point. This is also true for the "Dornbusch" Lighthouse on Hiddensee, built in 1888 (above left).

"Sanssouci" ("without worries") – that is how Frederick the Great wished to live in his summer palace in Potsdam. With that goal in mind, he had Georg Wenzeslaus von Knobelsdorff build him a graceful retreat (right top) among the vineyard terraces of Potsdam in 1747, partly according to his own designs. A single-story structure, it is considered a masterwork of the German rococo and the most important sight in Potsdam. Adorned with ornate sculptures and rich furnishings, the palace also bears witness to its occupant's lively interest in the arts: in his music room the king liked to play his flute; in his magnificent library he would hold debates with Voltaire, the French philosopher of the Enlightenment.

Maxims such as the following bear witness to his literary interests: "Thus do I say sedulously / Enjoy every moment / Today the heavens may smile upon us / We do not know if they will grumble tomorrow."

More buildings were added later such as the New Chambers and the New Palace (left bottom, with performers during the popular "Night of the Palaces"). Frederick's successors were active as well, adding the Orangery and the Charlottenhof Palace.

In 1816, landscape architect Peter Joseph Lenné began the elaborate transformation of the spacious park, which extends all the way up to the Pfaueninsel (Peacock Island) and the parks of Glienicke and Babelsberg.

The Chinese Tea House, built in 1757 by Johann Gottfried Büring, is a pavilion in Sanssouci Park. Outside, the rococo tea house is adorned with six groups of figures and twelve individual figures.

DRESDEN

Baroque and neoclassical buildings still characterize the cityscape of Dresden today. From down on the Elbe you get spectacular views of the Brühlsche Terrasse with the Academy of Art, the Ständehaus (Guild Hall), Hofkirche and Semper Opera House as well as of the rebuilt Frauenkirche.

"Venice of the East", "Saxon Serenissima", "Florence on the Elbe", "Pearl of the Baroque" – the epithets that have been used to describe the capital of the Free State of Saxony over the centuries are as numerous as they are effusive. And with good reason, for the former seat of the Great Elector is without doubt one of the great European centers of culture. Seat of the Albertiner government from 1485, it developed into one of the most magnificent baroque centers of power in the German states under Elector Augustus the Strong. In the late 18th and early 19th centuries, intellectuals even made Dresden a center of German Romanticism. However, the devastating bombing raids of World War II brought the glorious city to her knees.

In February 1945, Dresden's Old Town was irrecoverably destroyed. Thankfully, many buildings have been lavishly rebuilt including the city's most famous icon, the Frauenkirche (Church of Our Lady), the Zwinger, the Semper Opera House, the Residenz (Dresden Palace), the Hofkirche (St Trinitatis Cathedral), and the Brühlsche Terrasse on the banks of the Elbe.

Augustus the Strong commissioned architect Matthäus Daniel Pöppelmann and sculptor Balthasar Permoser to build the Zwinger (left), a masterpiece of courtly baroque in 1709. Completed in 1732, the palace gardens are framed by galleries and pavilions that today house museums.

Three words sum up Germany's westermost metropolis: churches, art and kölsch beer. A Roman settlement was the original nucleus of this cosmopolitan city on the Rhine. During the reign of Charlemagne, Cologne became an archbishopric, and by the early Middle Ages it had become one of Germany's leading cities.

Romanesque and Gothic churches still bear witness to the former spiritual and intellectual importance of Cologne, most of all of course the famous Kölner Dom (Cologne Cathedral). Art also seems more present here than anywhere else in Germany. Its important galleries and museums are numerous and include the Museum Ludwig and the Wallraf Richartz Museum. The local joie de vivre is also legendary all year round, not just during the Rose Monday (Carnival) celebrations.

People from Cologne often sum up their philosophy of life with two sentences: "Et kütt, wie et kütt." and "Et hätt noch immer jot jejange" ("Things happen the way they do" and "In the end things have always turned out alright"). People take things the way they come in Cologne because they are convinced that in the end all will turn out just fine. If you look back on 2,000 years of history, apparently you can afford such equanimity. After all, the locals have outlasted the ancient Romans as well as the occupation by the French in the 19th century.

Cologne's lifeline is the Rhine and its heart is the Cathedral. In the evening, the panorama is particularly beautiful and the view from the Deutzer Bridge to the church of Gross St Martin and the Cathedral is brilliant (main picture).

COLOGNE CATHEDRAL

Begun in the year 1248, the Kölner Dom (above, view over Hohenzollern Bridge) was not completed until 1880, after an interruption of more than 300 years from 1530 to 1842. It is considered a masterpiece of French Cathedral Gothic. The focal point of the cathedral is the Shrine of the Three Kings (left, priests celebrating holy communion), the largest reliquary ever created. It was made in around 1200 by Nicholas of Verdun, the most famous goldsmith of the Middle Ages, and holds the bones of the Three Magi. The Gero Cross is about 200 years older; its figure of Christ was one of the earliest monumental sculptures created after antiquity. Around 1440, Stephan Lochner painted the Altar of the City Patrons, a highlight of German Gothic art. When the sun shines, the interior of the cathedral is flooded with light thanks to its 10,000 sq m (107,600 sq ft) of windows.

Aachen's most important building is the imperial cathedral, whose history is closely connected with Charlemagne. The main picture shows the emperor's throne and the inset picture a painting of Charlemagne by Albrecht Dürer.

BRÜHL

The main sights in the town of Brühl, situated around 15 km (9 mi) south of Cologne, are the palaces of Augustusburg and Falkenlust. Construction on Augustusburg was begun in 1725, as a residence for Clemens August von Wittelsbach, Elector and Archbishop of Cologne. A unified work of art created by Johann Conrad Schlaun, François de Cuvilliés and Dominique Girard, the palace documents in detail the transition in style from baroque to rococo. The furnishings in the magnificent staterooms are of the most remarkable quality, and the imposing staircase was the work of Balthasar Neumann. All of the rooms in the palace face toward the gardens, which gives it the feel of a summer residence. The palace was restored after extensive destruction during World War II.

Falkenlust was begun in 1729 according to plans by Cuvilliés and Leveilly and was used for falconry, one of the elector's hobbies. The rooms are fairly private in character, but are nevertheless magnificently appointed.

AACHEN

Aachen, the former residence of Charlemagne, was one of the most important cities in Europe during the Middle Ages. The Romans had already settled here for the prized local hot springs, and those healing waters are probably the reason why, over 1,200 years ago, in the winter

Top: Exterior of Aachen Cathedral with the Hungarian Chapel.
Bottom: The octagonal interior.

of 794, Charlemagne decided to expand the existing royal mansion in Aachen. After his return from Rome in 800, Charlemagne was crowned emperor here and from then on Aachen was to remain the coronation site of German kings for more than 600 years.

Numerous historical buildings still bear witness to the great days of emperors and kings, for example the town hall and the octagonal Palatine Chapel, which forms the core of Aachen Cathedral.

The harmonious interplay of palace and baroque garden reveals the full grace and beauty of Augustusburg Palace (left).

MOSEL VALLEY

The Mosel is one of Germany's most capricious rivers, despite the fact that it rises in France, where it is called the Moselle. With its source in the heart of the Vosges Mountains, the Mosel snakes past Metz before reaching Luxembourg and finally enters German territory for the last 243 km (151 mi) of its 544-km (338-mi) total length. More than 2,000 years ago, the river was part of the Roman realm and called the Mosella. Caesar had conquered the land and mountains along its course at that point, but even earlier, the Celtic Treveri had named it Mosea. Indeed, the Mosel probably has a longer history than any other "German" river. After all, Germany's oldest town, Trier, was founded on its banks. The Mosel is a meandering river (left top, near Bremm) that flows past famously steep vineyards (left bottom, Landshut Castle near Bernkastel-Kues amid the vines) and numerous castles such as Cochem (above), originally built in 1100, destroyed by French soldiers in 1688, and rebuilt in its present neo-Gothic style in the 19th century. It sits perched above the town of the same name. The natural beauty of the region combined with the meandering river and its abundance of fish was even celebrated in song by the Roman poet Decimus Magnus Ausonius (310–395) in the 4th century.

Like in a fairytale, Eltz Castle sits enthroned in a misty valley near the Mosel. The medieval castle complex dates back to the 13th century and has been the property of the lords and counts of Eltz for the last 800 years.

TRIER

Records document that Trier was founded in the year 16 BC by the Romans during the reign of Emperor Augustus, and subsequently named "Augusta Treverorum," the town of the Treveri. Initially, Trier was the main town in the Roman province of Belgica, but during the reign of Emperor Diocletian it became the capital of the Westen Roman Empire and ultimately remained in Rome's possession until 475.

Numerous historical buildings in Trier were erected during that time, including the famous Porta Nigra (left), the best-preserved Roman town gate north of the Alps, the Roman bridge spanning the Mosel, the amphitheater, the basilica, the aqueduct from the Hunsrück Mountains, and of course the imperial thermae (below), begun in the early 4th century and one of the largest spas in the entire Roman Empire.

A setting for Romantics: Stahleck Castle,
first documented in the year 1102, stands
high above the Rhine near Bacharach.

"I don't know what it may signify," the poet Heinrich Heine wrote about the Loreley, a rugged rock towering 132 m (433 ft) over the Rhine. The question was born of a deep yearning in the German heart, and one from its most romantic place. For it is here on the Middle Rhine between Bingen and Koblenz that the origins of German Romanticism lie, with the glistening river winding through the narrow valley past medieval towns with half-timbered houses, castles on mountaintops, and vineyards clinging to steep slopes. No wonder the heart aches with a sweet melancholy, and not only the German heart. For it is by far the most attractive section of the Rhine (left the famous Pfalzgrafenstein, a river fortress built in 1326 to collect duties) ranking among the top destinations for visitors from all over the world. Truth be told, it is a remarkable landscape (left, the wine village of Bacharach tucked into a bend in the river), and the overall impression of beauty comes not just from the picturesque river scenery but also from the extraordinary wealth of historical and cultural monuments dating from several centuries (above, 12th-century Stahleck Castle).

Lake Constance is 64 km (40 mi) long, 14 km (9 mi) wide and 250 m (820 ft) deep. But it is more than the sum of its statistics. It is an enchanted region with places like the Church of St George on the Wasserburg Peninsula (main picture).

BIRNAU

The Birnau pilgrimage church is just a short distance above the lake, connected with Maurach Palace by a vineyard the skirts the shore. On clear days you can get magnificent views across the lake to Mainau Island and the foothills on the other side. And if you're lucky the panorama of the Alps will unfold as you stand on the terrace of the monastery. Enter the church through the main entrance and you will witness a unified work of art, architecture and sculpture full of baroque shapes and colors. The church was built between 1746 and 1750 under the direction of the master architect Peter Thumb from Vorarlberg and features pure rococo styling with rich furnishings. Seeing the church now makes it hard to imagine that it had been abandoned after secularization and was even used as a goat shed for a time until the Cistercians from Mehrerau Monastery in Bregenz took it over in 1919. The monks of the order look after pilgrims and hikers on the "Prelates' Path" that connects Birnau with the former Salem Monastery.

REICHENAU

Since the first monks arrived on this island in the early Middle Ages, Reichenau has been a textbook example of a "cultural landscape", in both senses of the term. The island features a matchless combination of historical monuments and refined agricultural cultivation. St George in Oberzell (above, amid fields), for example, is famous for the monumental Ottonic murals in its central nave. The old abbey church at Mittelzell has an open roof truss and contains a treasury with relics and shrines. Saints Peter and Paul in Niederzell harmoniously combines Romanesque and baroque styles.

CONSTANCE

The old town of Constance, which has been famous since the Council of Constance, is the "true" capital of the Lake Constance region. Positioned to link the northern and the southern shores of the lake, the Old Town is on the left bank of the Rhine. Its north side is especially well preserved with the cathedral, municipal theater, council building and medieval houses (above). On the right bank are residential and industrial areas where a number of solar technology companies are based. Higher up on Giessberg hill is the university, which is still dominated by the imposing youth hostel tower.

Baroque style among the vines – Birnau pilgrimage church (far left) has a picturesque location in a vineyard above the lake and features a magnificent interior (left, view through the main nave to the choir and the high altar).

MEERSBURG

On a clear day, the broad façades of the palaces of Meersburg can be seen from as far away as the foothills of the Swiss Alps. The complex comprises a medieval castle (above) and three baroque structures. The reddish domain building and the yellow former priests' seminary stand parallel to the lakeshore, while the mansion built as the new residence for the bishops of Constance between 1741 and 1750 is oriented exactly toward Constance Cathedral. Since secularization, the buildings have served multiple purposes, for example as a guesthouse, a state winery and a grammar school. The Old Town boasts attractive half-timbered houses hemmed in at a fair distance by 20th-century buildings, as well as the ferry buildings and a new hot springs facility.

LINDAU

Lindau owes its early prosperity in the Middle Ages to the "Milan Messenger" route, an important horse and carriage connection between southern Germany and northern Italy. The splendid merchants' mansions from the baroque period still bear witness to this affluence. Aside from the island, whose buildings are historic landmarks, Lindau also includes the districts on the mainland and a few villages farther inland. The Bad Schachen district was an elegant spa resort back in the mid-19th century and is known today for its hotels and the Peace Museum in Villa Lindenhof.

BAYREUTH

Wilhelmine von Bayreuth (1709–1758) was an enlightened margravine and active but cautious reformer of her small fiefdom, an architect and philosopher, a composer and writer, as well as the favorite sister of Frederick the Great. From her privileged position she was able to influence the look of her namesake town, Bayreuth, with her style of choice, rococo. From 1736, she enlarged the Hermitage, the Old and the New Palaces as well as the splendid palace gardens. It was on her initiative, too, that the Margraves' Opera House was built in 1748, a masterpiece of the European baroque built according to plans by Joseph Saint-Pierre. Its magnificence was what attracted Richard Wagner to Bayreuth when his own plans for a festival hall in Munich had failed. With the help of his patron, King Ludwig II of Bavaria, Richard Wagner was able to fulfill his dream in 1872. Every year since then, the international community of Wagner enthusiasts makes the pilgrimage to the festival with its important opera productions.

Goethe's enthusiasm for Franconia was not exhausted solely by his admiration for the natural beauty of the region between the Main and Danube. What he loved were the art treasures and Franconian wines, which he took to with gusto.

WÜRZBURG

In a beautiful location at the foot of Fortress Marienberg and the lovely municipal vineyards, Würzburg extends around the market square with its late-Gothic St Mary's Chapel and the House of the Falcon

Top: Würzburg's old Main Bridge dates back to 1133. In the 18th century, twelve statues, including St Kilian (here), were added. Middle: Fortress Marienberg. Bottom and right: The Würzburg Residence (palace).

with its rich rococo stucco work. Many of its treasures are hidden, for example the small Lusam Garden behind the baroque Neumünster, final resting place of the minstrel Walther von der Vogelweide.
The Residence (1720) is a masterpiece of the baroque built by Lukas von Hildebrandt and Johann Balthasar Neumann. Inside is a grand staircase with a ceiling painting by Giambattista Tiepolo.

The Margraves' Opera House in Bayreuth (left) is one of the most beautiful baroque theaters in Europe; another gem in the town is the Hermitage (far left).

BAMBERG

This town of emperors and bishops is more than 1,000 years old and cozily situated on seven hills in the valley of the river Regnitz. Unlike Nuremberg or Würzburg, the former "caput orbis" (head of the world) was only lightly damaged in World War II and in some ways still feels like an old engraving. This is why Bamberg and its Old Town with the world-famous symphony orchestra are certainly worth a visit. There are many sights to see, including the old town hall from the 14th century, the "little Venice" fishermen's quarter and the late-Gothic cathedral with the *Bamberg Horseman*.

Top: Bamberg's Saints Peter and George Cathedral is one of the most important churches of the German Middle Ages.
Above: The *Bamberg Horseman*.
Right top: View of the Old Town.
Right: The town hall on the Regnitz.

The Emperor's Tomb inside the cathedral was created by Tilman Riemenschneider between 1499 and 1513, and the Marian Altar is by Veit Stoss. In the west choir lies the only papal tomb in Germany (Clement II), and the Diocesan Museum holds precious cathedral treasures.

ROTHENBURG OB DER TAUBER, AUGSBURG

ROTHENBURG OB DER TAUBER

Rothenburg ob der Tauber is a gem of late-Gothic architecture, each square more romantic than the last, and crooked alleyways and buildings. The Siebersturm at the junction of Plönlein and Untere Schmiedgasse (main picture) is one of the towers in the old town wall.

This small town is the absolute epitome of German Romanticism. If a medieval European setting is required for a film, Rothenburg is often the town of choice. Its medieval ambience has remained more or less unchanged to this day and once inspired the painter Ludwig Richter to call it a "fairy-

tale of a town". The town's unique appearance, with its red tile roofs, towers and turrets, the town hall (left), large market square with fountain, town gates, churches, half-timbered houses, and a 2-km (1.5 mi) town wall simply transports you back to another time. And if that isn't enough, you can futher immerse yourself in the Middle Ages in one of the museums, for example in the Reichsmuseum, where the "Meistertrunk-Humpen", the elector's tankard from the Thirty Years' War, is on exhibit, or in the Medieval Crime Museum, where the darker sides of the Middle Ages are explained in lurid detail.

AUGSBURG

Augsburg is inseparably linked with the Fuggers, one of the richest merchant dynasties in history, to whom the city owes many celebrated buildings including the Renaissance town hall flanked by the Perlach Tower (left), and the magnificent Golden Hall ceiling in the town hall.

The first settlement in what is now Augsburg goes back to the year 14 BC making it Germany's second-oldest town after Trier. It had its heyday in the 15th and 16th centuries as an important trading city on the trans-Alpine route that served southern Germany, Italy and lands beyond.

WIESKIRCHE, NEUSCHWANSTEIN, LINDERHOF, HERRENCHIEMSEE

In a spectacular location upon a promontory at the foot of the Ammer Mountains near Füssen stands the "fairytale" castle of Neuschwanstein (main picture, upper left). Hohenschwanstein Palace (lower right) was bought by Ludwig II's father Maximilian II in 1832.

WIESKIRCHE

The "Wies" Pilgrimage Church is dedicated to a wondrous event: in 1730, monks from nearby Steingaden Abbey produced an image of Christ for the Good Friday procession on a farm near the hamlet of Wies that belonged to the abbey. Then, on June 14, 1738, the statue suddenly began to shed tears, a miracle that immediately transformed the church into a pilgrimage site. A cult soon developed around the Scourged Savior of Wies, resulting in the commissioning this church, perhaps the most exuberant rococo church in all of Germany. The architects were the brothers Dominikus and Johann Baptist Zimmermann and it was built between 1745 and 1754.

NEUSCHWANSTEIN

Ludwig II commissioned Neuschwanstein Castle in 1860. It was built in neo-Romanesque style according to plans by theater set designer Christian

Jank to replace the ancient ruins of Vorder-Hohenschwangau. Its model was Wartburg Castle in Thuringia – the setting for the famous Wagner opera "Tannhäuser". Ultimately, Ludwig would only spend a few days at the castle before being arrested and deposed, among other reasons because of the high construction costs of the castle and the resulting debts of the state. Today, Neuschwanstein is one of the most-visited castles in the world, and the income it generates has by far paid the debt it once created.

LINDERHOF

Linderhof was an agricultural estate near Ettal that King Ludwig II knew from hunting trips with his father Maximilian II. It became his wish to erect a copy of the palace and gardens at Versailles, but his plans proved far too ambitious for the narrow valley where Linderhof is situated. As a result, in 1869, construction began on his father's former hunting lodge, which at the time stood on the what is now the palace forecourt. Linderhof Palace is the only larger palace that Ludwig II was able to see completed. The grounds also include smaller "refuges" such as the Venus Grotto (above) and the Moorish Kiosk.

HERRENCHIEMSEE

The Old Palace on Herrenchiemsee, one of the two islands in Lake Chiemsee, is where the Basic Law of the Federal Republic of Germany was written in 1948. Far more famous, however, is the "fairytale King's" New Palace. The foundation stone for the building, whose garden façade is almost identical to that of the one in Versailles, was laid in 1878. But the project remained unfinished for financial reasons. Only twenty of the originally planned seventy rooms were completed, among them the impressive Hall of Mirrors (above).

Visible from a great distance, the Church of Wies (left) sits on a hill at Pfaffenwinkel, not far from Füssen. Its interior is exceptionally beautiful and features lavish stucco work and rich ceiling frescoes. The paintings are by Johann Baptist Zimmermann.

MUNICH

Founded in 1158, Munich owes much of its meteoric rise to Napoleon, who in 1806 made Munich the capital of Bavaria. King Ludwig I brought architectural splendor to the city while his son Maximilian II promoted the arts. The Alps seems to begin just beyond the city limits (main picture).

THE RESIDENZ

The Residenz is the historical seat of power in Munich and it is from here that Bavaria's counts, electors and kings ruled. It was built in the 16th century to replace the Neuveste Castle (from the 14th), which had replaced the Old Court as the ducal seat. Between 1568 to 1619, a Renaissance complex was built that was later expanded to include baroque, rococo and neoclassical styles.

Since World War II, the Residenz now comprises ten courtyards and 130 rooms. The Court Church of All Saints as well as the former Residenz Theater (now the Cuvilliés Theater), a splendid, newly restored rococo building, are also part of the complex.

The Residenz still plays an important role in Munich. It houses museums (including the Porcelain, Silver and Treasure Chambers in the Königsbau, Cabinet of Miniatures, State Collection of Coins, Collection of Egyptian Art) and is a prestige building for festive occasions and receptions, for example in the Antiquarium, the largest Renaissance hall north of the Alps.

MARIENPLATZ

Munich's urban center is framed by the neo-Gothic New Town Hall from 1909 (above) with its famous Glockenspiel, as well as the Old Town Hall from 1480. When Ludwig the Bavarian granted the market charter to Munich in 1315, he stipulated that the Marktplatz remain "free from building for all eternity". In 1638, Elector Maximilian I had the Marian Column erected there in gratitude for the city being spared during Swedish occupation in the Thirty Years' War. Since 1854, the center of Munich has been known as Marienplatz, named after the Madonna on top of the column.

FRAUENKIRCHE

The onion domes of the Frauenkirche are the most recognizable icons of Munich, the capital of Bavaria. They also mark an important limit: no building in the city center can be higher than their 99 m (338 ft). The Church of Our Lady, more accurately called "Cathedral of Our Blessed Lady", has ten bells. Susanna, the largest bell, dates back to 1490, and weighs eight tons. Built in what would have been a record time of twenty years by Jörg Halspach, the Gothic church is 109 m (358 ft) long, 40 m (131 ft) wide, and accommodates roughly 20,000 people. It has been the cathedral church of the archbishops of Munich and Freising since 1821.

The Antiquarium (far left, 1568–1571) is the oldest preserved room in the Munich Residenz. The name refers to the antique sculptures that decorate the space. The Cuvilliés Theater (left) is the most attractive loge theater of the Rococo age.

HOFBRÄUHAUS

Hundreds of visitors from around the world stream in and out of the Hofbräuhaus on a daily basis. It accommodates up to 1,300 guests and has become a venue of cultish proportions. The beer hall goes back to 1589, when Duke Wilhelm V had a brewery built to supply his court and servants. In 1828, Ludwig I began selling the beer at prices soldiers and working class people could afford, so they too could enjoy this "healthy" drink. The most famous regular here is an angel, Alois Hingerl, from Ludwig Thoma's 1911 story "Ein Münchner im Himmel". After too many beers he forgot his task and still sits there to this day.

NYMPHENBURG

In 1662, Electress Henriette Adelaide bore her husband, Elector Ferdinand Maria, a son and long-awaited heir to the throne of Bavaria, Max Emanuel. To show his gratitude, the ruler gifted her the extravagant Nymphenburg Palace. Unfortunately, she would not live to see its completion in 1757.
The palace's baroque façade is 700 m (766 yds) wide. Behind that, the palace park covers over 3 sq km (1 sq mi), with greenhouses, the Badenburg and Pagodenburg pavilions, and the Amalienburg hunting lodge. The summer residence of the Wittelsbachs and birthplace of Ludwig II, Nymphenburg boasts stately rooms, the Gallery of Beauties, a Nymphenburg Porcelain exhibit, and the Museum of Carriages and Sleighs in the former royal stables.

STEIN AM RHEIN, SCHAFFHAUSEN, ST GALLEN

The Rhine Falls near Neuhausen, with Laufen Castle on the southern side (main picture), are spectacular at any time of the year but they are especially impressive in early summer when the river is swollen.

STEIN AM RHEIN

Sometimes also called the "Rothenburg of the Upper Rhine" due to its medieval townscape characterized by timbered gables and bay windows, Stein am Rhein is situated where the Rhine exits the lower section of Lake Constance (Untersee). Its main gem is the town hall from 1539, which boasts a variety of painted motifs taken from the history of the region and the town. Stein's most striking appeal, however, comes from its numerous meticulously maintained medieval houses. Opposite the town hall, for instance, is the late Gothic Weisser Adler (White Eagle) with its painted Renaissance façade, while the Hirsch and Krone buildings feature magnificent five-sided wooden bays. The Rote Ochsen (Red Ox) was built in 1446 and painted in 1615. Also worth a visit is the former Benedictine monastery of St Georg, with buildings from the 14th to the 16th centuries that are open to the public. They give an impression of monastic life in the late Middle Ages. The real showpiece is Abbot David von Winkelsheim's picture gallery completed in 1516.

SCHAFFHAUSEN

The Rhine Falls are Europe's largest waterfall in terms of water volume – the drop in height is only 25 m (82 ft). Without the falls, Schaffhausen would not have developed into a town as it did early in the Middle Ages when the goods transported along the Rhine were off-loaded onto wagons here for a few miles, from which the waggoners, merchants, aldermen and toll keepers all profited. The large cathedral is testimony to the town's former

Top: View of the Old Town over the Rhine with the Munot fortress and the steeple of St John's Church. Bottom: The Fountain of the Moors on the central Fronwagplatz.

wealth and, dating from the 11th/12th centuries, it is a fine example of a very pure form of the Romanesque style. The former Benedictine All Saints Monastery, which today houses the comprehensive All Saints Cultural History Museum, was added later to the cathedral (large cloister and herb garden). The town's landmark is the Munot fortress dating from the 16th century.

Stein am Rhein is considered to be the best intact medieval town in Switzerland after Murten. It features a charming Old Town (far left) with painted façades such as this one on Rathausplatz (town hall square, left).

ST GALLEN

St Gallen has been an important cultural center in the Lake Constance region since the early Middle Ages, and the textile and weaving industries later made it an economically important town as well. The collegiate church and monastery were rebuilt in the mid-18th century in late-baroque style – only in the crypt can remains of the original 10th-century building still be seen – and the library contains books from the monastery's early days. The monastery was founded by Abbot

Top: Gallusplatz to the south-west of the cathedral is lined with magnificent townhouses.
Bottom: Room in St Gallen Abbey Library.

Otmar in the 8th century after the Irish traveling preacher and monk Gallus had settled here as a hermit in 612. The library's inventory has been expanded continuously since the early Middle Ages. Thankfully, the dissolution of the princely abbey in 1805 took place without incident and the library now contains more than 130,000 volumes as well as about 2,000 manuscripts, around 400 of which date back to before the year 1000. The most valuable of these include the "St Gallen monastery plan", a plan for the ideal monastery drawn up in about 820, as well as the Codex Abrogans, a Latin lexicon of synonyms named after its first entry and which, having been compiled in German in about 765, is considered the oldest known work in the German language.

Magnificent city gates and arcades are the landmarks of Bern's historic city center. The main picture shows the view along the Kramgasse and the Marktgasse to the Käfigturm (Prison Tower) and Zytgloggeturm (Clock Tower).

ZURICH

It is a cliché, and an incorrect one at that, to assume that the country's economic metropolis on Lake Zurich, with its more than 100 banking headquarters, is just a boring, old-fashioned financial center. Zurich boasts numerous architectural gems such as the Fraumünster church in the Old Town west of the river Limmat , which has a set of five windows by Marc Chagall. Next door is the 13th-century parish church of St Peter with Europe's largest clock face. The Grossmünster on the other side of the river, its neo-Gothic tower cupolas dominating the cityscape, entered the annals of church history as the domain of the reformer Huldrych Zwingli (1484–1531).

BERN

Once the largest city-state north of the Alps, Bern's historic center clearly depicts the chronological order of its different periods of expansion. The stately guild and townhouses with arcades extending for a total of 6 km (4 mi) are characteristic of the city center. Construction of the late Gothic St Vincent Cathedral began in 1421 and was only completed in 1573; the magnificent main portal was designed by Erhard Küng. The late-

The highly expressive Pfeiferbrunnen Piper's Fountain) in Bern.

Gothic townhouse was erected between 1406 and 1417 and renovated in 1942. The Heiliggeistkirche (Church of the Holy Spirit), from 1729, is one of the country's most important examples of Protestant baroque architecture. Bern's landmark, however, is the Zytgloggeturm (Clock Tower) city gate.
The ensemble of lovely historic residential buildings in the Gerechtigkeitsgasse stands out from the multitude of beautiful buildings in Bern, and some of them date back to the 16th century. Bern's Renaissance fountains with their lovely expressive figures are also worth seeing, three of them having been created by the Freiburg sculptor Hans Gieng.

The twin towers of Zurich's Grossmünster dominate the skyline of this, the "smallest large city in the world", situated at the northern end of Lake Zurich seen with the river Limmat – a tributary of the Aare – running through it (far left and left).

The Bernese Oberland is the cradle of Swiss tourism, which was instigated by three famous figures: Rousseau, Haller and Goethe. They sparked an enthusiasm for nature that became a trend among high society types to escape to the mountains. The Bernese were quick to react. The first official "Unspunnenspiele" (a festival uniting town and country) took place near Interlaken in 1805, set against the Alpine backdrop with yodelers, Fahnenschwingen (flag throwing), Steinstossen (stone throwing), and traditional garb – a huge open-air event two centuries ago! Visitors arrived via Lake Thun, some – like the Rothschilds for instance – with their own boats, and it is still a nice way to view the spectacular scenery. And by the time you reach Interlaken with the Eiger-Mönch-Jungfrau triumvirate, there is only one thing you will want to do: head off into the mountains!

GRINDELWALD

This health spa town nestled among the mighty Eiger at 3,970 m (13,026 ft), Wetterhorn (above) at 3,701 m (12,143 ft) and Schreckhorn at 4,078 m (13,380 ft) has been the main attraction in the Bernese Oberland for more than 150 years. A trip with the Jungfraubahn (above) from Kleiner Scheidegg through the Eiger and Mönch to Europe's highest train station, the Jungfraujoch tunnel station at an altitude of 3,454 m (11,333 ft), is a unique experience.

From left to right:
The Eiger (3,970 m/12,026 ft),
the Mönch (4,099 m/13,449 ft) and
the Jungfrau (4,158 m/13,642 ft), plus
the Männichen (2,345 m/7,694 ft) in
the foreground make up the Jungfrau
region of the Bernese Oberland.

LAKE LUCERNE

Lake Lucerne with its four cantons of Uri, Schwyz, Ob- and Nidwalden is the patriotic heart of Switzerland

and it was here on the Rütli that the oath of the Swiss Confederacy was taken in 1291, with William Tell allegedly bringing the bad bailiff to book. The lake is overlooked by the most famous viewing peak (Rigi, 1,797 m/5,896 ft) in the Alps, accessible via railway (the oldest in the world) since 1871. Lucerne, located where the Reuss River leaves the lake, boasts the famous Kapellbrücke (Chapel Bridge), a lovely promenade, and is one of the most attractive travel destinations in the country. The view over the lake takes in Titlis (3,239 m/10,627 ft), the highest mountain in the region. There is a cable car between the monastery village of Engelberg and the top of the glacier where, in this region of eternal snow, – a marketing "concept" by the resort director – Japanese and Chinese tourists like to get married.

LUCERNE

Mark Twain found Lucerne "very appealing" and added: "It begins with a fringe of hotels down at the water and crawls ... idyllically up three steep mountain slopes". The oldest town in the Swiss interior (Lucerne received its town charter in 1178) is also its cultural and economic center. Watched over by Pilatus Mountain and the Rigi peak, the town is tucked into the northern end of Lake Lucerne.

The Old Town with its picturesque squares and alleys simply compels you to take a stroll. Lucerne's landmark is the over 700-year-old wooden Chapel Bridge over the river Reuss. The Franciscan and Jesuit churches, the Ritterscher Palace as well as the Culture and Convention Center are on the left bank, while the court church and the town hall are over on the right bank.

UPPER ENGADIN, ST MORITZ, BERGELL, LOWER ENGADIN

The Morteratsch Glacier (main picture) is the largest glacier in the Bernina Range. It is framed by imposing mountains and the Piz Bernina which, at 4,049 m (13,285 ft) is the only mountain in Engadin over 4,000 m (13,124 ft).

UPPER ENGADIN

The Inn (Rhaeto-Romanic "En") Valley is lined with massive mountain chains and is around 90 km (56 mi) long. It extends from the Maloja Pass at the far eastern end of Switzerland to the Austrian border near Martina. Engadin (Rhaeto-Romanic "Engiadina") is generally taken to refer to Upper Engadin:

"This Upper Engadin is the loveliest stopover in the world," claimed Thomas Mann, who "almost" believed himself to be happy there. The Upper Inn Valley from Zuoz as far as Maloja is indeed a landscape beyond compare in the Alps. There is no oppressive sense of confinement even in the high mountains near the edge of the forest. It is a broad, open area and in the midst of

all this are the Upper Engadine Lakes which, together with the larch forests glowing golden in the autumn and the white snowcapped peaks beneath the bright blue sky, produce an alpine scenery that was a draw for nature enthusiasts even in the days of the stage coach, inspiring Nietzsche to the conclusion that: "All desire longs for eternity."

ST MORITZ

This upscale health resort in the heart of Upper Engadin enjoys special status: famous for having twice been the venue for the Winter Olympics (1928 and 1948), it has cleverly promoted itself as the "Top of the World". As the gateway to a unique landscape of lakes (Lake St Moritz, Lake Silvaplana, Lake Sils) the village, first documented in 1139, offers a wide range of sporting options with its much-lauded "champagne climate" in both winter and summer.

BERGELL

Two adjacent areas could hardly be more different than the Upper Engadine lake plateau and the Bergell valley: at the 1,815-m-high (5,955-ft) Maloja Pass, the wide valley, which rises no more than 50 m (164 ft) from the Inn ravine near St Moritz, suddenly drops dramatically to the south-east as far as the Italian border. The mountains then suddenly close up on one another, but not far away is the "threshold to paradise", as the painter Giovanni Segantini (1858–1899) named the village of Soglio (above), situated on a sunny peak above the narrow valley – one of the most popular tourist destinations in Bergell.

Nietzsche spent several summers at Lake Sils (left), where he wrote significant parts of his philosophical work *Also sprach Zarathustra* (*Thus Spake Zarathustra*). He said to a friend who visited him there that he needed to have the blue sky above him in order to gather his thoughts.

LOWER ENGADIN

The appeal of this wide valley landscape at the foot of the Silvretta Range lies in its primeval nature. Zernez, at the confluence of the Inn and the Spöl, was almost burnt to the ground in 1872 and has hardly any old buildings left at all. It is nevertheless a starting point for hikes into Swiss National Park (170 sq km/67 sq mi), which was opened on August 1, 1914, the first of its kind in Europe.

Guarda and Ardez are considered the loveliest towns in Lower Engadin. They are both subject to strict preservation orders and comprise exceptionally appealing Engadine buildings, many of which feature century-old courtyards

Tarasp Castle, built in around 1040 and towering atop a shale cliff top, is Lower Engadin's landmark.

with sophisticated scraffiti and bay windows, as well as tremendously thick walls protecting meticulously paneled living rooms and bedrooms. The valley broadens after Ardez and it is here that Scuol, its tourist center dominated by the Tarasp Castle, is situated. Until 1915, the village was considered the "spa queen of the Alps" thanks to its hot springs, but fell into oblivion thereafter only to be revived again in the 1990s with the opening of a modern version. The valley narrows again to the east and becomes more rugged and remote. A number of small villages such as Sent, Ramosch or Tschlin hug the narrow, sunny terraces before both the road and the river cross the Austrian border at Martina, close to the Finstermünz Pass ravine.

The "Top of Europe" (main picture): Europe's highest cog-railway station is situated on the Jungfraujoch (3,454 m/11,333 ft) and provides a fascinating view of the top of the Aletsch Glacier – the largest glacier in the Alps with a length of almost 24 km (15 mi) and a surface area of close to 118 sq km (46 sq mi).

The mighty flow of ice extending to the north-east between Konkordiaplatz (2,850 m/9,351 ft) near the Jungfraujoch and Riederalp (1,919 m/6,296 ft) reaches up to 1,800 m (1,968 yards) in width. What has been evident for a long while, however, is also to be seen at the Aletsch Glacier: reduction of mass, a visible sign of climate change. While the glaciers lost about one-third of their surface area and almost half of their total volume between the mid-19th-century and 1975, they have forfeited a further twenty-five per cent of their mass in the last thirty years. If the trend continues, then more than seventy-five per cent of the glaciers in the Alps will be gone by 2050. The ice does not only melt, however, it also migrates. The compacted ice moves down from the peaks and passes into the valleys, out of the so-called feeding areas and into the wear areas; a maximum of 1.5 m (5 ft) per day. A snowflake falling up on the Jungfraujoch onto the Aletsch Glacier will therefore become a drop of water again down below at the entrance to the Massa canyon after a journey probably lasting some 500 years …

The Aletsch Glacier is currently shrinking by around 50 m (55 yds) per year as a consequence of climate change. The worn shapes on the sides are easily visible in these pictures. From far left: View of the Wannenhorn; of Eggishorn with Jungfrau, Eiger and Mönch; the Jungfrau.

Enchanting in shape and with a magical light, it is no wonder that the Matterhorn is also referred to as the "crown jewel of the Alps". A particularly lovely view is with Riffel Lake in the foreground (main picture). The normal route up to the 4,478-m (14,692-ft) summit is via the distinctive Hörnligrat.

What hasn't already been written about this mountain! Bombarded regularly with superlatives, the Matterhorn's incomparable shape is much vaunted, having been referred to as the "advertising mountain" due to its use in promoting just about everything.

Who would have thought? The Matterhorn adorns not only Swiss yoghurt containers and Belgian beer bottles, it has also found itself on wine labels and on Japanese confectionery, on a cigarette carton from Jamaica and even on a poster for a Rolling Stones

European tour in 1976. Luis Trenker made a tearjerker of a film out of the tragic first ascent of the mountain (1865) by Edward Whymper, in which the four-man crew lost their lives, and in Zermatt the souvenir shops are full of Matterhorn kitsch. A mythical mountain and yet so much more than just pyramid-shaped rock?

Well, "Horu" (as it is called by locals) has brought great prosperity to the country village of Zermatt (1,616 m/5,302 ft). The hotel pioneer Alexander Seiler was the first to recognize the huge significance of this unique mountain backdrop for his tiny village. And indeed, the "mountain of mountains" has been captivating visitors since Whymper's time. They come from all over the world to marvel at this magnificent monument to Alpine altitudes, some of them even coming to climb it.

LAVAUX, GENEVA, LAUSANNE, CHILLON

Château de Chillon, the most frequently visited historical monument in Switzerland, is famous for its location upon a rock on the shores of Lake Geneva.

LAVAUX

Grapes have been cultivated on the Lavaux Vineyard Terraces for at least 1,000 years. This landscape, arguably one of the most beautiful in Switzerland, stretches roughly 30 km (19 mi) along the northern shore of Lake Geneva, from the eastern outskirts of Lausanne up to the Château de Chillon.

Three suns, so say the locals, warm the grapes there: the sunshine of the day, the reflection of the sun's rays on the lake's surface and the sun's heat that is stored by the stone walls during the day and released at night.

The present terraced landscape dates back to the Benedictine and Cistercian monks of the 11th and 12th centuries. The grape variety that is grown on the shores of Lake Geneva is called the Gutedel – a variety that is generally known as "Chasselas" or "Fendant" in Switzerland. The fourteen communes of the Lavaux produce exclusively white wines, all of them with one of the following "appellations contrôlées": Villette, Saint-Saphorin, Dézaley, Epesses and Chardonne. The wines are a major part of the economy here.

GENEVA

Geneva lies where the Jet d'Eau fires its plume of water 145 m (476 ft) into the sky, framed by the Jura and Savoy Alps and huddled into a bay on Lake Geneva. The "Protestant Rome", where around 450 years ago John Calvin propagated his rigorous ideas for reform and Henri Dunant founded the Red Cross in 1864, is today a truly international city. A third of its inhabitants are foreign; over 200 organizations including the United Nations (UN) and the World Health

Geneva is the second-largest city in Switzerland. It lies where the Rhône flows out of Lake Geneva.

Organization (WHO) have their headquarters there. But beyond the diplomats, expensive watches and Cuban cigars, there are also some worthwhile architectural attractions: St Peter's Cathedral including its archaeological excavations and adjacent Place du Bourg-de-Four; the richly stocked Museum for Art and History; the Palais des Nations – headquarters of the UN; and the memorial to philosopher and Geneva native son Jean-Jacques Rousseau. Geneva is also an Alpine city, as can be seen in the Geneva altar of Konrad Witz from 1444, in his painting *Petrus Altar* (today in the Museum of Art): depicted is a marvelous haul of fish from Lake Geneva with Mont Blanc as a backdrop.

The Lavaux Vineyard Terraces descend dramatically down to Lake Geneva (left). The lake and the Alps form a unique backdrop for the vineyards in this historic wine-growing region.

LAUSANNE

This city in Canton Vaud is on the north shore of Lake Geneva and is an important center of education and trade fairs as well as the seat of the Federal Supreme Court – the highest court in Switzerland – and of the International Olympic Committee. Scattered with villas and spread across several hills is the Old Town, which can also be reached cog railway from the port district of Ouchy. The main attraction is the early-Gothic cathedral. Consecrated in 1275, it was Switzerland's most attractive church in its day.

CHILLON

Château de Chillon, the epitome of a romantic moated castle, is roughly 5 km (3 mi) south-east of Montreux, the sophisticated holiday resort on the north shore of Lake Geneva that has become famous for its international jazz festival. Built in the 11th and 12th centuries by the counts of Savoy, the castle controlled the route from Burgundy over the Great St Bernard Pass to Italy. It became famous mainly thanks to Lord Byron's ballad, "The Prisoner of Chillon". The poet – who had visited the castle in 1816 – had been inspired to write the ballad by the fate of Geneva prior François Bonivard, who was imprisoned in Chillon for six years because of his reformist tendencies before being liberated from his chains in 1536.

TICINO

Ticino is known as the "sunny side of Switzerland", and every school-child there knows that on the other side of the Gotthard peak, the sun shines more often than in Zurich. Ticino is a popular holiday region, and some may ask themselves whether this is in fact the southern part of Switzerland or the northern part of Italy. At any rate, the Alpine world here already exudes an air of Mediterranean promise.

Hermann Hesse described Ticino, his adopted home, as "wonderfully rich and beautiful", and it is surely the diversity of contrasts that still fascinates visitors today.

LOCARNO

The heart of Ticino beats on the Swiss side of Lake Maggiore. One of the most beautiful towns on the north shore of the lake is Locarno, not far from where the Maggia River flows into the lake from its high mountain source. Locarno has been famous since 1946 for its annual film festival.

With approximately 2,300 hours of sunshine a year, the people of Locarno enjoy the mildest climate in Switzerland. The historic center of the town, first documented around the year 789, was originally directly on the lake, but over the course of centuries, the Maggia has deposited immense amounts of sediment between Locarno and Ascona that today occupies about half the former width of the lake. The icon of the town is the Madonna del Sasso Pilgrimage Church, situated on top of the wooded Belvedere Hill (above), where in 1480 the Blessed Virgin is said to have appeared to a monk, wearing a halo of bright light.

ASCONA

In around 1900, Ascona (above, view of the lakeside promenade) was still a peaceful, sleepy fishing village. But then two foreigners settled here, disgruntled with their hectic lives in the city – Belgian Henri Oedenkoven, son of an industrialist, and his partner, German pianist Ida Hofmann. They called Ascona's local mountain the "Monte Verità", or "the mountain of truth", and founded a "vegetabilist cooperative" to help in their individual quests for happiness. Light, air and love played an important role in their mission along with nudism, theosophy, emancipation and loads of raw foods. The days of the cooperative are long gone, but Locarno's much smaller western neighbor clearly still enjoys something of a reputation as a mecca for the avant-garde – and for art. It is also still a very good place to pursue happiness: the mountains, wonderful light and fresh air at least are guaranteed.

LAKE LUGANO, LUGANO

Etruscans and Gauls had already settled on Lake Lugano long before the Romans came. The lake is around 35 km (22 mi) long, up to 3 km (2 mi) wide and up to 288 m (945 ft) deep. A view of the lake from one of Lugano's two mountains – Monte Bré (above) at 925 m (3,035 ft) or Monte San Salvatore at 912 m (2,992 ft), which rises like a sugar-loaf out of the water – is spectacular. The largest part of the lake, which is 217 m (712 ft) above sea level, belongs to the Swiss canton of Ticino while the smaller part belongs to the Italian provinces of Como and Varese.

Lugano, whose Old Town square is surrounded by arcades, was the capital of Ticino from 1803 to 1878, alternating in a six-year cycle with Locarno and Bellinzona. Today it is considered the "capitale morale", the "heartfelt" capital of the Ticino, and the region around Lake Lugano, with its rolling hills and cypress trees, is known as "Tuscan Switzerland". Hermann Hesse spent almost half his life in Montagnola above the lake; a museum near his former home, the Casa Camuzzi, is dedicated to the Nobel Laureate in Literature.

Where today subtropical vegetation and the most northerly olive trees in Europe flourish, 15,000 years ago was permafrost. The basins of the lakes were dug out by glaciers, which then formed terminal moraines when they receded. That allowed the valleys to fill with water. The shores rise steeply here due to this glacial activity. The same is also true of Lake Maggiore, which is fed mainly by the Maggia, a river rising in the northern Ticino Alps.

Vienna is one of the continent's most historic metropolises and has been able to retain its splendor in the face of much adversity. The imposing St Stephen's Cathedral sits majestically in the heart of the city (main picture).

ST CHARLES' CHURCH

It is the symbolic building of those euphoric centuries after the second Turkish Siege in 1683, when Vienna was transformed into the elegant metropolis that it is today. St Charles' Church was commissioned in 1713 by the emperor of the same name, Charles VI, at the end of a plague epidemic. Its creators, Fischer von Erlach Sr and Jr, combined the classic forms of Greek, Roman and Byzantine architecture to construct the church. A temple portico rises up under the patina-green dome, while triumphal pillars decorated with spiral reliefs and a bell tower soar up on both sides. A magnificent dome fresco by J. M. Rottmayr adorns the oval interior.

ST STEPHEN'S CATHEDRAL

St Stephen's Cathedral, Vienna's most important religious building and the city's emblem, is visible from afar and affectionately known by locals as "Steffl". It is a masterpiece of stonemasonry made from 20,000 cu m (706,293 cu ft) of sandstone. It dates back a good 750 years. Its west front still originates from the previous Romanesque building; the rest is High Gothic. The

Top: The southern spire of St Stephen's Cathedral towers over Vienna.
Middle: "Pummerin", the third-largest church bell in Europe.
Bottom: The high altar, by brothers Tobias and Johann Jakob Pock.

southern spire, the third-highest in Europe, measures 137 m (449 ft) and soars gloriously towards the heavens. From its viewing deck, which is reached by climbing 343 steps, you get a panoramic view of the city. The solemn interior is peppered with artistic treasures from the past. The most prominent of these are the marmoreal tomb of Emperor Friedrich III, the New Town Altar, the so-called Servants' Madonna, and Anton Pilgram's pulpit and organ stand.

"I want to keep my vow before those who fear God" is the inscription on St Charles' Church (left). The monumental building is almost 80 m (262 ft) long, 60 m (197 ft) wide 72 m (236 ft) high at the top of the dome.

IMPERIAL CRYPT

An attraction just as curious as it is popular is the Imperial Crypt, also known as Capuchins' Crypt, on Neuer Markt square. From the early 17th century, the Habsburg rulers and their next of kin were buried in a total of 138 metal caskets in the deep vaults here, traditionally guarded by Capuchin friars, at the foot of the rather unimposing Ordenskirche. Maria Theresa and her husband Francis Stephen of Lorraine were laid to rest here – in

Behind the tomb of Emperor Joseph II is the double casket of Maria Theresa and Francis I Stephen.

a double sarcophagus that was lavishly adorned with life-size figures in rococo style. Next to them lies the reformist Emperor Joseph II in a simple copper casket much more in keeping with his humble character.
Emperor Franz Joseph I also has his final resting place here, as do his wife Elisabeth of Bavaria (known more commonly as "Sissi"), his son Rudolf, his brother Maximilian, who was murdered in Mexico, and, from 1989, Austria's last empress: Zita.

HOFBURG

The Hofburg was for many centuries the Habsburg monarchy's seat of political power and served as the imperial family's main residence. It also houses the present-day National Library (above, the ceremonial room), which Emperor Charles VI had built by Johann Bernhard Fischer von Erlach and his son in 1722. It was the first part of the court library.

COURT RIDING SCHOOL

The Spanish Riding School was not opened to the general public until after World War I. It is one of the oldest establishments for classic dressage. The performances of the legendary Lipizzaner stallions – elegant, snow-white horses originally bred in Spain – were one of the highlights of court entertainment from the 16th century.

The Hofburg, radiant in the evening light, still bears witness to the opulence with which the emperors of the Habsburg dynasty adorned their capital until the end of the monarchy in 1918.

MUSEUM OF ART HISTORY AND NATURAL HISTORY

The "twin museums" on the Burgring were designed in the early 1870s by Hamburg-born architect Gottfried Semper and Vienna native Carl von Hasenauer. The buildings look identical from the outside, but their content could hardly be more different: while the thirty-nine rooms of the Museum of Natural History (top right, a dinosaur skeleton) are home to great collections of minerals, meteorites, fossils, and skeletons as well as present-day plant and animal species, the Museum of Art History (top left, the Dome Hall) houses one of the most valuable painting galleries in the world – from Dürer and Breughel, to Rembrandt and Rubens and Tintoretto. Added to this are the Kunstkammer, coin cabinets, antiques and the Egyptian and Oriental collections.

The "Gloriette" (main picture) in the park at Schönbrunn Palace provides an excellent view over the vast "Austrian Versailles". The park is home to sculptures and fountains, as well as a Palm House and zoological garden.

SCHÖNBRUNN

The ultimate symbol of imperial, baroque Vienna will always be Schönbrunn Palace, located outside the city center in the western villa district of Hietzing. As an early 18th-century creation, it reflects the desire to express architectural exuberance, which inspired aristocratic builders after the triumph

over the Turks. In its current form, the sunny-yellow palace complex is the result of a massive renovation led by Nikolaus Pacassi and Fischer von Erlach between 1744 and 1749. Schönbrunn was the summer residence of the Habsburgs until 1918. Today, up to 11,000 admirers visit the magnificent imperial apartments, the historic coaches in the carriage collection, the Palm House, and the zoological garden every day during the high season. Like Versailles, a walk through the vast park with its artistically landscaped flower beds, hedges, ponds, fountains and statues feels simply decadent.

BELVEDERE

One of Vienna's main baroque monuments is the Belvedere, by Lukas von Hildebrandt. The legendary commander and conqueror of the Turks, Prince Eugene of Savoy, had this summer palace – actually comprising two palaces – built between 1714 and 1723. The more opulent Upper Belvedere (left) was once the scene of a significant moment in Austrian history: in 1955, in the Marble Hall, foreign ministers of the four occupying powers sealed independence for the young republic by signing the State Treaty. Masterpieces by Waldmüller, Klimt, Kokoschka and others in the palace's other rooms testify to the heyday experienced by the world of fine art in the 19th and early 20th century. The Lower Belvedere (right), which was clearly simpler on the outside but appointed almost as lavishly as its twin on the inside, is primarily reserved for special exhibitions.

KAISERGEBIRGE

What a contrast! At one end of the Kaisergebirge range are the bizarre pinnacles of the Wilder Kaiser (or "Wild Emperor", top), and at the other, the green ridges of the Kitzbühel Alps. Generations of climbers have left traces of their efforts in the light, firm limestone of the Kaisergebirge. Ludwig Purtscheller, the great alpinist, wrote about these fascinating mountains: "Other mountains may tower over them in terms of absolute height or sheer immensity, but the Kaisergebirge is unparalleled [...] when it comes to the wonderful arrangement of their bizarrely fissured peaks and horns."

KARWENDEL

This section of the Northern Tyrolean Limestone Alps, which soars up from the Seefelder Sattel in the west to Lake Achensee in the east, gets its name from the rocky gray walls and the hollows dug out of the stone by the glaciers – so-called cirques (or Kare). The highest peak in the Karwendel range, which includes the rock faces of the Laliderer (left) and the Überschalljoch (below) is the Birkkarspitze (2,756 m/9,042 ft). Cable cars are the easiest way to access the 2,334-m-high (7,658-ft) Hafelekar from Innsbruck, or the Karwendelspitze from Mittenwald in Germany. The massif, whose northern foothills transition into Upper Bavaria, is subdivided into four ranges, running from east to west. The valleys in between, with their mountain pastures covered in Swiss stone pine, are blocked off to private traffic. The region where the Isar (Munich's river) has its source is rather sparsely settled and, along with the peaks, is largely a nature reserve.

KITZBÜHEL

Geologically part of the schistous and greywacke zone, the Kitzbühel Alps, located in the Eastern Tyrol on the border with Salzburg, are a low mountain range characterized by forests and gentle grassy meadows. The name comes from the district capital of Kitzbühel, winter meeting place of the international jet set since the sporting successes of Toni Sailer, the "Blitz from Kitz". The famous Hahnenkamm Races come under the sporting and social media spotlight every year toward the end of January.

DACHSTEIN

where the three states of Styria, Salzburg and Upper Austria meet. The Dachstein group (left, the Bischofsmütze or Bishop's Cap) is a karstified limestone high plateau with several jagged peaks and the easternmost glaciers in the Alps.

HALLSTATT

This pretty little town (below) lent its name to an entire culture, the "Hallstatt Culture". When Johann Georg Ramsauer began the first excavations on the pre-history of Central Europe in the shadow of the Dachstein Mountains (left) in 1846, he and his team unearthed upwards of ten thousand priceless discoveries documenting the transition from the European Bronze Age to the early Ice Age.

The highest peak here – the Dachstein, at 2,995 m (9,827 ft) – towers over the extreme western end of the region of Styria. The mighty massif marks the point

Tavonaro Cross on the Stripsenjoch in the Wilder Kaiser range, the southern part of the Kaisergebirge mountains.

SALZBURG

Hugo von Hofmannsthal called the Salzburg state capital the "heart of the heart of Europe". This city not only produced Wolfgang Amadeus Mozart, but has also inspired artists from all over the world for centuries. Hohensalzburg Fortress, its Cathedral, Collegiate Church, residence, St Peter's and Mirabell Palace – the collective urban works of art on the Salzach between the hills of the Kapuzinerberg, Mönchsberg and Festungsberg dazzle the senses with their intense baroque atmosphere and fascinating range of cultural attractions. This urban gem that is the Getreidegasse (left) largely has Archbishop Wolf Dietrich von Raitenau to thank for its present-day appearance. Around 1600, the Archbishop had half of the city's medieval center demolished and the expansive central open spaces laid out. His successor, who was just as extravagantly minded, subsequently completed the unique architectural ensemble.

Hohensalzburg Fortress sits atop the Mönchsberg, below which nestles the charming Old Town.

MIRABELL

HELLBRUNN

Mirabell Palace (meaning nice view) was originally called Altenau, after Simone Alt, the mistress of Archbishop Wolf Dietrich von Raitenau, who had the palace built for his beloved in 1606. At the time its location was still outside Salzburg city limits. The palace (above, with Mirabell Garden), which was converted between 1721 and 1727 into a baroque complex by Lukas von Hildebrandt, Austria's most famous builder along with Fischer von Erlach, has been the registered office of the mayor and the magistrate since 1950.

Markus Sittikus, Count of Hohenems, the cousin and – from 1612 – successor of Archbishop Wolf Dietrich von Raitenau, built his "villa suburbana" between 1613 and 1615. It was a country pleasure palace with park complex and water features in the present-day district of Morzg. "May his successors have pleasure" is inscribed above the entrance. One of the murals in the Music Room (above), known as the "Octagon", which has ornate frescos by Donato Mascagni, depicts the Archbishop as a pink cavalier.

Lake Wangenitzsee (large picture) is at an altitude of 2,464 m (8,084 ft) in the Hohe Tauern National Park, a natural landscape and habitat for ibexes, marmots, bearded vultures, chamois and golden eagles (insets, from left).

GROSSGLOCKNER

The Grossglockner, Austria's highest peak, is a mighty 3,798 m (12,461 ft) and best admired from the lookout on Kaiser Franz Josefs Höhe. The high alpine road named after it, which leads into the Salzburg Fusch Valley from Heiligenblut, winds its way through twenty-six hairpin turns and over sixty bridges to an altitude of 2,500 m (8,203 ft). Built in the 1930s, it has brought more than fifty million visitors closer to these exhilarating mountains since its opening in 1935. The 50-km (31-mi) stretch of road is only open from April to November, depending on the snow conditions, and features a number of museums, educational tracks and signposted viewing points.

HOHE TAUERN

There are six national parks in Austria. The one in the Hohe Tauern is by far the largest (1,836 sq km/ 709 sq mi) and also the highest. Apart from the Grossglockner, the Grossvenediger checks in at 3,666 m (12,028 ft) some 30 km (19 mi) further west, armored with the largest interconnecting glacier district in the Eastern Alps. This region supplies the headstream of the Salzach (which flows through Salzburg) and the Isel, as well as

Top to bottom: Edelweiss, gentian and campion, the wonderful blossoms of the Hohe Tauern, give this landscape its unique appearance.

two of the mightiest waterfalls in Europe: the 380-m-high (1,247-ft) Krimmler Falls in Upper Pinzgau, and the Umbal Falls in the gorgeous Virgental valley.

Some 150 years ago, mountaineering pioneer Ignaz von Kürsinger described the Hohe Tauern as a "magical world" of mountain pastures, rock and ice, "full of great, wild natural scenery and beautiful flowers". The national park protects the last, pristine natural landscape in the Eastern Alps – and not least its unique flora and fauna.

A picture-postcard view: the Gross-glockner (left), located on the border between Carinthia and East Tyrol, with the Pasterze at its base, the largest glacier in the Eastern Alps (far left).

The Wachau Valley is known for Dürnstein, with its castle ruins, Renaissance palace, baroque monastery and former Poor Clare Convent (main picture). On a rocky promontory over the Danube is Melk Abbey, with its ornate baroque church and famous monastic library (inset).

The steep, narrow valley road that leads through Wachau begins in the west with the grandiose, baroque monastic residence of Melk which, with its imposing twin-spired domed church, is the "crown jewel" of this area. A number of castles, castle ruins, palaces and churches adorn the river valley between the pretty villages of Obstbauerndorf and Winzerdorf.

This area is also home to the small township of Willendorf, made famous by what was the most important discovery from the Old Stone Age – the Venus of Willendorf. After the wine-growing towns of Spitz and Weissenkirchen you reach Dürnstein, where a hike up to the monastery beneath the castle ruins is worth the effort. The slender late-baroque tower of the

monastery is one of the most elegant of its kind. The valley widens after Dürnstein, and provides a clear view as far as Krems, the medieval town with the Gothic buildings of the Gozzo-Burg, the Dominican Church and the Church of the Piarist Order. The Göttweig monastery perched ceremoniously on a hilltop marks the end of the Wachau Valley.

Just a short distance away from Dürn-stein is the wine-growing town of Weissenkirchen (left), dominated by a mighty fortified church dating back to the 14th century.

The view of castle hill in Graz from the Franciscan Church is dramatic. The Herrengasse (main picture) lies in one of the best-preserved Old Towns in Central Europe – an exemplary series of winding residential streets, bourgeois mansions and aristocratic palaces from the Renaissance and baroque periods. But this regional metropolis on the Mur, once an important bulwark against the Ottomans and today Austria's second-largest city with 250,000 inhabitants, has more than just a charming backdrop. At the base of the clocktower, the main icon of Graz located on castle hill, is an extremely vibrant cultural, spiritual and intellectual city, as demonstrated by reputable universities, theaters, festivals like the "Styriarte" or "Steirischer Herbst" ("Styrian Autumn"), and museums such as the Kunsthaus art gallery, the Joanneum with its Old and New Galleries, and the Landeszeughaus armory museum with its historic armatures and weapons. Tradition and modernity suggest a successful symbiosis in Graz, from the ornate Old Town to spectacular projects like the floating shell island in the Mur (below), an integrated work by New York artist Vito Acconci that is held in place with steel cables and accessible via bridges.

LAKE MILLSTATT, NOCKBERGE MOUNTAINS

A famous monastery, an ancient Roman settlement, and diverse fauna await visitors on the shores of Lake Millstatt (main picture, view toward Seeboden from Döbriach) and its surrounding area. Nearby Spittal an der Drau can lay claim to the most beautiful Renaissance building in the country: Porcia Castle.

A matchless ambience welcomes those seeking rest and relaxation in the Nockberge mountains (above), whose highlight is the Schiestlnock region at 2,206 m (7,238 ft), largely unsettled grassy mountains reminiscent of Scotland. The region is strictly protected in a national park covering 185 sq km (71 sq mi). Conversely, high alpine scenery characterizes the backdrop of the Malta Valley, which leads westward from Gmünd, the region's capital, into a world of thundering waterfalls and majestic ice-capped peaks towering up to heights of 3,000 m (10,000 ft). The Kölnbrein Dam – Austria's highest dam at 204 m (669 ft) – dominates the end of the valley.

KLAGENFURT

Klagenfurt is the region's cultural and political center. Art and pub scenes prove to be more urbane than one would expect from a city with not even 100,000 inhabitants. Its historic center has been lovingly renovated and exudes an almost Latin ambience in summer. The city's most recognizable icon is the Lindworm at Neuer Platz square and the "Wappensaal" in the regional parliament building (above).

LAKE WÖRTH

Near Klagenfurt, large stretches of the Lake Wörth (Wörthersee) shore-line radiated sophistication. The highlight and main cultural-historic attraction on the southern shore is the predominantly late-Gothic former collegiate church – today parish church – of Maria Wörth (main picture on the horizon). The Madonna on the high altar at this popular pilgrimage site is an exquisite piece from 1420.

ROME

The center of the present-day metropolis of Rome – located at a bend in the Tiber River – was first settled around 3,000 years ago. The people who settled here left traces of their civilizations from the very start, providing Rome with tremendous appeal for anyone interested in art, architectural and cultural history.

The presence of the city's mythical founders, Romulus and Remus, can be felt during a walk through its fascinatig streets just as much as that of the other well-known Roman emperors and popes who resided in this, the capital city of Christianity, during the Renaissance and baroque periods. More than any other city, Rome is testimony to the advanced development of European culture and it is indeed here that some of the deepest roots of western civilization are to be found.

THE CAPITOL

In ancient times, there was a temple on the Capitoline Hill that was dedicated to Jupiter, king of the gods. It was reached by a winding path leading south-east from the Forum. Today you climb the hill from the west on a flight of stairs designed by Michelangelo. At the top is a piazza, also designed by Michelangelo, and which is paved with a geometric pattern. The bronze equestrian sculpture of Marcus Aurelius in the center of the square (above, today a copy) is the only one of its kind to have escaped being melted down in the Middle Ages because the rider was thought to be Constantine I, defender of Christianity. The Palazzo Senatorio on the piazza is the seat of the mayor of Rome.

FORUM ROMANUM

Located between the Palatine Hill and the Capitoline Hill, the Roman Forum and the other buildings dating from the 6th century BC were the site of religious ceremonies and political gatherings. It was here, for example, that speeches were held and all manner of merchandise offered for sale. During the day it was said to have been a bustling areal full of buyers and sellers.

The fall of the Roman Empire saw the deterioration of Forum buildings (above) such as the triumphal arch of Septimius Severus, the Temple of Saturn and the Temple of Vespasian in front of the baroque Santi Luca e Martina Church, which then fell into disuse. In the Middle Ages the Forum was known as the Campo Vaccino, the cow's meadow.

THE COLOSSEUM

THE PANTHEON

Among the highlights on Capitoline Hill are the remains of a colossal statue from the 4th century BC in the courtyard of the Palace of the Conservators. It depicts Emperor Constantine I and once stood in the apse of the Basilica of Constantine on the Roman Forum. The unclothed body parts were made of marble while the rest was of bronze-clad wood.

The site where the towering ruins of the largest amphitheater in antiquity now stand was once occupied by a wooden construction that fell victim to the great fire of AD 64. Nero's included those grounds in his new palace and even had an artificial pond built. His successor Vespasian then commissioned a three-story stone arena in about the year AD 72, a magnificent building financed in part by the gold and other treasures that fell into Roman hands following the plundering of the temple in Jerusalem. The consecration of the colosseum was marked by games that lasted one hundred days during which a multitude of people and thousands of animals were killed in the name of mass entertainment.

The Piazza della Rotonda to the west of the Via del Corso boasts one of the most impressive buildings of antiquity: the Pantheon. Built in 27 BC, the Pantheon was a temple dedicated to all of the gods, as its name implies. The round opening in the dome was of mythical significance, creating a link with the heavens. Inside the former temple are the tombs of the painter Raphael and the first king of unified Italy, Victor Emanuel II.

Bernini's Allegory of the Ganges (main picture) is one of four allegories of the four main continents – in this case Asia – known to Renaissance geographers. It adorns the Fontana dei Quattro Fiumi (Fountain of Four Rivers) built in the middle of the Piazza Navona in 1651.

PIAZZA DI SPAGNA

This square is so named because it was here that the Spanish ambassador to the Holy See had his residence in the 17th century. This area was alleged to be unsafe for young Romans at the time, some of whom apparently disappeared without a trace here – presumably forced into serving in the Spanish army. The popular name "Spanish Steps", which refers to the first part of the staircase built in 1726 linking Piazza di Spagna with the Trinità dei Monti church higher up, is misleading because its construction was initiated by a French cardinal. The staircase in the middle of Rome was actually intended to proclaim the greatness of the French monarch.

PIAZZA NAVONA

This piazza was not originally built as such, but rather emerged as the result of organic growth over the centuries. Its oblong outline is testimony to the fact that this was once the site of a stadium built by Julius Caesar and subsequently expanded under Domitian in about AD 85. In the early Middle Ages a church was built here on the purported site of St Agnes' death as a martyr. Living quarters and shops eventually rose where the lower

The Fontana del Nettuno created by Antonio del la Bitta between 1873 and 1878 depicts the Roman god of the sea killing an octopus with a spear.

sections of the former grandstand lay, and they gradually developed into larger buildings. Sixtus IV established a market here in 1477, and in 1495 the square, which also used to be a horse racing venue, was paved over.
In the mid-17th century, Bernini and Borromini were commissioned with the expansion of the square. Bernini's creations included the Fontana di Quattro Fiumi while Borromini took on the construction of Sant' Agnese. The Fontana di Quattro Fiumi was financed by a special tax levied on bread, among other things, a measure that was wildly unpopular at the time.

The official name of the Spanish Steps (left) is "Scalinata della Trinità dei Monti". They are a popular meeting place. The Fontana della Barcaccia (far left) at the foot of the steps features a bark by Piero Bernini in commemoration of the flooding of the Tiber in 1598, when boat traffic was still possible.

FONTANA DI TREVI

Rome's most famous fountain is the Fontana di Trevi completed in 1751 by Nicola Salvi. In fact, Anita Ekberg's legendary "bath" in this fountain – from a scene in Fellini's film *La Dolce Vita* (1960) – made a significant contribution to the fountain's fame. There are also superstitions involving the fountain, for example, that anyone who throws a coin into the fountain, whose central figure depicts the god of the sea flanked by tritons, is sure to return to Rome. At around 26 m (85 ft) in height and 20 m (66 ft) in width, the Fontana di Trevi is the largest fountain in Rome.

PIAZZA DEL POPOLO

The Piazza del Popolo used to provide access to the city from the north. Having undergone several conversions, the appearance of the "people's square" is today the work of architect Giuseppe Valadier, who wanted to "open up" Rome. When he began the conversion of the piazza in 1816, Valadier left the 1,500-year-old Porta del Popolo gate and the adjacent Santa Maria del Popolo Church standing along with the two 17th-century churches Santa Maria in Montesanto and Santa Maria dei Miracoli. The center of the square is crowned by an ancient Egyptian obelisk that is around 3,200 years old.

ST PETER'S

Facing St Peter's Square (above) is the mighty façade of St Peter's Basilica, officially known as San Pietro in Vaticano and which was built in the 16th century on the site of the apostle Peter's cruci-fixion. It is also where Emperor Constantine built Rome's first basilica. The present-day building is some 45 m (148 ft) high and 115 m (126 yds) wide. The height of the lantern crowning the dome is 132 m (433 ft) and the interior covers an area of 15,000 sq m (16,145 sq ft). It can accommo-date around 60,000 worshippers. Naturally, the most famous artists of the age were involved in its construction: architects Bramante and Sangallo, sculptors Bernini and Maderno, and master painters Michelangelo and Raphael (both of whom were employed as archi-tects as well). St Peter's grave is said to be located in the so-called "grotto" beneath the church.

St Peter's Basilica is an oblong building in the shape of a Latin cross. The central dome high above the crossing lets in light.

THE SISTINE CHAPEL

The Sistine Chapel, commissioned in 1477 by Pope Sixtus IV, was not just a place of worship but also a fortress with walls that are 3 m (10 ft) thick. It also continues to serve as the venue for the papal conclave, in which the College of Cardinals elects a new pope. Upon the completion of construction work in 1480, Lorenzo de' Medici, the "ruler" of Florence, sent a number of his city's leading artists to Rome to decorate the interior of the chapel with frescoes. Having waged war against the pope in the preceding years, he now wanted to make a gesture of peace. The artists included Pietro Perugino, Sandro Botticelli and Domenico Ghirlandaio. The walls were decorated with scenes from the lives of Jesus and Moses, while the ceiling of the dome was transformed into a luminescent blue sky with golden stars. It was only later, from 1508 to 1512, that it was painted over by Michelangelo.

LAKE GARDA, LAKE COMO, LAKE MAGGIORE, LAKE ORTA

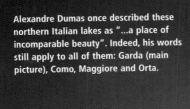

Alexandre Dumas once described these northern Italian lakes as "...a place of incomparable beauty". Indeed, his words still apply to all of them: Garda (main picture), Como, Maggiore and Orta.

LAKE GARDA

Lake Garda (above, the town of Gardone) was known as "Lacus benacus" in antiquity, after the Neptune-like divinity Benacus. The lake, which is 52 km (32 mi) long and up to 346 m (1,135 ft) deep, is fed by the Sarca, Ponale and Campione rivers. It has long been a popular holiday destination and is particularly popular among windsurfers.

LAKE COMO

Lake Como is 51 km (32 mi) long and 4 km (2.5 mi) at its widest point and is situated between the Lugarno and Bergamo Alps. Bellagio (above) is the loveliest town this stunning body of water, carved into the narrow valley by the Adda glacier and still fed by the Adda River. Comer divides into the Como and Lecco arms to the south.

LAKE MAGGIORE

LAKE ORTA

Lake Maggiore extends from the southern Alps to the Po River plain and is fed by the Ticino River, a tributary of the Po. Four-fifths of the lake are in Italy and the rest is in Switzerland. It is 66 km (41 mi) long and has four islands (Isole Borromee) situated in the Gulf of Verbania. The most famous of them is Isola Bella.

Measuring just 13 km (8 mi) in length, Lago d'Orta is one of the smallest, but also one of the most idyllic of the north Italian lakes. The resort town of Orta San Giulio (above) with its lovely Palazzo della Comunità – the old 16th-century town hall – is located on a narrow peninsula that extends far out into the lake.

South Tyrol is a region with a long history with its commercial heart Bolzano and its spiritual center at the Neustift Monastery.

BRESSANONE

At the confluence of the Rienza and Isarco rivers, the Isarco Valley widens to form a broad natural caldera that is home to the town of Bressanone, a bishop's see since 990, as well as the oldest and second-largest settlement in the region of South Tyrol. Bressanone remained the bishop's seat for nearly 1,000 years until 1964, when Bolzano took over for the then newly created diocese of Bolzano-Bressanone. The skyline of Bressanone is still one of the most beautiful in all of South Tyrol. Its historic center, which has been at least partially transformed into a pedestrian zone, is a perfect example of well-preserved alpine city architecture.

NEUSTIFT MONASTERY

Legend has it that the founding of Neustift Monastery can be traced back to the fate of bereaved parents: When their four-year-old son died, Reginbert and Christine of Sabiona are said to have given up all hope of earthly fortune and bequeathed their belongings to Bressanone's Bishop Hartmann, who founded an Augustinian choral monastery before the gates of the city in 1492. Since then, people have lived there according to the "Rule of St Augustine", which dates back to the Church Father, Augustine of Hippo (354–430), and

Above: In 1350, a cycle of frescoes was created in Neustift Monastery that included this portrayal of the Adoration of the Magi in Bethlehem. Right: The three-aisled monastery church, a baroque gem, was given its present-day appearance in 1753.

states: "First and foremost, you shall dwell together in unity, and be of one mind and one heart in God". As a popular resting stop for pilgrims on the way to Rome or the Holy Land, the monastery quickly became an important point of reference in European spiritual life. The "Wunderbrunnen" (miracle fountain) from 1508 in the monastery courtyard testifies to the confidence and humor of the Order, and its frieze not only depicts the seven ancient wonders of the world, but also the Neustift Monastery – as the eighth. Regarding earthly pleasures is a quotation from the South Tyrolean journalist and historian, Josef Rampold: "It has always been difficult to distinguish art connoisseurs from wine lovers in Neustift, and the fine line between them is often astonishingly blurred in the monastery cellar."

Bressanone was for centuries the seat of a powerful prince-bishop. The cloister of its cathedral (far left and left) is considered a compendium of the region's Gothic fresco painting.

BOLZANO

The main square in the capital of South Tyrol (Bozen, in German) is named after German minnesinger Walther von der Vogelweide, who has been looking out over Waltherplatz (right) from his pedestal since 1889. From then on, Bolzano developed into a big city. In the Mussolini era, it was given a more Italian look, with imperial features and heroic monuments around the Piazza Vittoria – and a growing industrial district. Nowadays, there is clearly more Italian than German spoken in the city.

MERANO

Merano is a popular health resort town (right) in the Adige Valley, with a mild climate, cozy loggias, elegant promenades, tiny alleyways, and the Tyrol Castle towering majestically over the city. The Adige has its source somewhat above Lago di Resia, which was dammed in 1950, and for which 163 houses in the villages of Curon and Resia had to be sacrificed. Today, only the tip of one church spire can be seen poking up out of the water. Italy's second-longest river, the Adige, flows through Merano, Bolzano, Trento and Verona before reaching the Adriatic.

TRENTO

A gem of a city, Trento is an ancient trading center situated in the wide valley where the Valsugana splits from the Adige Valley toward Bassano and Padua. The capital of Trentino, Trento's Old Town is characterized by Renaissance architecture. The Council of Trent was set up here in the 16th century and took almost twenty years to prepare the Catholic Church for the Counter-Reformation. The Romanesque cathedral (right) with its baroque dome was begun in 1212, and bubbling away in front of it in the Piazza Duomo is the baroque Fountain of Neptune.

TYROL CASTLE

The history of Tyrol Castle, first officially mentioned in 1140, also reflects the history of the region established in the 13th century under Count Meinhard II and named after this former ancestral seat of the counts of Tyrol. The heydays here were followed by years of decline. In 1347, the castle was besieged by King Charles of Bohemia, who was later unable to overcome the dogged resistance of Countess Margarete of Tyrol-Görz, known as Margarete Maultasch or Margarete "the Ugly". In the 16th century, when the Countess of Tyrol moved her residence first to Merano and then later

Tyrol Castle, which houses 13th-century frescoes, rises up on a moraine hill at the northern edge of the town of Merano.

to Innsbruck, Tyrol Castle went into noticeable decline. It was destined for the auction block to be sold "for demolition" and used as stone quarry. After a long hibernation, extensive restoration work became a necessity; it was only completed in 1984.

Since June 2003, Tyrol Castle has been the home of the South Tyrol Regional Museum for Cultural and Local History. When visiting the complex, located above the town of Merano, it is particularly worth admiring the ornately decorated entrances of the main building (great hall) and the frescoes in the castle chapel. The castle's great hall still has its old round-arched windows that provide a lovely view of the "Cradle of Tyrol" beyond the fertile Adige Valley.

THE DOLOMITES

The primeval Tethys Ocean is said to have once covered the area where the towering Dolomites now stand. It was a tropical region at that time and as a result, huge limestone coral reefs flourished along the flat coastlines. Over the course of the millennia this limestone changed into dolomite, a mineral named after the French mineralogist Dieudonné de Gratet de Dolomieu. Forty million years ago, the Tethys basin was thrust upwards and the Dolomites are one of the consequences of that momentous development. The high plateaus have huge peaks, some with craggy, blade-like pinnacles. The Marmolada is the highest of them at 3,342 m (10,965 ft).

"The loveliest mountains in the world? The Dolomites!" – Le Corbusier. Indeed, Mother Nature provided us with some truly magnificent shapes and colors here between the Isarco and Marmolada, and the Pusteria Valley and Feltre.

The Tre Cime di Lavaredo, Italian for "three peaks of Lavaredo" (on the right), form the most famous profile of the Dolomite Range.

Mantua is particularly picturesque when its medieval fortress walls are reflected in the three reservoirs of the Mincio. They too date back to the Middle Ages (main picture).

VERONA

Verona became popular among lovers thanks to William Shakespeare, before whom, admittedly, a half-dozen other authors had already told the melodramatic story of Romeo and Juliet. Fortunately for him, none had done it so touchingly as the Englishman. Many visitors still come to Verona's Casa Giulietta to stroke the right breast of the bronze figure of Juliet in the hope of finding luck in love. But it is not just because of the dramatic couple that visitors come to Verona. Thousands also come for the Opera Festival in the ancient arena, which of course goes well with Shakespeare: opera is often a feast of fantasy, frequently melodramatic, and very rarely without heartbreak.

Architecturally and artistically speaking, Verona is a virtual treasure trove. Sites worth seeing include: the Romanesque abbey church of San Zeno Maggiore with its masterly bronze reliefs on the doors; the Sant' Maria Matricolare Cathedral and the majestic Gothic church of Sant' Anastasia; the Piazza delle Erbe and the Triumphal Arch; and the Teatro Olympico. Make sure also to cross the Ponte Pietra to reach the north bank of the Adige, the oldest part of the city, with a Roman theater and some more interesting churches.

Left from top: The Ponte Pietro (the oldest bridge over the Adige), presumably built in the 1st century; the Arena di Verona at the Piazza Bra; the Piazza dell'Erbe; the Basilica di San Zeno.

MANTUA

The heart of Manuta is the Piazza Mantegna with the Basilica di Sant' Andrea, whose construction started in 1472, at the Piazza dell'Erbe. The Duomo Santi Pietro e Paolo is adorned with frescoes created between 1599 and 1605. Rising up at the Piazza Sordello is the Palazzo Ducale – a residence of the Gonzaga family. Its ornate rooms, lavishly decorated with frescoes and paintings, are now home to an antiques collection and a collection of paintings. The Castello San Giorgio, the oldest part of the palace, dates back to the 14th century. Its Camera degli Sposi contains particularly magnificent frescoes completed in 1474 – the impressively beautiful illusionist paintings on the ceiling are the oldest of their kind.

The Piazza Sordello (top) is bordered by the baroque façade of the cathedral, the Romanesque Campanile (bell tower) and the Palazzo Ducale. The fresco by Andreas Mantegna (above) adorns the Camera degli Sposi in the Palazzo Ducale and depicts the Duke of Mantua, Ludovico Gonzaga III, with his wife, Barbara of Brandenburg, their children and courtiers.

Padua's world-famous Arena Chapel (Cappella degli Scrovegni) was painted by Giotto di Bondone in the early 14th century (main pictures). Sponsored by banker Enrico Scrovegni, the vivid depiction of its figures was a novelty at the time.

VICENZA

Vicenza was founded back in Roman times and rose to architectural fame when it joined together with the Republic of San Marco – Venice, that is – in 1404. Gothic residences and Renaissance buildings have been lovingly preserved in the Old Town, in particular the works of Antonio Palla-dio, who was born in Padua in 1508. The artworks in the Museo Civico (in one of Palladio's former palaces) and the palaces along the Corso Andrea Palladio are also worth seeing.

Palladio made his breakthrough as the winner of a competition to redesign the Palazzo della Ragione, the town hall. His design surrounded the two levels of the building, also known as the "Basilica", with rows of arcades and the window that was later called the "Palladio motif". It has a wide central arch, flanked by two narrow vertical openings the same height as the arch impost. An extreme rarity is the Teatro Olimpico, Palladio's last work and a fascinating attempt at reconstructing and restoring such an old structure.

PADUA

In ancient times, Patavium was one of the wealthiest cities in northern Italy. After being totally destroyed by the Lombards in the early 7th century, Padua quickly recovered and in 1222, became one of the first university cities in Europe. It now has a population of around 210,000 today.

The Giotto frescoes in the Arena Chapel should be the first thing on any tour of the city. They depict the life of Mary and Christ, as well as the Last Judgment and allegories of virtue and vice – a realistic, religious cosmos created by the artist born near Florence in 1266.

Following a fire, the Palazzo della Ragione, the medieval town hall, was given the giant, almost 80-m-

The marshy plain of the Prato della Valle was drained through a canal in the 18th century. The banks are lined with statues depicting the city's scholars (above).

long (262-ft) and 27-m-high (89-ft) hall on the first floor in 1435 – an architectural feat so impressive that the entire building has been called "Il Salone" ever since. At the nearby university you can see the Teatro Anatomico, where medicine students have listened to lectures since 1600.

Farther west is the baptistery, built in 1260, with mysterious paintings by Giusto de' Menabuoi. Standing in front of the Basilica di Sant' Antonio is the Basilica of St Anthony, overarched by several cupolas and home to one of Italy's most famous equestrian statues: Donatello's Erasmo da Narni, known as Gattamelata. Padua is also home to the oldest botanical garden in Europe, with some plants that are well over one hundred years old.

The stage in Vicenza's Teatro Olimpico, designed by Palladio, is a unique production in and of itself. The set, which is modeled on Roman examples, takes the form of a palace façade adorned with sculptures, five entrances and wooden backdrops to create the illusion of an idyllic ancient city.

VENICE

SAN GIORGIO MAGGIORE

From the piazzetta at the Doge's Palace it is easy to see the San Giorgio Maggiore Church (main picture) situated on a small island in the Canale della Giudecca – one of more than 100 islands in Venice. The relics of St Stephanus of Constantinople are said to have been brought here in 1109, the result being that the church and monastery adjacent to the grave of the apostle Mark subsequently became an important pilgrimage site in the lagoon city. In 1223, the monastery was destroyed by an earthquake, but its buildings were rebuilt between the 15th and 17th centuries and those are what you see today.

ST MARK'S CATHEDRAL

St Mark's cathedral features five mosaic portal niches that form the eastern end of St Mark's Square. The close connections with the Byzantine Empire meant that Venice's main church, built between 976 and 1094, had the stylistic influences that region.

THE DOGE'S PALACE

Starting in 9th century, the Doge's Palace was the residence of the Venetian head of state and the seat of the Venetian government. The present day appearance of this marble and stone master-piece dates from the 14th and 15th centuries.

THE CANAL GRANDE, THE RIALTO BRIDGE

The Canale Grande is roughly 4 km (2 mi) long and lined with magnificent palaces built and owned by nearly five centuries, of merchants and nobility. It is the main traffic artery in Venice upon which a throng of gondolas and vaporetti ply their way. The end of the canal is marked on the right bank by the baroque Santa Maria della Salute Church with its wonderful dome. The roofed Rialto Bridge (above) spans the canal at about its halfway point. Originally a wooden bridge, between 1588 and 1592 it was built of stone with its present design, including two rows of shops.

THE CATHEDRAL, GALLERIA VITTORIO EMANUELE II, LA SCALA

The trio of Milan includes the cathedral (main picture), the Galleria (below) and La Scala (below, with the Leonardo da Vinci memorial statue on the left). During Late antiquity the Roman Empire was at times ruled from Milan, and the city became one of the focal points of the new Italy in the Middle Ages. Its greatest sightseeing attraction is the cathedral, a masterpiece of Italian Gothic 157 m (515 feet) in length and 92 m (302 feet) at its widest point. It is one of the world's largest Gothic churches and the marble façade is decorated with no less than 2,245 individual statues.
The Piazza del Duomo forms the heart of Milan and is linked to the Piazza della Scala by the Galleria Vittorio Emanuele II, which has been an exemplary model for many modern shopping center architects. The Teatro alla Scala is Milan's famous opera house, owing its reputation as the "best opera house in the world" to the wonderful acoustics, and its existence to Empress Maria Theresia.

SANTA MARIA DELLE GRAZIE

Santa Maria delle Grazie was constructed between 1465 and 1482 by Guiniforte Soari as a high Gothic Dominican convent. In 1492, Renaissance master builder Donato Bramante began work on a new choir with semi-circular apses. Just five years later, in 1497, Leonardo da Vinci then completed his monumental wall painting *The Last Supper* (below) in the abbey's refectory. The piece depicts the moment in which Jesus utters the famous words: "One of you will betray me".

THE CINQUE TERRE

The five villages (Cinque Terre) of Monterosso, Vernazza (main picture), Corniglia, Manarola and Riomaggiore are simply striking, clinging to the cliffs and bays of the steep Ligurian coast between Levanto and Portovenere.

Though hard to believe, there is still no direct road along the coast that connects the five sleepy hamlets. But perhaps it is for the better. In the past the impassable coastline was accessed using footpaths and steps. The Via dell'-Amore, which seems to hug the craggy rocks, links Riomaggiore (top), the most eastern Cinque Terre village, with Manarola (middle), where the Natività di Maria Vergine Church boasts a Carrara marble rose window on its façade. Corniglia (above) is the only one of the five villages about 100 m (328 ft) above the sea.

PORTOVENERE

Portovenere at the western end of the La Spezia Gulf is just one of the architectural gems to be found along the Ligurian coast. Situated on a cliff above the town is the 13th-century San Pietro Church with its black and white marble façade, as well as a Genoese fortress dating back to the 12th century. The Cinque Terre strip of coast extends to the north-west of Portovenere.

SAN VITALE

Ravenna was once the capital of the Western Roman Empire, later became the center of power of the Goths before developing into the focus of the Byzantine part of Italy until it was conquered by the Lombards in 751. A number of buildings from that era survive in nearly original form in Ravenna and feature fascinating mosaics. They are among the most important remnants of early Christianity. Close to the old city wall is the San Vitale Church (main picture, the capped vault of the presbytery), which was built between 525 and 547, based on the Hagia Sophia in Constantinople (now Istanbul).

The church is a plain, octagonal brick building from the outside, but the interior boasts surprisingly lavish décor. The unique mosaics depict scenes from the Bible as well as of the imperial couple Theodora and Justinian with their entourage. The dome vault of the apse features Christ seated on a luminescent blue globe framed by two angels, Bishop Ecclesius and the church's namesake, St Vitalis.

SANT'APOLLINARE IN CLASSE

The Basilica of Sant'Apollinare in Classe, situated about 5 km (3 mi) outside of Ravenna and built between 533 and 549, has an especially impressive interior consisting of twenty-four columns made of Greek white marble, each linked via arches that separate the nave (above) from the side aisles. The mosaics in the apse dome are from the 6th century are definitely worth taking a look at. They depict an intaglio cross in the night sky symbolizing Christ's transfiguration, flanked by the Old Testament prophets Moses and Elias. Beneath that is St Apollinare, to whom the church is dedicated, standing in the midst of a blossoming paradise landscape.

PISA, LUCCA

PISA

LUCCA

The cathedral, the baptistery, the Camposanto, and the Leaning Tower ("Campanile") constitute a unique ensemble in Pisa known as the Piazza del Duomo. The tower here began to lean in 1185, due to the marshy subsoil, twelve years after construction had begun – and with only the first three floors completed. One hundred years passed before efforts were made to counter the leaning by means of a significant slant in the opposite direction.

The cathedral exhibits the characteristic light and dark stone stripes of the Pisan style. The most eye-catching feature of the nave (above) is the mosaic by Francesco di Simone and Cimabue in the apse depicting the seated Christ, flanked by Mary and John. The large image shows the grand façade with the Campanile and the Fontana dei Putti.

Lucca originally developed on a tiny island in the marshes of Serchio – "luk" means marsh in the Ligurian language. Situated on the Via Francigena, Lucca enjoyed economic importance even as a Roman colony. The fortifications of the town began in 1544, and anyone wanting to reach the city center today has to pass through one of the eleven fortified gates. The city wall, which is 4 km (2.5 mi) in length and up to 30 m (98 ft) thick, has trees growing on it. The buildings around the Piazza del Mercato (above) were originally built around the former Roman amphitheater.

The Tuscan capital on the Arno River (right) is considered the birthplace of the Renaissance and of humanism, which began around 600 years ago and is of paramount importance for the history of European art. The elevated Piazzale Michelangelo provides an overwhelming view (main picture) of the city including the mighty red dome of Santa Maria del Fiore built by Filippo Brunelleschi between 1420 and 1436 as a central highlight of the center.

THE BAPTISTERY, CATHEDRAL, AND CAMPANILE

Upon seeing the baptistery (top left) Michelangelo is purported to have said that, "only the gates of paradise could be so wonderful." The church, which dates back to the 4th century and is the location of Dante's baptism, is among the oldest buildings in the city. Magnificent 13th-century mosaics (right) adorn the cupola above the baptismal font. The baptistry is also renowned for its splendid portals depicting scenes from the Old and New Testaments.

Construction of the Santa Maria del Fiore Cathedral began in 1296. Consecrated in 1436, Florence's most famous landmark is 153 m (502 ft) long, 90 m (295 ft) wide in the transept and, with the lantern on the octagonal dome, 116 m (381 ft) high, making it the fourth largest church in the Occident after the cathedrals in Rome, London and Milan. Construction of the freestanding bell tower, almost 85 m (279 ft) in height and clad in marble of different hues, was begun by Giotto in 1334.

FLORENCE

PIAZZA DELLA SIGNORIA, PALAZZO VECCHIO

The secular center of Florence is the Piazza della Signoria, home to the Loggia dei Lanzi, with its priceless sculptures, and the Palazzo Vecchio, the seat of the mighty Medici government completed in 1322.

The foundation stone for the Palazzo Vecchio (top) was laid in 1299. Sculpture later enjoyed a golden age in the Florence of the Medicis, and Michelangelo's world-famous *David* puts in two appearances in the city: the original in the Galleria dell'Accademia (middle left) and a replica in front of the Palazzo Vecchio (middle right shadow). Ammannati's *Fountain of Neptune* (bottom left) and Bandinelli's *Hercules and Cacus* at the Piazza della Signoria are also masterpieces to behold.

THE UFFIZI

The Medici family determined the city's fate for generations. Their rise began with Giovanni (1360–1429), who was able to increase his fortune through banking, the pope being his best customer. The Uffizi, begun in 1560, was initially used as administrative buildings for the Medicis.

Today, the buildings of the Uffizi (top) are testimony to both the Medici passion for collecting art and to their generous patronage of the arts. Middle: A sculpture gallery. Bottom left: Lorenzo de' Medici, also known as "il Magnifico". Bottom right: Duke Cosimo I, who commissioned the construction of the building, designed by Giorgio Vasari.

PONTE VECCHIO

PALAZZO PITTI

Only goldsmiths used to be permitted to ply their trade on this world-famous bridge with its tiny shops. In Roman times a wooden bridge spanned the Arno here.

The Palazzo Pitti (top, with a sculpture by Roberto Barni; bottom, a bedroom) was built between 1457 and 1819 for the banker Luca Pitti. It combines several styles due to its centuries of building phases. In 1550, the Medicis made the palace their main residence. The adjacent Boboli Garden from 1590 is a gem of Italian garden design. Today the palace and garden are home to seven museums and galleries, including the world famous Galleria Palatina.

The Salone dei Cinquecento, 1495 (main picture) on the first floor of the Palazzo Vecchio is decorated with city views and images of battle by Vasari and his atelier. Six freestanding sculptures by Vincenzo de' Rossi in front of the walls represent the deeds of Hercules. Michelangelo's sculpture *Genius of Victory*, originally created for the tomb of Pope Julius II in Rome, was displayed here in 1565.

FLORENCE

SANTA MARIA NOVELLA

SAN LORENZO

CAPPELLE MEDICEE

This Dominican church was built in the 13th century and is famous for the many frescoes in its choir chapel. From top to bottom: The main choir chapel dedicated to the Virgin Mary and St John the Baptist; view of the nave; the Chiostro Verde, "green cloister"; view of the exterior façade.

San Lorenzo is one of the oldest churches in Florence. The first structure was consecrated in AD 393; the second was built in 1059; and Brunelleschi renovated the church in 1419. From top to bottom: View of the dome; fresco by Agnolo Bronzino; the nave; view of the unfinished exterior.

This complex is the final resting place of the many members of the Medici family. It includes the Cappella dei Principi, designed in 1604, and its crypt, as well as the Sagrestia Nuova, the new sacristy – Michelangelo's answer to Brunelleschi's Old Sacristy in San Lorenzo.

SANTA CROCE

Legend has it that the great St Francis of Assisi himself laid the foundation stone for the construction of Santa Croce (main picture and above). The Franciscans did have a monastery here in 1221, during the lifetim order's celebrated found erous famous artists, s and politicians such as Macchiavelli and Mich are buried here in Santa

SIENA

Siena was originally an Etruscan settlement, later became a Roman colony (Saena Iulia), and eventually sided with the Ghibellines in the Middle Ages, thus becoming Florence's arch rival. The city reached the height of its political power in the 13th century, after which it was ruled by a council

of nine merchants between 1287 and 1355. Siena was conquered by the Spanish in 1555, who then ceded it to the Grand Duchy of Tuscany. The city is dominated by the Gothic cathedral with its interior of black and white marble (left and main picture). The Piazza del Campo (below) has been the

venue of the biannual Palio since the Middle Ages, a horse race with a magnificent medieval ambience that always takes place on July 2 and August 16. Siena's opposing city districts compete against one another in the race, and the residents don historic costumes.

CHIANTI

The center of the Chianti region lies north of Siena. The area is famous for its idyllic, gently undulating landscape (right). Extensive vineyards, wine estates and attractive cypress and pine alleys characterize the scenery. And yes, Chianti Classico wine estates with their Gallo Nero – black cockerel – emblem as a quality guarantee are everywhere, tucked into misty valleys down narrow country roads. The word "chianti" originally stems from the ancient Etruscan language and referred then to a

high-quality product before it became synonymous with an entire wine-growing region. The turning point came in 1841, when Bettino

Ricasoli developed his idea of an "original" chianti at Brolio Castle, and it was he who established the best ratio of grapes.

SAN GIMIGNANO

VOLTERRA

This area was once the scene of civil war and the families had tower houses built in order to outdo one another. Of the original seventy-two towers only fifteen are still standing. They guard over the Piazza della Cisterna in the center of the Old Town and give San Gimignano its characteristic skyline.

The former Etruscan town of Volterra is situated about 45 km (30 mi) from the coast on a cliff amidst the Tuscan hills. Excavations indicate that the town was extremely prosperous during the 4th century BC. A 7-km (4-mi) wall encompassing fields and pastures surrounded Volterra at the time, meaning the residents were able to fend for themselves when under siege.

MAREMMA, MASSA MARITTIMA

Maremma, the coastal region between Livorno and Monte Argentario, has been settled since Etruscan times. The Romans also knew how to make use of this area but their drainage systems were later forgotten. Parco Naturale della Maremma was set up in 1975 and reforestation with pines, poplars and cork oaks has ensured beneficial water circulation and also created an appropriate habitat for deer, badgers, foxes, wild boar – and the wild Maremma horses. Massa Marittima (left) lies on the edge of the Maremma region at an altitude of about 830 m (2,723 ft). It became a bishop's see in the 12th/13th centuries, to which a number of magnificent medieval buildings remain testimony to this day.

PIENZA, VAL D'ORCIA, MONTEPULCIANO, CRETE

VAL D'ORCIA

PIENZA

Situated between Montepulciano and Montalcino in the Val d'Orcia, Pienza was designed by Bernardo Rossellino on the orders of Pope Pius II as the "ideal Renaissance town". The focal point of the historic center is the Piazza Pio II, which is lined with a number of impressive buildings. You can see the cathedral (above) through the colonnades of the Palazzo Civico. The square is bordered to the left and right by the Palazzi Vescovile and Piccolomini.

The Val d'Orcia – roughly 50 km (31 mi) south of Siena– embodies a Renaissance landscape. Over centuries, graphic depictions of this area had a major influence in the history of European art with regard to our notions of the ideal landscape.

MONTEPULCIANO

CRETE

Situated on top of a picturesque hill between Valdichiana and the Val d'Orcia, Montepulciano (top) at 605 m (1,985 ft) is one of the highest towns in Tuscany. As is often the case in this area, Etruscans first settled here in 715, calling the town "Castrum Politianum". Although mostly famous for its wine, Montepulciano is also home to a classic example of a centralized Renaissance church, situated somewhat outside of the town: San Biagio (above).

"Crete", not to be confused with the island, designates an area to the south-east of Siena, between Vescona and Asciano. It is an area that has unfortunately been heavily deforested and overgrazed, but the grey and yellow boulders, a result of erosion, are still a beautiful feature of this surrealist lunar landscape. Here – and a little further south in the Val d'Orcia (main picture) in particular – was where the first landscape artists found the inspiration for their frescoes. Cypresses, isolated farmhouses and a little church on a hill like the one close to Pienza (above) are considered typical of Tuscany.

ORVIETO

Orvieto's origins go way back to Etruscan times when the town was settled on the 200-m-high (656-ft) block of tuff stone above the Paglia Valley, where it remains today. During the course of some 3,000 years of human activity here, a labyrinth of caves both large and small has developed within the depths of the mountain, interconnected via stairs and passages. The first to dig their way into the mountain were of course the Etruscans. The town's inhabitants later dug into the soft rock to remove "pozzolan", which can be mixed with water to make a cement-like material. The subterranean columns and vaults were simply a side effect. The town's focal point is now the piazza with the cathedral (main picture), considered to be one of the loveliest Gothic churches in Italy. Its construction went on for around 500 years up until the end of the 17th century.

ASSISI

Assisi lies on a hillside below Monte Subasio and is Umbria's most important pilgrimage destination. St Francis of Assisi was born here in 1182 into a wealthy family of cloth merchants and founded the mendicant Franciscan order in 1210. He was canonized in 1228, two years after his death, the same year that work began on the construction of the Basilica di San Francesco where he was buried in 1230. The church, which consists of an upper and lower

URBINO

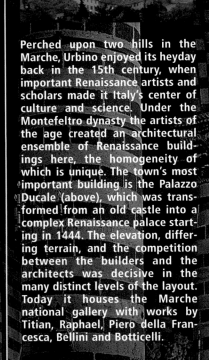

Perched upon two hills in the Marche, Urbino enjoyed its heyday back in the 15th century, when important Renaissance artists and scholars made it Italy's center of culture and science. Under the Montefeltro dynasty the artists of the age created an architectural ensemble of Renaissance buildings here, the homogeneity of which is unique. The town's most important building is the Palazzo Ducale (above), which was transformed from an old castle into a complex Renaissance palace starting in 1444. The elevation, differing terrain, and the competition between the builders and the architects was decisive in the many distinct levels of the layout. Today it houses the Marche national gallery with works by Titian, Raphael, Piero della Francesca, Bellini and Botticelli.

basilica, is decorated with magnificent frescoes and is the town's most important attraction. It is considered to be Italy's largest church of artworks, and most of the famous painters of the age created significant works of art here: Cimabue, Giotto, Simone Martini and the Lorenzetti brothers. Giotto's *St Francis preaching before the Pope* fresco (below) from the end of the 13th century can be seen in the upper basilica.

Perugia, the capital of Umbria, is situated on a range of hills between the Tiber Valley and Lake Trasimeno. It was an important town even in Etruscan times and remains so today, a fact evidenced by the historical buildings that give Perugia's Old Town its very special flair, with narrow, often covered alleyways and splendid squares. Now a modern university city, the Piazza IV Novembre with the Palazzo dei Priori (above) still forms the center of the Old Town. The Fontana Maggiore (also above) has been in existence here since 1278, the fountain being fed with water from the hills around the town by means of a sophisticated system of pipes. The towering Gothic San Lorenzo Cathedral stands opposite the Palazzo dei Priori.

NAPLES

CASTEL NUOVO, PALAZZO REALE,

The Castel Nuovo, residence of the Neapolitan kings and viceroys, dates back to the 13th century. The city councilors today meet in the castle's Sala dei Baroni, with its ornate star vault where, during a wedding, Ferdinand I of Aragon once arrested all the barons who

In the Palazzo Reale (top and middle), visitors can see Bourbon furniture and paintings; it is also home to the national library. The mighty Castel Nuovo, a fortress and royal residence (above), is a genuine masterpiece of the Italian early Renaissance.

had participated in a conspiracy against him. After their arrest they were then placed in chains, tortured and executed.
Between 1600 and 1602, the Palazzo Reale was built based on designs by Domenico Fontana as the new residence of the kings from the dynasty of the Spanish Aragonese and Bourbons.

HISTORIC CENTER

The historic center of Naples, capital of the province of the same name, dates back to the Greek settlement of Partenope, whose Old Town was eventually expanded with a new town ("Neapolis"). Numerous Mediterranean cultures – from the Greeks to the Normans and the Spanish Bourbons – have made their mark on this city, allowing Naples to form its very own microcosm within Italy.

Time seems to have stood still in some areas of Naples, and the fact that the city dates back to a Greek settlement from the 5th century BC can be seen in the remains of a market from ancient Neapolis, the ruins of which were found under the Gothic San Lorenzo Maggiore Church. Next to the Chapel of St Januarius is the 6th-century Santa Restituta Basilica, a proud testament to the early prevalence of paleo-Christianity belief in the region. Located inside the San Gennaro Church, the basilica features ancient columns and a baptistry from the 4th century. San Gennaro also has important catacombs.

The view over the Bay of Naples, the yacht marina and Mt Vesuvius. Italy's third-largest city, it is probably the most hectic, but also one of the most endearing Italian metropolises.

CASERTA

In the 18th century, Luigi Vanvitelli built a palace complex in Caserta for King Charles VII of Naples that was comparable in size and grandeur to Versailles. Located around 40 km (25 mi) north of Naples, the palace of Caserta was constructed between 1752 and 1775 and intended to display the power and confidence of the Bourbons, who ruled Naples from 1734 to 1860. The irony of the story is that, Charles VII left Naples to become Charles III King of Spain before the palace was completed.

The enormous dimensions of the complex are breathtaking, with a floorplan measuring 253 x 202 m (830 x 663 ft)

The Palazzo Reale in Caserta is also known as the "Versailles of the South". The staircase (top) gives an idea of the complex's colossal dimensions. Hardly less fascinating is the castle park, with its fountains and sculptures such as the hunting scene above.

and 1,217 rooms on five levels. The main attractions are the monumental staircase, the castle chapel and the court theater with the grand park as the backdrop. The park covers roughly 80 hectares (198 acres) and primarily impresses visitors with its various fountains and pools. At the time, extensive naval battles were staged on the water basins along the 3-km-long (2-mi) central channel.

When the crater of Mt Vesuvius exploded after centuries of tranquillity, hot magma rolled into the valley and covered Pompeii in lava and ash. A surprising number of wall paintings were preserved under the volcanic ash, as is the case with this depiction of two gods (main picture).

Vesuvius erupted on August 24 of the year AD 79, completely covering the Roman town of Pompeii under a layer of ash within roughly six hours. The neighboring town of Herculaneum was also smothered under glowing lava. After the eruption, the towns were not rebuilt and eventually forgotten. However, Pliny the Younger (ca. AD 61–113), whose uncle and adopted father were killed by the eruption, had described the event, which led the archaeologists in the right direction. The first excavations began in 1748, and today they provide an invaluable impression of life in antiquity. The remains of shops and the painted walls of splendid villas were still left standing; even petrified bread was found in the bakeries. Other discoveries included a mill, a latrine and some "graffiti" on the walls. The stepping stones that enabled passersby to cross the street without getting their feet are even still visible. The dead people are the most impressive, however, their bodies forming hollows of volcanic ash. Filled with plaster, the human figures are now visible again as silent witnesses of the eruption.

The portrait of Paquius Proculus and his wife (top) also survived and can be seen in the National Museum in Naples, as is the case with the delicate angel (middle). One of the loveliest wall paintings can be found in the Triclinium of the Villa dei Misteri (above), depicting the initiation of a young woman in the cult of Dionysus.

Around 15 km (9 mi) outside of Naples, Mt Vesuvius (left) is mainland Europe's only active volcano. Since the 18th century, excavations beneath the volcano's crater have been revealing remains of settlement in the lava layer, which is up to 7 m (23 ft) deep in places.

Excavations in Pompeii began in 1748, and since then entire streets including the buildings and the Forum (above) have been exposed. Today archeologists are primarily focused on preventing the deterioration of the ruins.

AMALFITANA

The small town of Amalfi on the Gulf of Salerno was once one of Italy's leading seafaring republics. Today the name is associated with one of the loveliest stretches of Mediterranean coastline. Cut straight into the cliffs in places, the Amalfitana coastal road connects the villages between Nerano and Salerno. It follows winding stretches of the shoreline for around 45 km (30 mi), continually providing spectacular panorama views of the azure-blue ocean and the Costiera Amalfitana. The view from the garden of the Villa Cimbrone is especially lovely, as is that from the Villa Rufulo, both in Ravello (above). The villages are strung together like pearls with lemon groves and vineyards scattered between them. The charming houses are built in precarious positions along the steep cliffs and cling to the slopes to create a picturesque scene.

AMALFI

The world's oldest maritime law – the Tavole Amalfitane – has its origins in Amalfi (main picture), the most important town along this stretch of coast. The 9th-century cathedral, which can be reached by a magnificent flight of steps from the Piazza Duomo (above), is a source of local pride.

POSITANO

"I have the feeling," wrote John Steinbeck of this seafaring town founded in the Middle Ages, "that the world is vertical in Positano. An unimaginably blue and green ocean washes up on the fine pebble beach in the bay." There are crossings to Capri from this splendid town.

CAPRI

Capri is made up of pure limestone and the island's geological landmark, the three Faraglioni in the south-east, is the result of erosion of that limestone. The island is relatively small, just 6 km (4 mi) long and a maximum of 2.5 km (1.5 mi) wide. Ferries from the mainland dock at the Marina Grande. Sights include the villages of Capri and Anacapri on the slopes of Monte Solaro, as well as the cliffs of the Arco Naturale in the east. The Blue Grotto, a karst cave that is thought to have been known to Emperor Tiberius, is 54 m (175 ft) long, 15 m (50 ft) wide and up to 30 m (98 ft) high can be accessed through an entrance located just above water level. It owes its name to the mysterious blue color of the water – sunlight enters through the water creating a reflection that lights the cave.

PALERMO

Palermo was the main base for the Carthaginian fleet in the First Punic War and went on to enjoy exceptional periods of cultural prosperity under the Moors, Normans and the Hohenstaufens of Germany. Thankfully, a tremendous number of historic buildings have survived from all of these epochs. In the Old Town, Byzantine churches stand next to Moorish mosques and baroque and Catalan palaces are juxtaposed with classical barracks and Arabian-style pleasure palaces. Highlights here include the splendid cathedral (above right); the Norman Palace with the mosaic-embellished Cappella Palatina (main picture), and the 16th-century Piazza Pretoria with the mannerism-style Fontana Pretoria (below). The San Cataldo, La Martorana (right) and San Giovanni degli Eremiti churches, the La

Zisa Palace, the Teatro Massimo, the catacombs of the Capuchin monastery, and the National Gallery and the Archaeological Museum are all worth seeing as well.

The lively Vucciria market (above left) on the Piazza Caracciolo is nicknamed the "belly of Palermo". It is the town's best-known market and one of the oldest in Europe. The kiosks and shops selling fish, meat, fruits and vegetables are all strung together like an oriental souk along the narrow alleyways.

MONREALE

Situated around 8 km (5 mi) from Palermo is the small episcopal town of Monreale. Monte Caputo provides fabulous views of the Sicilian capital with its bay that looks like it was drawn with a compass, the Conca d'Oro. The main sightseeing attraction here, however, is the world-famous cathedral. Wilhelm II, King of Sicily, was the original benefactor of a Benedictine abbey that was built on these lofty heights in 1172, which sooned formed into a town. Seeing the growth, he had a cathedral built at its center – a basilica intended to symbolize the triumph of the Christians over the Moors. With a length of 102 m (112 ft) and a width of 40 m 140 ft, Sicily's largest church is supported by eighteen antique columns. It houses the sarcophaguses of Kings Wilhelm I and II and has a magnificent bronze portal and marble floors. The mosaics (above) in the cathedral cover 6,300 sq m (67,788 sq ft) and depict stories from the Bible in incomparable splendor. The cloister – the only surviving section of the monastery – is also worth seeing with its many differently designed column pairs.

MOUNT ETNA

Unlike the highly explosive Vesuvius near Naples, Mt Etna (above and main picture) is a "good mountain": it erupts consistently and calmly instead of unexpectedly and intensely, and its lava contains little in the way of gases, making the volcano less explosive. Provided one sticks to the sign-posted paths, it is safe to make an excursion up to the 3,000 m (9,843 ft) peak – an unforgettable experience. Anyone looking to keep more of a distance can enjoy a wonderful hike around its lower slopes. The region was declared a national park in 1981.

TAORMINA

The whole east coast of Sicily is dominated by the silhouette of Etna, and the town of Taormina (above), the most frequently visited hamlet on the island. Its idyllic location on a cliff high above the ocean and its ancient amphi-

theater ensured that Taormina was to become a popular destination as far back as the 19th century. Founded in the 4th century BC, Taormina was Greek for more than 200 years before ultimately falling to Rome in 215 BC. From the Teatro Greco, built in the 2nd century BC on the foundations of

an existing Hellenistic structure, the view extends as far as Etna – easily one of the loveliest theater settings in the world (left). The terrace of the Piazza IX Aprile (above) situated 200 m (656 ft) above the sea provides a very good viewing area.

SARDINIA

Sardinia is the second-largest island in the Mediterranean after Sicily and has a tremendous cultural heritage to match its magnificent natural splendor. Over thousands of years, the Phoenicians, Romans, Vandals, Byzantines, Moors, Pisanese, Genoese, Aragonese, Spanish and naturally mainland Italians have all left their mark here. Nevertheless, Sardinia was able to maintain its own language and culture.

The north is the most popular region with magnificent diving and sailing options. It features quaint villages with ancient, labyrinthine town centers, good infrastructure, and a romantic landscape with granite cliffs and dark maquis shrub land in the interior. The "Costa Smeralda", the Emerald Coast where the Aga Khan created an exclusive holiday resort in the early 1960s, is of course legendary.

COSTA SMERALDA

The Capo d'Orso rock formations (top) are one of the landmarks of the Costa Smeralda, with its clear blue bays and idyllic landscape.

CAPO TESTA

Just a few miles wide, the Bocca di Bonifacio (above) separates the Capo Testa from the bizarre rock formations of the island of Corsica to the north.

MADDALENA

This group of tiny islands belong to the Parco Nazionale dell'Arcipélago de la Maddalena to the north-east of Sardinia. There are sixty-two in total.

CAPO CACCIA

The Capo Caccia (main picture) is Sardinia's westernmost point. The Grotta di Nettuno (above) can be reached via the Escala del Cabirol with its 656 steps.

St. John's Co-Cathedral (main picture) is Valletta's main church. It has very elaborate interior decor (right, an image of the Madonna).

Control over the town of Valletta changed hands for centuries starting with the Phoenicians and moving on to the Greeks, the Carthaginians, the Romans, Byzantium, and the Moors until it was finally handed over to the Order of St John following the Turkish siege of 1565. It then grew into a fortified town that was characteristic of the 16th century. The Order of St John proceeded to construct a series of Renaissance and baroque palaces, churches and hospices within its walls, the Order's newly-found confidence and wealth being expressed in the magnificent décor of the Grand Master's palace and its two courtyards. The baroque church of Our Lady of Victory was built as a sign of gratitude for the endurance during the siege of 1567. St. John's Co-Cathedral, built between 1573 and 1578 as a burial place for the knights of the Order, was decorated with ceiling frescoes and magnificent side chapels. The library founded by the order in 1555 houses valuable manuscripts. The Manoel Theatre dating from 1731 can be found within the labyrinth of alleys and steps and is one of the oldest stages in Europe.

Surrounded by the sea on three sides, Valletta (far left and left) is situated on a 60-m-high (199-ft) cliff on Malta's north coast. The large dome of the Carmelite church dominates the town.

GDANSK

Gdansk has a history going back more than 1,000 years, when it maintained close trade relations with Flanders, Russia and Byzantium continuing into the 12th and 13th centuries. Gdansk was a member of the Hanseatic League from 1361 and was assigned to the Polish crown in 1466. With ninety-five percent of the city in ruins at the end of World War II, Gdansk has since become a model of reconstruction work.

The most important attractions are naturally in the city center. St Mary's Church, for example, is the largest medieval brick church in Europe, its most striking feature being the 82-m-high (269-ft) bell tower. The city's Old Town comprises Long Street and the streets

The port crane on the Motlawa River in Gdansk used to be a city gate.

adjoining it. Influential patricians built magnificent palaces like the 17th-century Hans von Eden House for themselves in the heart of the Old Town. The 15th-century Arthur's Court is among the finest examples of late-Gothic architecture in Northern Europe; the town hall, the Golden House and the Torture House are also worth seeing. One city gate from the Middle Ages has been converted into a port crane. In the northern part of the Old Town there is a series of churches, the Old Town Hall, the Small and the Large Mill and the Old Castle, which are worth visiting. The Vistula Spit, on the delta, is south of Gdansk. You can reach Malbork by crossing the spit to the south-east.

TORUN

The knights of the Teutonic Order once built a castle here, at the foot of which a town developed that went on to become a thriving commercial center in the 14th century. It even maintained its own merchant fleet for the purposes of trading with the Netherlands. The First and the Second Peace of Torun were concluded here in 1411 and 1466 between the Teu-

tonic Order and Poland. In 1454 the Teutonic Order castle was burnt down by the citizens of Torun (only remnants survive to this day) and the town became an independent city-state under the sovereignty of the Polish king. The town continued to change in appearance over the centuries, as is evidenced by the Gothic patricians' houses, the baroque and classic town houses and the opulent palaces of the 19th century. Construction of the Old Town Hall was begun in 1259, and Copernicus's birthplace dating from the 15th century has remained intact. The Cathedral of St John the Evangelist and John the Baptist as well as St Mary's Church (above left) are also worth seeing.

FROMBORK

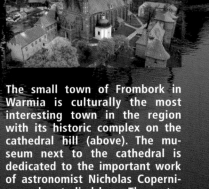

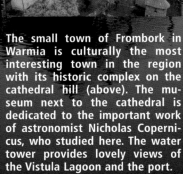

The small town of Frombork in Warmia is culturally the most interesting town in the region with its historic complex on the cathedral hill (above). The museum next to the cathedral is dedicated to the important work of astronomist Nicholas Copernicus, who studied here. The water tower provides lovely views of the Vistula Lagoon and the port.

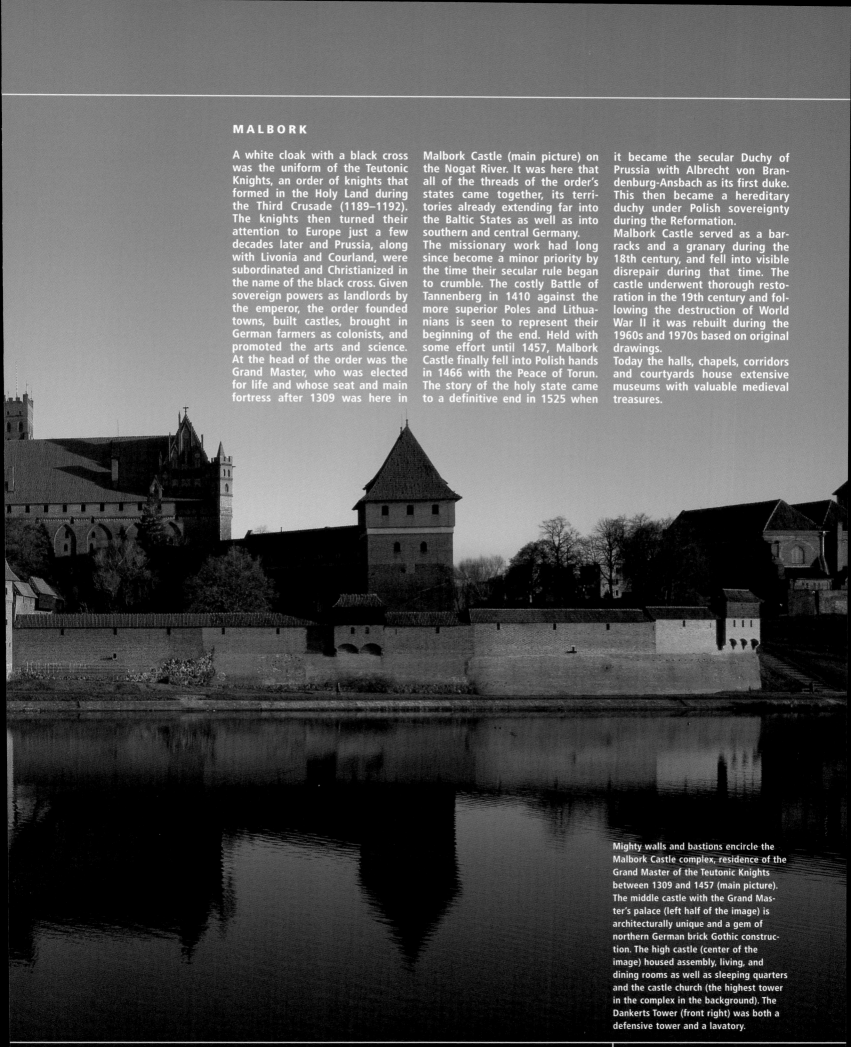

MALBORK

A white cloak with a black cross was the uniform of the Teutonic Knights, an order of knights that formed in the Holy Land during the Third Crusade (1189–1192). The knights then turned their attention to Europe just a few decades later and Prussia, along with Livonia and Courland, were subordinated and Christianized in the name of the black cross. Given sovereign powers as landlords by the emperor, the order founded towns, built castles, brought in German farmers as colonists, and promoted the arts and science. At the head of the order was the Grand Master, who was elected for life and whose seat and main fortress after 1309 was here in

Malbork Castle (main picture) on the Nogat River. It was here that all of the threads of the order's states came together, its territories already extending far into the Baltic States as well as into southern and central Germany. The missionary work had long since become a minor priority by the time their secular rule began to crumble. The costly Battle of Tannenberg in 1410 against the more superior Poles and Lithuanians is seen to represent their beginning of the end. Held with some effort until 1457, Malbork Castle finally fell into Polish hands in 1466 with the Peace of Torun. The story of the holy state came to a definitive end in 1525 when

it became the secular Duchy of Prussia with Albrecht von Brandenburg-Ansbach as its first duke. This then became a hereditary duchy under Polish sovereignty during the Reformation.

Malbork Castle served as a barracks and a granary during the 18th century, and fell into visible disrepair during that time. The castle underwent thorough restoration in the 19th century and following the destruction of World War II it was rebuilt during the 1960s and 1970s based on original drawings.

Today the halls, chapels, corridors and courtyards house extensive museums with valuable medieval treasures.

Mighty walls and bastions encircle the Malbork Castle complex, residence of the Grand Master of the Teutonic Knights between 1309 and 1457 (main picture). The middle castle with the Grand Master's palace (left half of the image) is architecturally unique and a gem of northern German brick Gothic construction. The high castle (center of the image) housed assembly, living, and dining rooms as well as sleeping quarters and the castle church (the highest tower in the complex in the background). The Dankerts Tower (front right) was both a defensive tower and a lavatory.

Early morning in the Masurian Lake District. This idyllic landscape of eastern Poland is also referred to as the "Land of a Thousand Lakes."

The Masurian Lake District is a refuge for more than 350 bird species including Steppe Eagles, Mute Swans and the Common Merganser (from top).

THE MASURIAN LAKE DISTRICT

There is no denying the magic of this landscape. Hikers, cyclists and canoeists alike can all enjoy the thoroughly fascinating water landscape here. More than 3,000 lakes are linked via rivers and canals, all mingling with wonderful forests. Gnarled trees shade cobblestone alleys that are still traveled by horse-drawn carts, while storks build their nests in the tops of the steeple. A visit to Masuria is like taking a journey back in time to the early 20th century.

Olsztyn is the main center of the Masuria region as well as the perfect starting point for excursions to a number of different sightseeing attractions, including Lidzbark Warminskj with its mighty castle that used to be the seat of the Warmia bishops. Reszel Castle nearby dates back to the 13th century.

The powerful Teutonic Knights built a castle in Kętrzyn in 1329. Beyond Kętrzyn there is a sign pointing to the north-east indicating the "Wolfsschanze" (Wolf's Lair), which Hitler built in 1939, as his headquarters. The pilgrimage church of Święta Lipka is a baroque gem.

Top to bottom: The collegiate church in Dobre Miasto north of Olsztyn; the pilgrimage church Święta Lipka; and a panje horse cart.

BIAŁOWIEŻA

Despite the extreme temperatures here, which often sink well below the freezing point in winter, this cross-border national park possesses an astounding level of biodiversity. There are some 3,000 types of mushrooms and more than a dozen species of orchids. The heavily protected central zone of the park is home to the highest trees in all of Europe: 55-m-high (180-ft) spruces and 40-m-high (131-ft) ash trees. The Polish government began using zoo animals to breed European bison (left, also known as wisents) in the 1920s, with a scheduled program of reintroducing them to the wild as of 1952. Hunting had made these primeval oxen almost extinct by the end of the 19th century, but today there are around 300 of them wandering the vast forest areas again. They are the largest species of big game in Europe.

The wild horses that used to be found throughout Eurasia and which no longer exist in the wild have also found a refuge in this protected area. In addition to rare mammals such as bears, moose, lynxes and wolves, the area is also home to more than 220 different bird species.

KRAKOW

The 13th-century textile halls stand in the center of the Rynek, Krakow's market square (main picture). The ensemble originally comprised just a double row of small cloth merchants' shops, which were then amalgamated into a hall in the 14th century.

THE MARKET SQUARE, JEWISH QUARTER

Krakow was the capital of the Polish kings until 1596, and their coronation venue from the 11th to the 18th centuries. Wawel Hill with its royal castle and cathedral remains testimony to this bygone era. The Old Town here was designed by master builders and artists from throughout Europe from the 12th to the 17th centuries. The market square, one of Europe's largest medieval town squares, is the site of the textile halls and the Gothic St Mary's Church, converted in the 14th century. The famous high altar by Veit Stoss, who created his most important works in Krakow between 1477 and 1496, can be found here. Pivotal medieval intellectuals taught at the university, founded in the 14th century. A number of Gothic, Renaissance and baroque buildings including many churches and monasteries testifying to the city's rich history. The Kazimierz Quarter was once home to a thriving Jewish community where the Old Synagogue is worthy of special mention.

St Mary's Church opposite the main market square has an especially impressive interior with magnificent wall paintings and stained glass windows (far left). Corpus Christi Church in the former Jewish Quarter of Kazimierz (left) is one of the loveliest churches in Krakow.

PRAGUE

The Charles Bridge is 500 m (547 ft) long and its sixteen arches are supported by fifteen pillars. Master builder Peter Parler based the bridge on the Stone Bridge in Regensburg, Germany.

The unique beauty of the historic buildings in the "Golden City", combined with centuries as a European intellectual and cultural capital have made Prague a truly wonderful place to visit. Despite having been spared much of the reckless destruction of World War II, the ravages of time have nevertheless left a definite mark on the city. Thankfully, however, competent renovations have seen this more than 1,000-year-old city on the banks of the Vltava River restored to its former glory. Indeed, the Czechs have every reason to be proud of their lovely capital city, which was formerly a grand residence of the Bohemian kings and seat of the Habsburg emperors. Their former place of residence, Vyšehrad, also provides the best views of this marvel of historical urban development.

VYŠEHRAD HILL

Vyšehrad Hill with St Veit's Cathedral towers over Prague. It is a castle complex that has been the country's political, intellectual and cultural center for more than 1,000 years. Formerly the royal residence, it is now the official residence of the Czech president. Access to the complex is via the first of the inner wards (above).

ST VEIT'S CATHEDRAL

Emperor Charles IV commissioned St Veit's Cathedral on the grounds of Prague Castle in 1344, as Prague was being made into an archbishopric. The nave and the choir are supported by twenty-eight pillars. The largest church in the Czech Republic, it is the burial place of emperors and kings as well as the repository for the crown jewels.

CHARLES BRIDGE

Construction on the grand Charles Bridge began in 1357. It was later embellished with its masterful baroque statues between 1707 and 1714. the bridge takes you from the Lesser Quarter, the area beneath Vyšehrad Hill, over the Vltava River to the Old Town. Its decor is based on the baroque figures of the saints on the Ponte Sant'Angelo in Rome, the oldest and best known of these being the bronze statue of St John of Nepomuk dating from 1683. It commemorates the preacher and saint, John Nepomuk, whom King Wenceslas IV had tortured and thrown from the bridge into the Vltava River at this spot.

The bridge is named after King Charles IV (1316–1378), who inherited the kingdom of Bohemia in 1346, and was elected German king and crowned emperor in 1355. The first German university, the Charles University founded in 1348, is also named after him. He made Prague into an important city of the Holy Roman Empire.

THE GOLDEN ALLEY

Franz Kafka lived for a number of years in one of these cottages in Golden Alley on the castle grounds. The cottages were built along the castle walls in the 16th century to provide lodging for watchmen and tradesmen. The assertion that alchemists were at work here under Rudolf II has not been historically proven.

The Old Town Square (main picture) was originally established as a central marketplace and a part of the traditional coronation route for the Bohemian kings. It was also a place of execution.

THE OLD JEWISH CEMETERY

The Old Jewish Cemetery was established in the 15th century, the oldest tombstone belonging to the scholar and writer Avigdor Karo, who wrote an elegy on the occasion of the 1389 pogrom and who died in 1439. The most recent grave is from 1787, that of Moses Beck. Since then, no further burials have taken place here.

In total, there are some 12,000 Gothic, Renaissance and baroque tombstones to be seen here under the elder trees. The fact that the Jewish faith does not allow the destruction of grave sites means that there are up to nine burial levels on top on one another in some places.

The most famous is the grave of Rabbi Loew (ca. 1525–1609), the creator of the "Golem" (in Hebrew, "Klumpen"), a homunculus formed of clay and brought to life by means of Cabbalistic rituals. Loew was a Jewish theologian and Cabbalist whose real name was Juda ben Bezalel. He was the regional rabbi of Moravia from 1553 to 1573 and rabbi in Prague from 1597.

THE OLD TOWN SQUARE

The Old Town Square, a marketplace dating from the 12th century, is one of Prague's central attractions and is a key focal point for both visitors and locals with its cafés, street performers and musicians. It is dominated by the towers of the Gothic Tyn Church, which also houses the tomb of the Danish astronomer Tycho Brahe.

Today street performers turn the Old Town Square into an open-air stage.

THE ASTRONOMICAL CLOCK

The astronomical clock on the south side of the old city hall is the third-oldest of its kind. The Twelve Apostles appear in its windows every hour and the clock shows the phases of the moon, the position of the sun and the planet constellations – and of course the time.

Prague's astronomical clock is decorated with wooden figures, one of which symbolizes Death.

Small stones are traditionally laid on Jewish graves instead of flowers (left, Old Jewish Cemetery in Prague). The custom is said to date back to the era of desert migrations when the dead were covered with stones in order to protect them from wild animals.

THE OLD NEW SYNAGOGUE

The Old New Synagogue was built in 1270. Its name derives from the legend of the angels said to have brought stones from the ruins of the destroyed temple in Jerusalem to Prague for its construction, albeit only "on condition that the stones be taken back to Jerusalem some day" for the coming of the Messiah in order to then rebuild his temple. "Altnai" is the Hebrew term for "on condition that" and from which "old new" is derived.

The Old New Synagogue in Prague is the only one from this era in Europe where Jewish services are still held.

THE CLEMENTINUM

The Clementinum, built between 1578 and 1726, was once a Jesuit college. A colossal complex of buildings surrounding five large courtyards, it is now home to the national library, among other things, whose priceless inventory includes historic globes and incunabula.

With its wonderful long galleries, the Clementinum's library has one of the loveliest baroque halls in Prague.

FRANTIŠKOVY LÁZNĚ, KARLOVY VARY, MARIÁNSKÉ LÁZNĚ

"Here, the guest is king" a phrase to take literally at the Nové Lázně (New Spa) health resort. England's King Edward VIII (1841–1910) held the Roman bath (main picture) in high regard in his day. There are of course Junior and Imperial Suites if you can't afford the Royal Suite.

KARLOVY VARY

Emperor Charles IV (1316–1378) was allegedly the first to dicover the salt springs here in Karlovy Vary, formerly called Carlsbad, while out on a stag hunt. Some 500 years later, Bohemia's most extravagant health resort had

Karlovy Vary, one of the world's most famous health resorts, lies where Teplá creek flows into the Ohfie.

developed around the site and the political, artistic and social elite of Europe began meeting here.
In 1989, after fifty years of decline, the resort experienced a dazzling rebirth and most of the grandiose Wilhelminian buildings are once again resplendent, from the Mühl-brunn colonnade to the city theater and the Grand Hotel Pupp.

FRANTIŠKOVY LÁZNĚ

People have been aware of and enjoying the healing power of the waters at Františkovy Lázně baths since back in the 15th century. The springs are some 5 km (3 mi) north of the town of Cheb, which is also referred to as Eger and was Bohemian regional capital and fortress town.

In 1661, the first filling house was built at the mineral water source, and a bathhouse was later added in 1694. A town was officially founded in 1793 and was initially named "Kaiser Franzendorf" after the Austrian Emperor Franz II (1768–1835). It was renamed "Franzensbad" (now "Františkovy Lázně"), the name for which it is famous.

In 1852, it became independent from Cheb, obtaining its town charter in 1865. The health resort facilities were nationalized in 1946, but it was not until 1989 that it was re-privatized, and a Spa Františkovy Lázně Company was founded. Twelve of the original sources are still used, mostly for the treatment of rheumatic, heart, stomach, liver and circulation conditions.

Františkovy Lázně was one of the first mud baths in Europe, but gone are the days when women scooped carbonated spring water from the nearby river Ohfie, directly at the source, in order to sell it in the city and eventually all over Germany.

MARIÁNSKÉ LÁZNĚ

Mariánské Lázně is a spa resort town nestled into green mountains and surrounded by parks and mansions. It is also where Goethe wrote his Marienbad Elegy, a pained farewell by the poet to his "last love", Ulrike von Levetzow, after their final breakup.

The Nove Lázně health resort was opened in 1896 (top: an exterior view; above: the kings cabin – previously only reserved for the nobility). Second and third picture from the top: the cast-iron colonnade in Mariánské Lázně.

The baths have been completely restored, with pretty stucco façades painted in the "emperor's yellow" color of Vienna's Schönbrunn castle. Particularly magnificent is the 120-m-long (394-ft) colonnade made out of cast iron.

ČESKÝ KRUMLOV, ČESKÉ BUDĚJOVICE HOLAŠOVICE

All of the buildings around the central market square boast arcades (main picture) in the home of "Budvar," the original Budweiser beer. The Old Testament's Samson battles with a lion atop the fountain, which bears his name.

ČESKÝ KRUMLOV

The very location of this town is simply enchanting, situated as it is on both sides of a narrow bend in the Vltava River. The Old Town's labyrinthine alleyways like those in the Latrán quarter, with its lovely shingled-roof houses, could hardly be more picturesque. The Gothic St Veit's Church and the Schiele Center form the highlights of any tour of the more than 700-year-old downtown area. Painter Egon Schiele lived and worked in Krummau for a few months in 1911.

The main attraction, however, is the glorious castle, Bohemia's second-largest after Vyšehrad in Prague. The complex belonged to the Rosenbergs for around 300 years before coming into the possession of Emperor Rudolf II and ultimately to the princes of Schwarzenberg in the early 18th century.

In the upper section of the castle complex, visitors are able to view the original furnishings from the 16th to the 19th centuries. The fabulous collection of Flemish tapestries is particularly valuable, while the large painting gallery is also worth a look.

ČESKÉ BUDĚJOVICE

The town of České Budějovice is of course famous for its beer, but the market square with the Samson Fountain has formed the focal point since it was founded by King Ottokar II in 1265. The viewing platform of the 72-m (236-ft) bell tower also provides views of the town's other attractions: the baroque St Nicholas Cathedral, the town hall, the Dominican monastery, St Mary's Church, and the Salt House.

HOLAŠOVICE

Bohemian King Wenceslas II donated several villages to the Abbey of Vyšší Brod in 1292, including the small village of Holašovice, which retained a close link with the monastery for over five centuries. Its records show that both Germans and Czechs lived in Holašovice during this time.

It was only at the beginning of the 19th century that the first stone buildings were built on the site of this medieval village, and it was between 1840 and 1880 that the buildings acquired their present-day appearance. It is not known who the builders were or where they came from, but their efforts remain among the loveliest examples of baroque architecture in southern Bohemia today.

Most of the houses grouped around the Holašovice main square date back to the second half of the 18th century. The imaginative gables are a characteristic feature.

With an area of around 7 ha (17 acres) the Ceský Krumlov castle (1257) is one of the largest in Central Europe. It comprises forty buildings as well as five courtyards and a baroque garden. The castle tower dominates the town and the rest of the complex (left).

SPIŠ CASTLE

Spiš Castle, one of the largest castle complexes in Europe, towers over the Spiš basin in north-eastern Slovakia (main picture).

Medieval Spiš Castle (Spišský hrad), one of the largest of its kind in Central Europe, was built on the site of an earlier Slavic fortress in Spiš, a scenic region and historic administrative district in the foothills of the High Tatras. Following its sudden collapse, the 13th century tower house was replaced by a two-story Romanesque palace with a new round tower.

The castle chapel also dates back to the 13th century, when the castle survived an attack from the Mongolians almost without damage. Another fortress was built beneath the castle in the 15th century and both complexes underwent a Renaissance makeover in 1540. Spiš Castle declined in importance after its capture by Habsburg troops in 1710.

It was from the castle that Spišský Podhrahie ("church on top") and the Spišská Kapitula ("The Spiš Chapter", provost's residence), were founded. Located just a few miles away, they boast a number of buildings under historic protection including churches, a baroque monastery, a Renaissance town hall and some manor houses. The early-Gothic Church of the Holy Spirit in Žehra is also worth seeing.

BUDAPEST

BUDA, ÓBUDA, PEST

Buda, Óbuda (Old Buda) and Pest were all joined in 1872 to form "BudaPest," the new capital of the former Kingdom of Hungary. The royal castle town of Buda has largely retained its medieval character, with numerous Gothic and baroque buildings lining the narrow streets. Trinity Square lies at the center of the castle hill, which has been a municipality since the 17th century, and is dominated by the Church of Our Lady. Originally built in 1250, the church underwent a neo-Gothic conversion in the 19th century. Its south portal now features a tympanum relief comprised of original pieces from the high-Gothic building.

The royal castle, built on the site of a structure that was destroyed in the great siege of 1686, was begun in 1749 and is located just to the south of the castle hill.

The excavation sites of the Roman settlement of Aquincum, with its large amphitheater that accommodated some 13,000 spectators, can be found in Óbuda. The monumental, classical-style synagogue was erected in 1820 and is also worth visiting.

Pest is situated on the other side of the Danube. This commercial town was a center of middle-class and intellectual life in the 19th century. The buildings around the city ring are especially impressive.

ST MATTHEW'S CHURCH

Construction of St Matthew's (below and inset right) took place between 1255 and 1269 and was commissioned by King Béla IV. King Louis the Great converted it into a Gothic hall church with a nave and two side aisles at the turn of the 15th century. King Matthias Corvinus then expanded the church with a five-floor tower and the royal oratorio in 1470.

FISHERMEN'S BASTION

The Fishermen's Bastion was built between 1895 and 1902 on the site of the old fish market in Buda. The architect Frigyes Schulek, who was also responsible for the neo-Gothic conversion of St Matthew's Church, based the building's conical towers on the tents of the Magyar people.

The Danube is Budapest's main artery. Today, Buda (including ÓBuda) and Pest are linked by nine bridges.

The steam baths in the Gellért complex spa and hotel are a mosaic vision in turquoise. The main picture depicts one of the two pools in the men's steam bath, which differs little from that for women.

THE CHAIN BRIDGE

The Chain Bridge is the oldest and most famous of the nine bridges in Budapest. Its construction was initiated by the Hungarian reformer István Széchenyi who had also pioneered the founding of the Budapest Bridge Society in 1832; the English engineer William Tierney Clark was given the job of drawing up the plans. Preparations for the first pillar began on July 28, 1840, with wooden pickets first being driven into the bank to cordon off the construction site. The classic-style construction is still supported by two buttresses that resemble the Arc de Triomphe and contain the cables of the bridge body, which measures a total of 375 m (410 yds).

PARLIAMENT

The parliament building is based on its counterpart in London and was built between 1885 and 1904 according to plans by Imre Steindl. It features a magnificent staircase and has been the seat of the Hungarian parliament since 1989.

From top to bottom: The parliament buildings; the Dome Hall with the Holy Crown of St Stephen with the imperial insignia; the staircase; the gilded assembly hall.

THE GELLÉRT BATHS

Built in the Secessionist (Art Nouveau) style and opened in 1918, the Gellért Hotel and the Gellért Baths are the most famous in Budapest. The men's baths, the outdoor pools, and the thermal and steam baths for women are opulent in their design and decorated with lovely mosaics. Above the baths on Gellért Hill is a monument commemorating the baths' namesake, the martyred Bishop Gellért who, according to legend, was rolled into the Danube in a sealed barrel at this site.

Budapest's most famous bridge is the Chain Bridge built between 1839 and 1849 (left). The mighty pillars form two towers. The Danube is more than 300 m (328 yds) wide at this point, making the bridge an engineering masterpiece at the time. It quickly became the city's landmark.

ST STEPHEN'S, OPERA HOUSE, HEROES SQUARE

St Stephen's Basilica near the Chain Bridge was consecrated in 1905. The impressive dimensions of this magnificent church, which can accommodate around 8,500 people, become apparent with one glance up at the roughly 100-m (328-ft) dome with its wonderful mosaic styling. Heroes Square marks the entrance to the city park. The Hungarian State Opera is a magnificent neo-Renaissance building and a venue for extravagant musical productions.

Top to bottom: St Stephen's Basilica is named after the first Christian king of Hungary, Stephen I, and houses the king's embalmed right hand; interior of the basilica; the state opera; Heroes Square.

ESTERHÁZY

Esterházy Castle is located just a few miles south of Lake Neusiedl on the outskirts of the small town of Fertőd, where it forms part of the Fertő-Hanság National Park. It was originally built at the beginning of the 18th century as a small hunting lodge and later expanded by Prince Nicholas I who took his inspiration from a visit to Versailles. In 1764 he commissioned the royal Viennese builders Ferdinand Mödlhammer and Melchior Hefele with the conversion, which was to take almost half a century. Esterházy is also famous for having been the home of composer Joseph Haydn for several years. In fact, his famous Symphony No. 45 in F sharp minor was performed in the concert hall of the rococo castle for the first time in 1772 – his legendary "Farewell Symphony", at the end of which the musicians leave the stage one by one. Today the middle wing of the castle is a public museum while one of the side wings is now home to various schools.

Esterházy, one of the country's loveliest rococo castles, is often referred to as the "Hungarian Versailles", while parts of it also resemble Schönbrunn Castle in Vienna.

PANNONHALMA

The former Benedictine abbey of St Martins in Pannonhalma, roughly 30 km (19 mi) south-east of Győr, is one of the centers of Christianization in Hungary and is still inhabited by monks today. The monastery was founded by Prince Géza (940–997), became an archabbey under King Stephen I, and has been the center of the Benedictine Order in Hungary ever since then.

The oldest part of this sizable monastery is the collegiate church, consecrated in 1225 and constructed on the site of two previous buildings. With its strictly configured architecture, the complex remains impressive despite a number of extensive conversions. The crypt under the elevated choir was probably built on the foundations of the original church. In addition to lovely baroque stucco work and other classical elements, the collegiate church also houses a number of Romanesque and Gothic artworks. The sculptures in the late-Gothic cloister vault are said to symbolize human virtues and

Prince Géza Pannonhalma founded the Benedictine arch abbey in 966. The library room houses a plaster statue commemorating King Stephen I.

vices. The 55-m-high (180-ft) west tower was only built in 1830 during the classical conversion of the complex. A particular gem from this era is the ceremonial room of the Classical Library, built between 1824 and 1832, with its valuable manuscripts and incunabula.

The Porta Speciosa (left) is the main entrance to the monastery church, the interior of which is decorated in the late-Romanesque and early-Gothic styles (right).

THE JULIAN AND KAMNIK ALPS, BLED, LJUBLJANA

THE JULIAN AND KAMNIK ALPS

The massive limestone pinnacles of this beautiful region appear as if out of nowhere during the winding journey over the Carinthian border passes. It is immediaetly clear that the Julian and Kamnik Alps are still very much a part of the High Alps, their peaks simply bearing more exotic names such as Skrlatica, Jalovec or Prisojnik. Almost all of the roads here lead directly into the wilderness and to Triglav National Park, which encompasses almost all of the Julian Alps. Parts of the Kamnik Alps (Grintovec, at 2,558 m/8,393 ft) north of the Slovenian capital Ljubljana are also now protected by parks.

Bled's landmark is the truly idyllic church island with the ancient Church of the Assumption in the middle (main picture).

BLED

The Karawanken Tunnel, roughly 8 km (5 mi) long, provides easy access from Carinthia (Austria) to Slovenia, where the spa resort of Bled on the shores of the lake of the same name is worth a quick first stop. It is a well visited spot, but almost unbeatably charming: an island with the baroque Church of the Assumption, the Karavanke Mountains towering in the background, the castle perched on a bare rock face, and white sailboats

Bled is at the foot of the Julian Alps. The stately Bled Castle towers above the spa resort.

scattered around the blue waters of this idyllic alpine lake.

The island has been a popular Christian cult and pilgrimage destination for more than 1,000 years. It also became a beloved spot for those seeking rest and recuperation in the late-19th century when a resourceful Swiss spa physician set up shop here. By about 1900 it had become a fashionable meeting place for high society types. Bled's most prominent attraction is the castle, whose Romanesque tower has held up since 1004. The baroque wing houses an informative regional museum.

Back in the valley it is worth circling the lake on foot and making the crossing over to the island on board a wooden "pletna."

The mightiest of the peaks in the Julian Alps is the Triglav at 2,865 m (9,400 ft). Its name means "three-headed" (left and far left). It is situated in the national park of the same name and towers almost 2 km (1.2 mi) above the Vrata Valley. It was climbed for the first time in 1776.

LJUBLJANA

Although it has less than 300,000 residents, Slovenia's capital boasts all of the structural symbols of national sovereignty: the parliament building, various ministries and embassies as well as the national museum, gallery and library. Indeed, Ljubljana enjoys a very vibrant cultural ambience but it is the city's charm and grace that really make it special. Like Salzburg, the historical center is dominated by a castle from which the imperial Austrian governors administered the Duchy of Carniola for centuries.

To be certain, there is no denying the influence of the imperial Habsburgs on the overall appearance and character of Ljubljana, a city that is often still underestimated by many visitors:

Like Salzburg, Ljubljana has a pedestrian zone in its historic center on the Ljubljanica River. "Salzburg of the South" is one of the town's other names. Above: A view from the west bank of the river towards the three bridges and the old market).

pastel-colored baroque palaces, Wilhelminian buildings, Art Nouveau edifices, as well as older structures with quarry stone walls and shingled roofs. In many places it gives the impression of an accomplished miniature combination of Budapest and Vienna. The promenades along the Ljubljanica River and the alleyways lined with boutiques, souvenir and handicraft shops in the Old Town have something of a southern European flair. When the tables are set out in the open in front of the bistros and cafés, pivnicas and restavracijas, when the town's more than 50,000 students take a break from studying and go out on the town, the pedestrian zone is transformed into a Mediterranean parade.

THE PLITVICE LAKES

The sixteen lakes of Plitvice Lakes National Park, close to the border with Bosnia-Herzegovina, are connected by terraces, cascades and waterfalls and are testimony to the constantly changing yet pristine natural panorama of Croatian limestone. The chain of lakes extends over about 7 km (4 mi) and owes its existence to calcification and sinkholes.

Over several thousand years the limestone sinter has formed barriers and dams behind which the water pools up: algae and mosses are the reason for the shimmering blue and green hues of the twelve larger lakes.

The most impressive waterfalls, with drops of up to 76 m (249 ft), are near the four lower lakes. The lime-enriched water plunges over numerous terraces, themselves constantly collapsing and reforming, into the tiny ponds (left and main picture). The Korana is the end of the lakes where the Plitvica flows out.

The region at the foot of the mountain range known as the Small Kapela was declared a national park in 1949 and boasts rich flora and fauna. The dense forests are home to about 120 bird species as well as to deer, wolves and brown bears.

KORČULA

The capital of the island of the same name is proud of the fact that it is Marco Polo's birthplace. The idyllic, outstandingly well-preserved Old Town (main picture) is situated on a small peninsula. The late-Gothic Sv. Marko cathedral boasts modern sculptures that contrast with the Gothic tracery. The bishop's palace and treasury are home to valuable artifacts relating to the town's eventful history. Renaissance and baroque palaces line the alleyways of the Old Town and the Marco Polo House documents the life of the legendary sea voyager. The residents of the island put on a display of their famous Kumpanija dance during the sword dance festival at the beginning of July.

TROGIR

Trogir's beach promenade and Old Town are dominated by the St Nicholas tower of the Benedictine monastery and the clock tower of the St Laurence Cathedral (above). The Dalmatian port dates back to a Greek colony founded in 385 BC. The town, built on an island, fell under Byzantine control in the 6th century (until 1000), after which the Croats, Bosnians, Hungarians and Venetians then disputed its possession, with the Republic of Venice ultimately gaining the upper hand from 1420 to 1797.

The Benedictine monastery is home to reliefs and inscriptions dating from the 3rd to 1st centuries BC. The St Laurence Cathedral, a Romanesque-Gothic work, houses masterpieces of medieval painting and its West portal, built in around 1240 by master builder Radovan from Trogir, is one of the most important stone works in Croatia. The town hall and the loggia with the clock tower date from the 15th century.

Camerlengo Castle and the Markus Tower are part of the Venetian fortifications from the 15th and 16th centuries. Numerous Late Gothic as well as Renaissance and Baroque palaces and townhouses have also been preserved.

SPLIT

SIBENIK

HVAR

In just ten years the Roman Emperor Diocletian had a palace built for the period following his abdication in 305. His design was based on the example of a Roman castrum. His retirement home near the Roman town of Salona covers an area of about 215 by 180 m (705 by 591 ft) and was fortified with battlement walls. Following the Avar and Slav incursion (615) some of the residents of Salona fled into the ruins of the ancient Roman palace, the grounds of which came to form the core of what is now Split (above, seafront promenade; right

the imperial palace). Diocletian's octagonal mausoleum was turned into a Christian cathedral through the addition of an entrance hall and a bell tower, but the tomb's priceless decoration remained untouched. The Jupiter Temple was converted into the baptistery. There are vaults, columns, arches and frescoes dating back to the Roman palace complex all over town. The late-Gothic Papaliç Palace, the Cindro, the Agubio Palaces, and the loveliest baroque palaces in Split all date back to the golden age of this medieval trading town.

This attractive port is dominated by the white St Jacob's Cathedral (above). The low side aisles extend all the way to the crown height thanks to the Dalmatian master builder and sculptor Juraj Dalmatinac, who also built the baptistery and the apses in 1441. Niccolò di Giovanni Fiorentino completed the side aisles starting in 1477 and fitted the roof with a self-supporting barrel vault made of stone slabs that also support the exterior: a technical masterpiece at the time. Construction was completed as of 1505 by Bartolomeo and Giacomo dal Mestre.

This long, narrow island is a sight to behold in the summer, in particular when the lavender is in bloom. The main road leads to Hvar, a truly romantic town with a main square lined with Venetian and Classical buildings such as the loggia, the cathedral and the arsenal. The 16th-century Croatian poet Petar Hektoroviç lived in an attractive Renaissance castle in Stari Grad, the island's second town. This "old castle", Stari Grad, is the main attraction in the peaceful little hamlet.

DUBROVNIK

Dubrovnik is a city of breathtaking beauty with the old port, the Sveti Ivan fortress and the imposing town walls (below left). The fortress walls facing the sea are up to 6 m (20 ft) thick (below right).

Dubrovnik was one of the most important centers of trade with the Eastern Mediterranean (the Levant) during the Middle Ages. Known at the time as Ragusa – Dubrovnik being its official name only since 1919 –, the town successfully fended off claims to power in the 14th century by the Venetians and the Hungarians. Officially under Turkish rule as of 1525, it determined its own fate as a free republic up until the annexation of Dalmatia by Napoleon in 1809. Its mighty fortresses, with walls up to 6 m (20 ft) thick and 25 m (82 ft) high remain a testimony to its strength.

Ragusa was a bastion of Humanism in its time and had a tremendous influence on Slavic literature and painting. It was here that Croatian developed as a literary language between the 15th and 17th centuries. The town was almost entirely destroyed by an earthquake in 1667, but the large medieval buildings like the Rector's Palace and the monastery have been renovated. Most of the structure, some of the interior decor, and the imposing cathedral were rebuilt in the baroque style.

The Old Town, surrounded by the Sveti Ivan fortress, lends itself to a stroll. Stradun – the town's main trading street in the Middle Ages – leads to the clock tower, with the Roland Columns (far left). Left: A view from the portico of the Sponza Palace of Sv. Vlaho.

The bay of Kotor resembles a fjord cutting deep into the Montenegrin coast. The limestone slopes rise 2,000 m (6,562 ft) out of the sea here. The Church of Our Lady of the Rock was built on the Island of Gospa od Skrpjela in the early 17th century.

KOTOR

BUDVA

SVETI STEFAN

Founded by ancient Greek colonists, Kotor with its large natural port was on a par with Venice in the 13th and 14th centuries as a seafaring power and trading center. The town retains its historical character today, enclosed by 5 km (3 mi) of mighty walls with covered battlements, situated 260 m (853 ft) up on the cliff, and guarded by the Sveti Ivan fortress.

According to Greek legend, Budva was founded more than 2,500 years ago by Kadmos – son of the Phoenician King Agenor and brother of Europa. Originally situated on an island, today Budva is connected to the mainland via a causeway. The picturesque historic Old Town is surrounded by an imposing fortress.

Sveti Stefan lies in the middle section of the Budvanska Riviera. Today, the medieval fishing village, which dates back to the 15th century and was initially built on an island to afford protection against pirates, is a comfortable hotel town with around 250 beds. Its facilities also include a casino, which is why Sveti Stefan is often referred to as "Monaco on the Adriatic".

This unusual fresco is in a side cupola of the Naum monastery church in Ohrid and is thought to depict Jesus as world ruler with a child in his arms (main picture). He is surrounded by two angels and by saints of the Orthodox Church.

Founded by the Illyrians as Lychnidos, the Romans were also quick to recognize the strategic position of the town that later would be called Ohrid. Situated on the Via Egnatia, the main arterial road between Byzantium and the Adriatic, the town quickly developed into an important staging post. Klement and Naum, followers of the Slavic apostles Kyrill and Method, then founded several monasteries here in the late 9th century. The town became a Greek Orthodox bishop's see at the end of the 10th century as well as the imperial capital of the Bulgarian Czar Samuil for a spell. Subsequent Serbian rule under the auspices of Dushan was ended by the Ottomans in 1394, who then remained in Ohrid until 1913.

The Church of St Sophia was built by Archbishop Leo in the 11th century. It was converted to a mosque by the Ottomans and lost its dome, bell tower and interior galleries. The Church of St Clement houses the region's most valuable collection of icons. The historically protected Old Town boasts numerous Macedonian-style buildings of particular appeal.

Lake Ohrid is considered one of the oldest and deepest lakes in the world and is home to a number of endemic fish species. The Church of St John at Kaneo (left) was built on its steep shores in the 13th century, the octagonal tower being easily visible from the lake.

During the 15th and 16th centuries, Moldovan Prince Stephen III (Stephen the Great, 1457-1504), his successors and other high-ranking dignitaries founded some forty monasteries and churches in the north of the country around the capital Suceava. The exterior walls of the religious buildings in Humor, Voronet, Moldovita, Sucevita and Arbore were painted up to their overhanging eaves. The tradition, which began in Humor after 1530, came to an end with the ornamental painting in Sucevita in around 1600. The probable intention was to provide an object of worship for the faithful for whom there was no room in the church. The images also brought the Christian content to ordinary people, who may not have understand the offi-cial Slavic language of the church. The images included legends of the saints, scenes from the Bible such as The Last Judgment, the genealogy of Jesus and the Hymn to the Mother of God. There are also references to political events such as the siege of Constantinople by the "non-believers". The paintings in the church in Arbore date back to 1541 and are of particular artistic value.

The ornate Late Byzantine outer façades of the monastery churches in Moldova (main picture, Voronet) were more than just decoration – they were a "Bible for the Poor".

VORONET

Voronet, the oldest of Moldova's monasteries, was built in 1488 by Stephen the Great. The image above (a copy of Voronet in the Royal Palace, Bucharest) depicts the founder with his family. The artistic quality and vibrant display of what are still the original outside frescoes have earned the church the title of the "Sistine Chapel of the East".

HUMOR

Hardly a centimeter in Moldovan monasteries remained unpainted. The southern façade of the Humor monastery (top), for example, is a vivid interpretation of the Akathist Hymn, one of the oldest Eastern Orthodox hymns dedicated to the Virgin Mary. The interior is a blaze of bright hues (above).

The interiors of Moldova's monasteries (far left Voronet, left Sucevita) also reveal an overwhelming grandeur and a wealth of images. These were places for the faithful to pray and to receive religious instruction.

SUCEVIȚA

The Moldovan monasteries were not just places of pious contemplation and higher education, they were also safe havens against the Turks. The magnificent painted church in Sucevita has a distinctly fortified character.

MOLDOVITA

The Moldovita monastery was founded by Prince Petru Rares (1532-1546). The images depicted in the frescoes on the southern façade (above, the south-east side) include the genealogy of Jesus (the "Jesse Tree") and the rescue of the besieged Constantinople by the Mother of God, the teaching being that orthodoxy brings victory.

One of the highlights of a trip to Romania is an excursion through the Danube Delta. This mighty river divides into three main arms close to Tulcea, more than 2,800 km (1,740 mi) from its source in Germany and almost 80 km (50 mi) before its estuary on the Black Sea coast. The three broad waterways encompass a wetland of around 4,500 sq km (1,737 sq mi), a unique ecosystem that is home to the world's largest cohesive reed cluster (over 800 sq km/309 sq mi). This vast network of waterways, backwaters, canals, lakes, islands, floodplain forests and marshes is also home to a huge diversity of animals and plants. The mighty gallery forests of oaks, willows and poplars are overgrown with lianas and creepers, an especially impressive sight. Water lilies and floating reed islands (Plaurs) cover vast expanses of the water. The diversity of the bird life is also particularly striking, with huge flocks of pelicans and cormorants, for example, and fish eagles and egrets – so rare elsewhere.

Gliding slowly through the narrow channels in a boat or crossing one of the lakes is a wonderful experience in this seemingly forgotten natural paradise. Only seldom do you get a glimpse of the reed-covered huts, which serve as seasonal homes for the fishermen, beekeepers and reed cutters. A fishing village will occasionally crop up, typically inhabited by Romanians as well as Ukrainians and Lipovans, the descendants of 17th-century Russian immigrants. The impression of a fully intact wilderness is deceptive, however. Now protected as a biosphere reserve, the natural equilibrium of the delta also suffered massive disruption, particularly in the 1980s, as a result of haphazard tree felling, irresponsible drainage practices, hunting and livestock farming.

The floodplain forest along the Danube estuary on the Black Sea coast is flooded in the spring (main picture); water chestnuts cover large areas of its surface (right).

The bird life of the Danube Delta includes members of the egret family such as the Squacco Heron (right, a courting display). This is also the main breeding ground for the endangered White Pelican (far right).

RILA

The hermit Ivan withdrew to the inaccessible forests of the Rila Mountains in the 9th century. The monks who followed him soon began construction of a monastery in the vicinity of his cave, a monastery that was later awarded extensive privileges by the Bulgarian czars and which enjoyed a golden age in the 14th century. The Rila monastery fell into disrepair following Bulgaria's conquest by the Ottoman Empire. After being restored to its former glory between 1816 and 1862, it again became a cultural center and a "national sanctuary". The pride of the complex is the Nativity of the Virgin Church, a domed basilica with three naves and surrounded by an open colonnade (left and main picture).

PIRIN

The craggy landscape of the Pirin Mountains, which boasts forty-five peaks above the 2,600 m (8,531 ft), mark, includes the expansive national park of the same name. The park is dominated by Wichren, the third-highest mountain on the Balkan Peninsula at 2,914 m (9,561 ft). Characteristic of this limestone soil region are the approximately seventy glacial lakes – remnants of the last ice age – as well as the many waterfalls and caves. The diverse flora includes conifers such as the Red-Listed Black Pine and the Silver Fir. This pristine landscape is also home to the protected Eurasian Brown Bear (above left) as well as endangered wolves and rare bird species.

ATHENS

ACROPOLIS

Settlement on the fortress hill in Athens can be traced back to the New Stone Age. The former royal fort was converted into a religious site as far back as the 6th century BC. After being destroyed by the Persians, the sanctuaries were quickly rebuilt in the second half of the 5th century BC. The image of Athens' Acropolis is now dominated by the Parthenon.

This temple, built between 447 and 422 BC, was dedicated to the goddess of the city, Pallas Athene. The structure is flanked by a series of mighty columns with eight across the ends and seventeen along the sides. The cult image of Athena once adorned the interior of the temple, the so-called Cella. The inside and outside of the building were decorated with elaborate, three-dimensional marble statues, of which only part still exist today. The gable reliefs in the west, for example, depict Athena's birth, while those in the east illustrate her epic battle with Poseidon.

The Erechtheion, named after the mythical king of Athens, was built between 421 and 406 BC. It is home to several cult sites, which explains the unusual layout of the complex. The structure is surrounded by three large porches; the roof of the Caryatid Porch is supported by columns in the shape of young women (left and below). The Propylaea are the monumental gate complexes of the walls surrounding the Acropolis. They are considered the masterpiece of architect Mnesikles and were built between 437 and 432 BC. The variety of column arrangements here are remarkable. While the entire façade is Doric, the slender Ionic columns rise up in the central passage. Kallikrates' temple of Athena Nike was built between 425 and 421 BC, and is one of the oldest remaining buildings in Ionic style. The small but elegant temple has porches on both the eastern and western side.

Athens is the capital of Greece and a fast-paced international metropolis of five million people overlooking the Aegean. The sea of white houses is surrounded on three sides by mountains up to 1,413 m (4,636 ft) and scattered with bare cliffs poking up like islands. One of these rises bears the heart of ancient European culture, the Acropolis. At its feet, modern life pulsates, stretching as far as Piraeus, the port city on the Saronic Gulf.

PLÁKA AND PSIRRÍ

DIMOTIKÍ AGORÁ

The "Dimotikí Agorá" market is over 100 years old and still the best address for fresh meat and fish. Although the products are now displayed in glass freezers and include everything from hen and sheep tongues to cow hearts and lamb cutlets, they are always artistically organized on their various shelves. The market halls are also a popular meeting place for both night owls and early risers – the market's taverns are open around the clock. Cheese, nut and olive dealers have their stalls outside while fruit, vegetable, sausages and stockfish are traded on the opposite side of the road.

Athens' most beautiful historic quarter is the Pláka, right below the Acropolis. You'll find eateries, small hotels and of course a slew of souvenir stores here among the stately neoclassical villas from the 19th century. Folklore is the focus in the music taverns of the steep "Odós Mnisikléous" alleyway. Hollywood stars act on the screen of the "Cine Paris" rooftop garden cinema, flanked by the illuminated backdrop of the Acropolis, while priests purchase their liturgical accesories and robes at Athens' Orthodox cathedral. The adjacent merchant and handicrafts quarter, Psirrí, has become the hip place to be, but many artisans and merchants still pursue their trade here during the day.

View of the Acropolis from the south, with the mighty Parthenon in the center of the complex. Lykabettos Hill is in the background on the right.

MOUNT ATHOS

Moní Esfigménou Monastery (main picture) is located on the north-eastern coast of the Athos Peninsula. The chapel is home to an icon of a supposedly miraculous disposition, and the monastery library is located in the watchtower.

The first monastery was built on Mt Athos in 963, a holy mountain at the southern tip of the Chalcidice Peninsula. The monks' republic proclaimed here was declared autonomous as early as Byzantine times. Men under the age of twenty-one and women are still forbidden from entering. The monastery's quarters are currently inhabited by some 1,400 monks.

Athos has been an important center of Orthodox Christianity since 1054. Over the centuries, its scope of activities also included some 3,000 farmers working for the monastery in the 14th century; at its height, the republic's estate covered around 20,000 hectares (49,420 acres). The Athos school of icon painting had a significant influence on Orthodox art history, and

the typical monastery architecture left its mark in regions as far away as Russia. Each of the twenty main monasteries – seventeen Greek, one Russian, one Serbian and one Bulgarian – has a cross-in-square church in the center of the courtyard, with apses on three arms of the cross. Other buildings as well as the residential cells are located around the courtyard.

The autonomous monastic republic of Mount Athos, one of the most important centers of Orthodox Christianity, covers a total of twenty main monasteries (far left Vatopediou; left Hilandari) and twenty-two sketes (monastic villages). The minster of the Romanian skete Prodromou (center) is lavishly decorated.

METEORA

The **Meteora monasteries (main picture; insets, Roussanou and Varlaam)** were previously only accessible by makeshift rope ladders or simple cable pulls, but today they can be reached more easily by bridges, paths and steps hewn into the rock.

The name Meteora means "floating", which is a good description of the location where these monasteries are perched: the seemingly impossible Meteora formations soar out of the glacial valley of the Pínios like bizarre bowling pins. Hermits settled on the pillars in the 11th century, and a monk from Mount Athos founded the first of these rock monasteries in the 14th century. A total of twenty-four were eventually built. The Megalo Meteoro was founded by St Athanasios, Bishop of Alexandria, around 1360 and is the highest, and other monasteries were subordinate to it after 1490. The walls of the St Nikolas Anapavsas Monastery, founded around 1388, rise up on one of the other high cliffs. The Varlaam Monastery, named after the hermit who had built a church here back in the 14th century, was completed in 1517. The Roussanou Monastery has recently been re-inhabited by nuns and looks like a smaller version of Varlaam with its octagonal church. Agia Triada, or Holy Trinity, was established as early as 1438 and is accessed via 130 steps. It also featured in James Bond's *For Your Eyes Only*.

The Orthodox frescoes on the church dome (far left, the Meteora monastery of Varlaam) are always dedicated to Jesus, often depicted as a world ruler. The frescoes (left) in Meteora's Monastery of the Holy Trinity were created between 1692 and 1741.

DELPHI, OLYMPIA, EPIDAUROS, MYKENE, SOÚNIO

The Poseidon Temple, built on Cape Soúnio between 444 and 440 BC, is visible from great distances rising up at the southern tip of the Attic Peninsula.

DELPHI

From the 8th century BC, Delphi was one of the most important sanctuaries of ancient times. In the center of the holy district was a temple for Apollo (below)

where Pythia, a divine priestess, presided over the famous Oracle of Delphi. The Pythic Games were held every four years, with the musical and literary competitions held in the now well-preserved theater, and the athletic disciplines were held in the stadium, located at the highest part of the sanctuary perched above the Corinthian Gulf. A large monastery was built east of Delphi in the 10th century. Its church is one of three places of worship in Greece whose magnificent mosaic decorations were largely preserved from the time around the year 1100.

OLYMPIA

An ancient document registers the name of the first winner of a track race in the Sanctuary of Zeus in Olympia in the year 776 BC, a date that has since been considered the date of the first Olympic Games. They were held every four

years for over 1,350 years until a Byzantine emperor forbade them as heathen practices. Near the village of Olimbía, German archaeologists have been excavating the stately remains of this ancient cult district, including its sporting sites, for more than 100 years; the Olympic flame for the modern Olympic Games is always lit here at the Temple of Hera. Three museums display masterpieces of ancient art and sporting aspects of the Olympic Games in both ancient and modern times. The Nike of Paionios (top) is one of the things to be admired there.

EPIDAUROS

The complex of Epidauros, located in a narrow valley in the far eastern reaches of the Peloponnese, spans several levels. It is of key importance to the Asklepios cult, which spread throughout all of Greece in the 5th century BC. In Greek mythology, the god of medicine was the son of Apollo, whose powers of healing were also channeled through him.

Epidauros was an important cult town and health resort at that time. The complex included a spa, clinic and even hospitals. Aside from the Temple of Asklepios, the most important monuments are the Temple of Artemis, the Tholos, the Enkoimeterion, and the Propylaea. The most impressive example of classic Greek architecture in Epidauros is the theater (above), dating back to the early 3rd century BC. It is the best preserved building of its kind in Greece, and is particularly remarkable because of its excellent acoustics.

MYKENE

The Mycenaean culture, which dominated the entire eastern Mediterranean from the 15th to the 12th centuries BC, played an invaluable role in the development of classical Greece. Its name was taken from the Bronze Age fort, Mycenae, in the eastern Peloponnese. The region had already

been settled since 4,000 BC, but greater development did not start until the late Bronze Age. According to Greek tradition, the ancestral seat of the Atrides family was established by Perseus, son of the god Zeus. The main gate, commonly known as the "Lion's Gate", is impressive with a relief of two mighty – now headless – lions (top). Just behind that is the royal graves district where German archaeologist Heinrich Schliemann found the gold funeral mask of Agamemnon, who led the Greeks against Troy.

SOÚNIO

The Temple of Poseidon in Soúnio, whose sixteen remaining Doric marble columns still support the epistyle on which the temple's roof once rested. The location marks the southern border of Attika, which starts in the north near Egósthena at the Corinthian Gulf and Skála Oropoú at the Southern Euboean Gulf. In ancient times, Attika was basically the bread basket of Athens' agricultural hinterland. Slaves originally laid the foundations for Athens' wealth in the silver mines of Lávrio near Soúnio. In the Demeter Sanctuary of the present-day industrial city of Elefsína, free citizens wanted to demand better conditions for the afterlife by participating in this mysterious cult. In ancient times, the crews of Athenian war and trading ships thanked the temperamental god of the sea for their safe return at the Temple of Poseidon, partly decorated in gaudy colors. People hoped to be healed of illnesses in the Amphiáreion, while pregnant women made pilgrimages to Brauron to ask for assistance from the Goddess Artemis.

ZÁKINTHOS

The southernmost of the Ionic islands was once called "the Flower of the Levant" by the Venetians. With its cobbled streets and squares, arcades and the free-standing church spires, the island capital still bears clear Venetian traces, although it had to be completely rebuilt after a severe earthquake in 1953. At that time, only a bank and the main church had withstood the fierce seismic shocks and subsequent fires. The wide Bay of Laganás has been declared a marine national park where giant sea turtles lay their eggs on the beaches. Near Kerí, liquid pitch, which was used to caulk boats until very recently, still springs up from underground sources. The main tourist attraction here is the Blue Grotto, whose light effects are equally as impressive as those of the Blue Grotto of Capri.

Shipwreck Beach near Anafonítria in the north-west of the island of Zákinthos can only be reached by boat.

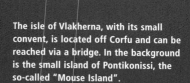

The isle of Vlakherna, with its small convent, is located off Corfu and can be reached via a bridge. In the background is the small island of Pontikonissi, the so-called "Mouse Island".

CORFU

Corfu, with more than 100,000 inhabitants, is the most densely populated island of the Ionic Archipelago. Referred to as Kérkira by the Greeks, it is a charmingly green island characterized by rolling hills and beautiful coastlines (right, Cape Drástis). Its more than 100 villages have managed to retain much of their historic flair, and the island's capital is considered one of the most beautiful towns in Greece. Its Old Town quarter (top) is towered over by the Old Fort and the spire of the Spyrídon Church. On the eastern side of Corfu, facing the Albanian and Greek mainland, the beaches are long, narrow and pebbly. Long sandy beaches line the northern coast. Closer to the open sea, the shore is rockier, but many sandy beaches sprawl below the bluffs here, or are nestled between bizarre rock formations. Archaeological sites are scarce, but Corfu has two small castles: British prince consort Philip was born in Mon Repos Castle, while Empress Sissi of Bavaria and later Emperor Wilhelm II spent many holidays in Achillío Castle.

SANTORINI

The island also known as Thíra by the Greeks is truly unique in the world. Until some 3,600 years ago, a mighty volcano soared out of the sea here. When it erupted, only the edges of the island remained. The Aegean branched into the resulting crater and later people built quaint whitewashed villages on the more than 300-m-high (984-ft) crater rim. The hamlets stretch far down the steep lava wall and use all available space for small terraces. Anyone who spends a few days here, or even just enjoys a sunset, will be spending time between heaven and earth. Santorini was already settled before the volcano erupted. Merchants and sailors, who had their houses decorated with artistic murals, lived in a city near present-day Akrotíri. Archaeologists discovered it under a thick layer of ash and lava.

Filigree bell towers and blue church domes are as characteristic of the island's architecture as its charming windmills. The curious stray cats add a little flair as well.

All of Santorini's villages – like here on the main island – are located on the rim of a crater formed by an eruption some 3,600 years ago. The Aegean branched into it, creating the archipelago.

The mosaic floor of a house on the island of Delos depicts Dionysus (main picture), the Greek god of wine, inebriation and plentifulness riding a leopard.

MYKONOS

One hundred years ago, admirers of Greek antiquities stopped on the Cyclades island of Mykonos to visit the sites of Apollo's cult on nearby Delos. They also had eyes for the hamlet of Chora, with its Old Town quarter. Artists and bohemians soon moved in. For fifty years now, the rich and beautiful of Europe have been frequenting Mykonos and, although the long beaches near town as well as those on the southern and south-eastern coast are often quite crowded, the largely treeless coasts and bays still boast long sections where you can still find yourself all alone. There are at least four museums worth visiting here as well: the Nautiko Moussio (seafaring since Minoan times), the Archaeological Museum, the Folklore Museum and the House of Lena (civilian life in the 19th century). The most unusual architectural gem on Mykonos is the Panagia Paraportiani church. Additions have been made since the Middle Ages, merging oddly with one another under a constantly re-applied coat of whitewash.

DELOS

Settled since the 3rd century BC, the island of Delos first appeared in historical texts in the 14th century BC. It then became an important cult center and pilgrimage destination in the 7th century BC as the "birthplace" of the god Apollo. In the 5th century BC, the island was the focal point of the First Delian League, and later became an important trading site deemed useful even by the Romans in the 2nd century BC.

The emergence of new trading centers, pirate raids and attacks by the soldiers of Mithridates of Pontos in the 1st century BC finally

Marble lions, which guard the mythical birthplace of Apollo, are the symbol of Delos. Two headless statues stand in the House of Cleopatra.

resulted in Delos' collapse, but excavation work has unearthed the ruins of numerous houses whose inhabitants had laid mosaics in their interior courtyards depicting different images such as dolphins, tigers and a variety of religious idols. The three temples of Apollo, reached via the holy road, are probably the simplest of all the sanctuaries dedicated to this god. To the west is the Artemision, the temple to Apollo's sister.

Cyclades means circular islands, from the ancient Greek word "kyklos" (cycle or circle). Náxos is the largest island of the Cyclades. Delos is a lesser-known island gem, and Mykonos (left, the island's capital of the same name) is considered a particularly chic jet-set isle.

NÁXOS

The Portara, a monumental marble gate on the Palateia Peninsula north of the port, is the symbol of Náxos and the only remains of a giant temple project that had been planned to honor the god Apollo in the 6th century BC. Also revered in Náxos is a mountain grotto beneath Mt Zas ("Zas" is Modern Greek for Zeus), where Crete-born Zeus is said to have grown up. The "local god" on Náxos is considered to be Dionysus, god of wine. The Bronze Age culture of the Cyclades in the 3rd millennium BC saw the emergence of a special form of marble idols. The slender, usually female and often creatively abstract

Spectacular in both morning and evening light: the Portara marble gate on Náxos.

figures range from a few centimeters to life-size and were an earlier highlight of European art. The collection in the Náxos Museum is the second largest after that in the Museum for Cycladic Art in Athens. Until it was destroyed by the Persians in 490 BC, Náxos was the power center of the Aegean. Thereafter, the island had to conform to Athenian rule. Náxos did not experience another boom until the arrival of the Venetians, who made it into the center of the "Duchy of Náxos" and built the fort, which can still be seen today. The Catholic cathedral in the highest part of the fort quarter was also built at this time. To the north, in the Bourgos quarter, are more than forty Greek Orthodox churches and chapels.

Particularly worth seeing is the approximately 6-m-long (20-ft) sculpture of the "Kouros of Flerio" in Melanes, and the Panagia Drossiani church in the mountain village of Moni, which is home to some of the oldest Byzantine wall paintings.

RHODES

Greece's fourth-largest island (bottom, Mandraki Harbor) was once considered a possession of the sun god Helios. In ancient times, Rhodes was home to four important cities and, for a short time, even one of the seven world wonders: the Colossus of Rhodes.

The main island of the Dodecanese group, which belongs to the Southern Sporades, has seen many a ruler come and go. The island, which was settled early on, fell under Macedonian hegemony during the time of Alexander the Great before a spell of independence and later rule by Byzantium.

From 1310, Rhodes fell under the rule of the Order of St John, and then in 1523 under Ottoman control. The Turkish rule lasted until 1912, when Italy conquered the island and held on to it until 1943. It was not until 1948 that the island became part of Greece. Rhodes City owes its present-day look to the Crusaders. Knights Road is a well-preserved example of a road in

the 15th century. Around it are the "hostels", the hospices of the knights' regional associations. The road begins at the Byzantine cathedral and leads to the residence of the Grand Master of the Order of St John, which was rebuilt by the Italians according to old engravings. The knights' hospital, built between 1440 and 1489, is today an archaeological museum.

The minaret of the Ibrahim Pasha Mosque, built in 1581, towers over the city wall of historic Rhodes (far left). Knights Road, with its cobblestones and two-story houses built from natural stone on either side, transports you back to the Middle Ages (left).

KARPATHOS

The second-largest island of the Dode-canese is still very pristine. The white-washed and pastel-colored houses, churches and windmills of what is arguably Greece's most beautiful mountain village are nestled tightly onto a steep slope. The town of Olym-bos was founded in 1420 by inhabi-tants of the now orphaned neigh-boring island of Saria, and the ancient Vrykos, who sought protection from pirates in the mountains.
Nowhere else in Greece has retained so much of its original culture as Kar-

None of the islands of the Dodecanese celebrates Easter with as much verve and color as the village of Olymbos on Karpathos.

pathos – thanks to its isolation, which the village maintained until well into the 1980s. The houses are built in the traditional style, the ancient Doric dialect is still spoken here and, partic-ularly charming, the women still wear their traditional garb. Bread is also still baked in collective stone ovens, and centuries-old customs are maintained. Naturally, tourism motivates these traditions as visitors expect that rustic ambience from the locals. Indeed, the main source of income today apart from cattle breeding is tourism. All the same, the festivals in Olymbos are colorful and celebrated with gusto, particularly the traditional Easter festival.

CRETE

Knossos (main picture, northern wing of the palace) is one of Crete's most important Minoan sites. Only copies remain of the most precious findings – the originals can be seen at the Archeological Museum in the island capital of Heraklion.

KNOSSOS

Crete is roughly 260 km (162 mi) long and 60 km (37 mi) wide and situated between the Aegean and the Libyan Sea. Three mighty mountains, each of them over 2,000 m (6,562 ft), cut through the island and represent a continuation of the mountain range of the Peloponnese towards Asia Minor. This was where Europe's first civilization was created 4,000 years ago. Those enigmatic Minoans were, for over 500 years, able to pacify the eastern Mediterranean and operate a flourishing trade with Egypt and the kingdoms of the Middle East. From 1900 to 1941, English archaeologist Sir Arthur Evans excavated the economic and religious center of the Minoans some 5 km (3 mi) south-east of the island capital of Heraklion: Knossos, a building complex up to four stories high with 1,400 rooms and covering 20,000 sq m (215,200 sq ft). Many of the corridors and halls in Knossos were adorned with artistic frescoes. Drinking and sewage problems were solved with clever pipe systems. The Minoans also already had their own script.

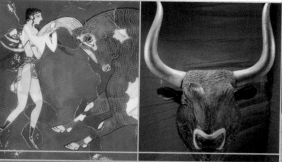

The Bull Leaper (far left, an excerpt) and the three Ladies in Blue (left) are famous Minoan frescoes found in Knossos along with the Rhython (center), a drinking vessel in the shape of a bull's head made from soapstone, gold and quartz.

ISTANBUL

GOLDEN HORN, GALATA BRIDGE, YENI CAMI MOSQUE

This city with three names – Byzantium, Constantinople and Istanbul – has experienced two empires in its history that significantly shaped the success of the Mediterranean for almost 2,000 years: the East Roman, or Byzantine, Empire and its direct successor, the Ottoman Empire. According to legend, the Byzantines fleeing the Ottomans threw so many treasures into the port basin that the water glistened gold. The "Golden Horn" (main picture with the Galata Bridge and the Yeni Cami Mosque, completed in 1663) was born. Istanbul has a unique relationship with the sea. The waters flow from the Black Sea through the Bosporus Strait, into the Sea of Marmara and the Dardanelles and out into the Aegean Sea. Indeed, a sought-after piece of real estate.

BLUE MOSQUE

The foundations of the Sultan Ahmed or "Blue" Mosque were laid in 1609, and the massive project was completed relatively quickly by 1616. Sultan Ahmed I, its sponsor, died one year after the mosque was finished. The colossal mosque, whose interior is decorated with predominantly blue Iznik tiles – hence its name – owes its spaciousness to the 43-m-high (141-ft) dome. It rests on four striking pillars, as well as four ascending half-domes, and has a diameter of 23.5 m (77 ft). The Mihrab, the prayer room, is made of marble and adorned with precious stones.

HAGIA SOPHIA

The Hagia Sophia was built in the 6th century in a remarkable five years during the reign of Emperor Justinian I. The main Orthodox church in the Byzantine Empire as well as the coronation site of its emperors, it was converted to a mosque by the Ottomans in 1453 after their conquest of Constantinople. Today it is a museum (main picture).

The highlights at Hagia Sophia include mosaics such as the one from in the 10th century (bottom right) in the southern vestibule. It depicts the Virgin Mary with her child. She is enthroned between Emperors Justinian I and Constantine the Great. Justinian rightfully presents her with a church, the Hagia Sophia, while Constantine gave her his city, Constantinople. Another splendid mosaic, no longer fully preserved, is the Great Deesis, an image of intercession with Jesus raising his hand in blessing (top right) in the southern gallery of the Hagia Sophia. The mosaic is from the 13th century.

TOPKAPI PALACE

After a fire in the Old Palace in 1540/1541, Sultan Süleyman had his residence moved to the Top-kapi Saray, which had been built on the site of the old Acropolis in the 15th century and provided a stunning view over the Bosporus. The complex stretches over an area of 6 hectares (15 acres) and is made up of numerous pavilions grouped around four spacious interior courtyards. The roof also forms a varied landscape (above). The Harem is made up of 300 rooms in a maze-like arrangement, at the centre of which is the festi-val room of the Padishah (below).

GRAND BAZAAR

The Grand Bazaar, where visitors can haggle for whatever their hearts desire, stretches over more than 32 hectares (79 acres) in the Beyazit district. There are over 4,000 stalls in some sixty malls. Built as a wooden structure under Sultan Mehmed II in 1461, it was rebuilt in stone in the 17th cen-tury following several fires.

EGYPTIAN BAZAAR

Also worth seeing is the covered Egyptian Bazaar, located in the Eminönü district near the Galata Bridge and the Yeni Cami Mosque. More than 100 merchants trade their goods there. The sites, sounds and smells are beguiling: nowhere else in the city will you find a richer selection of spices, sweets, dried fruit and tea.

PERGAMON

The cliffs, soaring to heights of over 300 m (984 ft), were used by the rulers of Pergamon for their capital city's acropolis (main picture). The awe-inspiring Altar of Zeus is now actually housed in the the Pergamon Museum in Berlin, but extensive remains of the royal city can also be seen on the original site and in the modern city of Bergama at the foot of the castle hill. The Temple of Emperor Trajan was completed by the emperor's successor, Hadrian, at the highest point of the ancient royal city of Pergamon — on the castle hill of modern-day Bergama.

MILETUS

Along with Ephesus and Priene, the ancient city of Miletus owes its wealth to sea trade, but had to be relocated several times due to the threat of silt buildup in the port. The old Lions Harbor is hardly recognizable among the ruins, which largely disappears in the wetlands of the Büyük Menderes river. A field of ruins, with the mighty theater building, the agora, and the walls of the thermal baths has been preserved. Today, frogs and storks make their home in the compound, which was formerly the largest city in ancient Greece, a region that comprised some eighty daughter cities and was where Thales, Anaximander and Anaximenes developed the basics of philosophy and mathematics. Miletus was famous for the woolen materials dyed with purple from the murex snail.

The ancient theater of Miletus (top) once seated up to 15,000 spectators. Bottom: The Temple to Athena in Priene.

PRIENE

Just like Miletus and Ephesus, the ancient city of Priene, located on the spectacular southern slope of the Mycale Mountain, was also a member of the mighty Ionian League, which was made up of twelve city-states and presumably founded by Greek colonists sometime before the year 1000 BC. The city was created around 450 BC by master builder Hippodamus of Miletus. The Temple of Athena, built in the 4th century BC to honor the city's tutelary goddess, is considered a masterpiece of Ionian architecture, and Alexander the Great continued to fund the construction after capturing the city. As Priene had already lost importance during Roman times, and had been uninhabited since the Middle Ages, the ruins provide an authentic picture of Hellenic city culture.

EPHESUS

This ancient city of ruins lies not far from the town of Selçuk. Long before Greek merchants and settlers arrived here on the Ionian coast, the Carians and Lydians considered it a holy place for the Great Mother Goddess Kybele. Its Temple of Artemis was part of the long tradition of the mother cult. In around AD 129, Ephesus became the capital of the Roman province of Asia and was home to an astounding 200,000 inhabitants at the time. Archaeologists have been able to reconstruct more of this ancient city's temples, grand boulevards, baths and residential dwelllings than any other site in Turkey. Only the

port has disappeared through centuries of silt deposits – the sea is actually several miles away from the city today.

Modern library buildings can hardly compete with the grand pillared architecture of the Celsus Library (left). Originally built as a memorial tomb for the Roman proconsul Tiberius Julius Celsus in the 2nd century AD (his sarcophagus is under the library), it is probably the most intact library from ancient times. Some 12,000 scrolls were stored within its walls back in the day. The Temple of Hadrian (right) was built in AD 123, on the occasion of a visit by the Emperor himself.

BODRUM

This former fishing village is like a whitewashed island in a blue lagoon. The center of Bodrum is the Johannite Castle from 1413 (above). Those who wish to can take a gulet, the traditionally high-built sailing ship, out for a picnic in a sheltered bay.

FETHIYE

Fethiye is famous for the magnificent blue lagoon of Ölü Deniz (main picture) and the Lycian tomb monuments hewn into the rock above the town (above). With their roofs, doors and protruding lintels, they are similar to Lycian residential architecture – a final resting place for the dead.

KAUNOS

The peculiar rock graves in the south-west of Turkey date back to the Lycians, who likely migrated here from Crete before the Greeks. These monumental rows of graves on the eastern bank of the Dalyan (above) were built in the 4th century BC for the citizens of the ancient city of Kaunos.

HIERAPOLIS

There have been settlements in the hot springs district of Pamukkale for thousands of years. The area was part of the Roman province of Asia in the 2nd century BC, and King Eumenes II of Pergamon had the city of Hierapolis built here in 190 BC. It was mainly planned as a fort complex. Along with the town came the first construction of thermal baths. Residential buildings, temples, a theater, as well as other Hellenic buildings. Some early Christian churches, whose ruins can still be seen today, were built in the area around the baths.

On the mountain above what is now Pamukkale are the ruins of the ancient Greek -Roman city of Hierapolis. The ruins feature city gates and cobblestone-paved streets.

PAMUKKALE

In addition to the remains of ancient buildings erected here until well into the 4th century, Pamukkale also has a magnificent and unusual natural spectacle to offer: hot springs rise to a height of roughly 100 m (328 ft) from a ledge in the Çökelez Mountains and flow down into the valley. Over time, the sediments (sinter) of the water, which was very rich in minerals, formed petrified waterfalls, forests of lime stalactites, and terrace-like basins, transforming Pamukkale into the surreal landscape you see today.

Pamukkale means "Cotton Fort" or "Cotton Castle" – a name that aptly describes the natural wonder of sinter lime created here from a hot spring. The warm healing waters pour from one limestone basin into another, leaving bizarre formations between the steps.

KYKKOS

Kykkos Monastery (main picture with its spacious cloister) is located near the town of Pedoulas. It is the most famous and also the mightiest monastery on Cyprus. It was founded by Alexios Komnenos toward the end of the 11th century, the Byzantine emperor who also donated his most precious treasure to the church, the icon of St Mary painted by the Apostle Luke.

Cyprus' first president, Archbishop Marakios III, who is buried in the nearby town of Throni, was a neophyte in the Kykkos Monastery during his younger years. The complex was completely burned down several times over the centuries. The present-day buildings are all recent works, but the ancient findings and liturgical devices displayed in the monastery's museum are priceless antiques.

ASINOU

The Church of Our Lady of Asinou (top), or "Pangia Forviotissa", stands alone on a wooded hill near Nikitari. From the outside, it appears to be a simple and basic facility, but inside it is home to what is probably the most beautiful Byzantine fresco treasure on the island. The Last Supper, Annunciation and Nativity, the Vita Jesu and the dozens of pictures of martyrs display the complete spectrum of exhilarating imagery from the Orthodox faith. Most of the murals date back to the 11th century. Despite having never been restored, they still look amazingly fresh.

ST SOPHIA

Kiev was named after the city's alleged founder, Ki. The first official documented mention of the city dates back to 860. Yaroslav the Wise laid the foundation stone for the city's most important church, the St Sophia Cathedral, in 1037. The exterior of this, the oldest eastern Slavic church (above), is a highlight of Ukrainian baroque style, while the interior (main picture) features a domed structure that exhibits Byzantine styles, with open galleries, gilded pillars, iconostases, as well as a number of wall paintings and frescoes. The church has thirteen domes and originally comprised five naves with five adjoining apses. Extensive conversions over the course of time, however, have changed the cathedral's external appearance.

With a width of 55 m (180 ft), a length of 37 m (121 ft) and a height of 29 m (95 ft), the interior has imposing dimensions and has retained its original Byzantine character. The 11th-century frescoes and mosaics depict scenes from the Gospel and portraits of the saints. The extensive gallery was once intended for the royal court.

MONASTERY OF THE CAVES

The Monastery of the Caves on the banks of the Dnieper was founded by hermits who submitted to a monastic regime in around 1050. Construction of permanent monastery buildings within the cave system began shortly thereafter. The caves subsequently served as tombs for these monks.

While the damaged buildings above ground were redesigned and expanded in the 17th and 18th centuries, the caves have more or less remained in their original condition. Three of these 12th-century underground places of worship have survived to this day. The grandest effort in the monastery complex is the Dormition Cathedral, rebuilt after suffering war damages (main picture).

THE KREMLIN

Russia's capital lies on the Moskva River, a tributary of the Volga. First mention was made of it in 1147, and by 1325 it had become a grand ducal residence. During the reign of Czar Peter the Great, Moscow lost its capital city status in 1713 to newly founded St Petersburg. It was the Bolsheviks who made Moscow the political center of Russia again in 1918. Over the course of its history the city has been plundered repeatedly as well as suffering devastating fires. At the beginning of the 20th century Moscow boasted 450 churches, twenty-five monasteries, and 800 charitable institutions. After the disintegration of the USSR, the metropolis (with more than 10 million residents) still has an impressive cultural complement. With over sixty theaters, seventy-five museums, 100 colleges and about 2,300 historic buildings, Moscow maintains a leading position among the world's cities.

For centuries, historical and political events in Russia have been inextricably linked to the Moscow Kremlin, seat of the czars and the metropolitan bishops since the 13th century. Architecturally speaking, the Kremlin had already attained its current size at the time of Grand Prince Ivan IV, known as Ivan the Terrible, who had himself crowned as czar in 1547. First mention of the city's defensive wall was documented in 1147; it was still a wooden construction until the 14th century. Ivan the Terrible gradually had the city walls and the numerous churches almost entirely rebuilt by the leading Italian and Russian master builders of the time, preferring instead to have more ostentatious buildings constructed in their place. These grand edifices were continuously expanded and remodeled until well into the 20th century. They now house priceless works of art. The Kremlin is still Russia's seat of government, for which the term "Kremlin" is synonymous. Within its walls are magnificent palaces, armories, senate buildings, as well as cathedrals and churches with characteristic gilded domes. The Church of the Deposition (Zerkov Rispoloscheniya) was constructed by Russian builders in 1485 and is the seat of the Russian patriarchs and metropolitan bishops. The name derives from a Byzantine feast day celebrating the arrival of the Mother of God's robes in Constantinople. The valuable interior decor includes a 17th-century icon wall (above left).

RED SQUARE, ST BASIL'S CATHEDRAL

Red Square (below) is roughly 500 x 150 m (1,640 x 492 ft) and was built at the end of the 15th century as a market and gathering place, in addition to its use as a place of execution. The famous St Basil's Cathedral (right) was built by Ivan the Terrible after his victory over the Mongol Golden Horde. The cathedral, consecrated in 1561, is considered an outstanding masterpiece of Old Russian construction. The central, steepled church is surrounded by eight chapels on a single foundation and arranged in the shape of a cross. It was the addition of the St Basil's Chapel that gave the whole complex its name. The central building with the pavilion roof is dominated by the nine differently designed chapels.

GUM

At the time of its completion in 1893, GUM, which was designed as a marketplace and today one of the largest department stores in the world, was considered one of the most advanced buildings in Russia with its steel and glass roof. Architect Pomeranzev combined both Renaissance and traditional Russian architectural elements in the building, designing it as a shopping center with the shops strung together.

THE GOLDEN RING

The Golden Ring is the absolute zenith for fans of Old Russian art and architecture. The term Golden Ring, which was first coined in Russia at the start of the 1970s, refers to a ring of enchanting old towns north of Moscow – Old Russian gems, places that could be the setting for the tales of Russian writers. The main towns are Vladimir, Suzdal, Yaroslavl, Rostov Veliky, Sergiev Posad, Pereslavl-Zalessky and Kostroma.

What began in the Middle Ages as fortresses providing protection against the Mongolian hordes from Central Asia, has developed into a series of Old Russian towns with mighty kremlins, defensive monasteries and quaint churches whose magnificent mosaics, icons and invaluable treasures stood in stark contrast to the misery of everyday life in these poor rural towns. While the term "golden" is a reference to the striking, gilded

domes of the medieval churches, the word "ring" denotes the close cultural and historic ties that bind the individual towns. They still stand today as testimony to a bygone era – that of "Old Russia", which existed up until the October Revolution of 1917 and which was a deeply religious nation.

SERGIEV POSAD

The Monastery of the Holy Trinity and St Sergius (above) is without doubt one of Russia's most important religious sites. The monastery complex, dating back to 1340, is a significant pilgrimage destination for Orthodox Christians. Enclosed by a mighty defensive wall that is 1600 m (1,750 yds) long, the complex was besieged in vain by Polish troops for sixteen months between 1608 and 1610. Sergiev Posad, referred to as Sagorsk between 1931 and 1991, was a national sanctuary even during the czarist era, enjoying support from the rulers who had had their own residence, the Chertogi Palace (17th century). The Russian state closed the monastery in 1920 and declared it a museum.

PERESLAVL-ZALESSKY

Founded in the 10th/11th centuries as a trading town on the shores of Lake Pleshcheye, Pereslavel-Zalessky is one of the oldest towns in Russia and has a wealth of churches and pretty wooden houses. The walls of the white cathedral (1152) on the Red Square inside the Kremlin are decorated with semicircular ornaments. One of the few older surviving Kremlin buildings is the Church of the Metropolitan Peter from 1585. The Annunciation Church (mid-17th century) boasts a spacious nave. The Goritsky Monastery (above) dates from the first half of the 14th century, and the Danilov Monastery, located in the south-western part of the town, is from the 16th century.

ROSTOV VELIKY

A panorama of rare beauty: the city with its cathedral of seven silver roofs, the walls of the Kremlin and the towers of the Monastery of Our Saviour and St Jacob as they rise up beyond picturesque Lake Nero. The name Rostov Veliky has a special significance in the colorful history of Old Russia. In Czarist times, only Novgorod and Rostov were entitled to use the adjunct "veliky" – meaning great. This town, established in 862, had already become a flourishing trading center by the Middle Ages. The Kremlin is protected by a wall over 1 km (0.6 mi) in length that features eleven towers. Domes decorated in silver and gold crown the Metropolitan's residence.

JAROSLAVL'

Prince Yaroslav founded this fortified town at the confluence of the Kotorosl and Volga rivers in 1010. Despite its age, many of the original historical buildings have actually survived the destruction of numerous wars. Having enjoyed its golden age in the 17th century, the buildings from this era are among the loveliest in Russia. The Monastery of Our Saviour (12th century) houses the 16th-century Cathedral of the Resurrection of Christ (above). The town's most magnificent church bears the name of the Prophet Elias. It was built in the 17th century, is decorated with wonderful frescoes and is located on the central town square, where the roads radiate out in a star pattern.

KOSTROMA

Kostroma represents the northern-most point on the Golden Ring and is a classic drawing-board town. It was built in its current manifestation following a devastating fire in 1773. A number of significant monasteries such as the Ipatiev Monastery, as well as the Resurrection Church, are among the few surviving witnesses to the period prior to that unfortunate year. A collection of wooden buildings typical of the region are on display in the Museum of Wooden Architecture, including a windmill, a farmhouse and some churches. The museum is located in the Monastery of St Hypathius, which is dominated by the Holy Trinity Cathedral with its golden towers.

SUZDAL

This unique museum town with over 100 historic buildings is the most intact Old Russian town. The monastery became the religious center of medieval Russia after the fall of Kiev. In the 11th century the small town housed the residence of the most powerful principality in Russia, before being destroyed by the Mongolians in 1238. The Kremlin, the market square, the open-air museum of wooden architecture, the monasteries and the traditional wooden houses stand out among the attractions. Some of the 18th- and 19th-century houses are adorned with wood or stone carvings. The 600-year-old Spaso-Yevfimiev monastery in the east of town is the largest in Suzdal.

VLADIMIR

This town on the Klyazma River was founded in 1108 by Vladimir Monomakh, the Grand Prince of Kiev, and was also named after him. The earthen walls and the Golden Gate from the 12th century have managed to survive and the magnificent churches here are well able to compete even with those of Kiev. Prince Andrei Bogolyubsky had the town's most famous landmark built in 1160, the Assumption Cathedral, with its three grandiose domes. A two-floor gallery, crowned with four golden domes, was later erected around the main building. The St Demetrius Cathedral is also worth visiting. Above: A large Easter procession with Russian Orthodox dignitaries.

After Czar Peter the Great had forced the Swedish King Karl XII to part with a strip of coastline along the Gulf of Finland, he finally gained his long-awaited access to the Baltic Sea, and thus to the West. He then built his new capital there, St Petersburg, which was intended to outmatch the splendor of other European cities. A great number of master architects and builders from Western and Central Europe such as Bartolomeo Rastrelli, Domenico Trezzini and Andreas Schlüter were involved in the construction of St Petersburg, a city that is particularly impressive with regard to the harmony created between its baroque and classical styles, grandiose squares, and numerous canals with more than 400 bridges. Nevsky Prospekt, St Petersburg's magnificent promenade, is lined with ostentatious buildings such as the Anitchkov and Stroganov Palaces.

THE WINTER PALACE

The Winter Palace (main picture and above: the splendid Jordan Staircase) is one of the most significant buildings in Russian baroque style. Begun in 1754 based on plans drawn up by Bartolomeo Rastrelli, it was intended as be an imperial residence directly alongside the Neva River. The Winter Palace is the largest component of the Hermitage complex.

THE HERMITAGE

The Hermitage is one of the most important art museums in the world. It comprises the Winter Palace, the Small, the New and the Old Hermitage, as well as the Hermitage Theater. The Hermitage art collection, which was started by Catherine the Great, is a museum of superlatives (right). The more than 1,000 magnificently designed rooms display around 60,000 exhibits, while the archive encompasses three million items. In addition to the archaeological section with exhibits dating back to antiquity, visitors can also enjoy a massive collection of classical European art.

PALACE SQUARE

The Winter Palace owes its current design to Peter the Great's successor, Empress Elizabeth. In fact, the building where the Emperor died in 1725 – on the site that is now occupied by the Hermitage Theater – was torn down completely to make way for the new palace. The square in front of the Winter Palace with the Alexander Column (right) has been the scene of key historical events. It was here that more than 1,000 demonstrators were murdered by czarist troops in 1905, and it was here that the October Revolution began in 1917, when the Bolsheviks stormed the grounds.

PETERHOF

LOMONOSSOV

PAVLOVSK

TSARSKOE SELO

The Peterhof residence (main picture) was built in 1714. It has an ornately designed garden and is indubitably the most elegant of the imperial residences around St Petersburg. Particular attention was paid during its planning to sophisticated water features including decadent fountains for which special wells were built (above, the Samson Fountain). A canal runs from the Golden Cascade, underneath the terrace used for musical and ballet performances, out to the Baltic Sea.

The suburb of Lomonossov, once referred to as Oranienbaum, is home to an extensive complex of palaces and parks built for Prince Alexander Menshikov in the 18th century by Italian and German architects. It was later converted into a summer residence. The interior of this rococo palace boasts magnificent decor: furniture and parquet flooring of the finest wood, silk wall hangings, embroidery, porcelain vases and lacquer work as well as wall and ceiling paintings.

Just 5 km (3 mi) away from Tsarskoe Selo is another imperial palace in the midst of Europe's largest landscaped park: Pavlovsk Palace. The name goes back to Czar Paul I, who commissioned Scottish architect Charles Cameron with this classic summer residence in 1780. Above: Czar Paul I's four-poster bed.

The colossal Catherine Palace, based on plans by Bartolomeo Rastrelli, has a 300-m-long (984-ft) baroque façade and forms the heart of the Tsarskoe Selo (Pushkin) palace and park complex about 25 km (16 mi) outside of St Petersburg.

THE AMBER ROOM

This gift to Peter the Great simply had to be monumental. At that time, the Prussians were keen to garner Russia as an ally in the costly war against Sweden. To this end Emperor Frederick Wilhelm I made the decision to sacrifice his extravagant Amber Room. After all, the czar had been very impressed by the chamber during his visit to the city palace in Berlin.

This truly imperial gift – with magnificent amber paneling shimmering in shades of warm gold – was ultimately brought to St Petersburg in 1716 and initially installed in the Winter Palace. Later, it was moved to the Catherine Palace in Tsarskoe Selo, the imperial summer residence south of St Petersburg. The brilliance of the amber room was dazzling, having been built in 1701 in Danzig and Königsberg by the best amber cutters and turners in Europe. The design was originally drafted by German sculptor Andreas Schlüter, but it was only after World War II that the Amber Room achieved real international fame – when it disappeared. In the hope of saving it from the ravages of war, German soldiers actually dismantled the panels in 1941 and stashed them away in Königsberg. The unique work of art remains at large to this day. In 1997, a commode and a mosaic were found in Germany – the only original parts of the now reconstructed Amber Room. They form the key attraction in the Catherine Palace. The painstaking reconstruction work began in 1979, and was finally completed in 2003. The newly created Amber Room was then presented to the international public in the presence of President Vladimir Putin and German Chancellor Gerhard Schröder.

Picture Credits

Abbreviations:
A = Alamy; BB = Bilderberg; C = Corbis; G = Getty Images;
Ifa = IFA-Bilderteam; JA = Jon Arnold Images; L = Laif;
RH = Robert Harding

Pictures listed in clockwise order starting at the top left.

S. 2/3 A/Peter Horree, 4/5 G/National Geographic/Paul Nicklen, 6/7 Bildagentur Huber, 8.1 G/Altrendo Panoramic, 8.2 G/Wilfried Krecichwost, 8.3 A/Mikael Utterström, 8.4 G/The Image Bank/Harald Sund, 8/9 Schapowalow, 9.1 G/Arctic Images, 10.1 A/Phil Degginger, 10.2 G/Panoramic Images, 10.3 G/altrendo panoramic, 10/11 G/The Image Bank/Steve Allen, 11.1 G/The Image Bank/ Hans Strand, 11.2 G/Panoramic Images, 12.1 Martin Schulte-Kellinghaus, 12.2 L/Reiner Harscher, 12.3 A/graficart.net, 12/13 H/Pinn, 14 Erich Spiegelhalter, 14/15 Erich Spiegelhalter, 15.1 Alimdi.net/Christian Handl, 15.2 Schapowalow/Huber, 15.3 BB/Christophe Boisvieux, 15.4 Erich Spiegelhalter, 16.1 Erich Spiegelhalter, 16.2 ifa/JA, 16.3 Reiner Harscher, 16/37 C/Carmen Redondo, 17 G/Panoramic Images,18/19 Erich Spiegelhalter, 19.1 L/Heuer, 19.2 Erich Spiegelhalter, 19.3 Peter Mertz, 19.4 A/OJPHOTOS, 19.5 Helga Lade Fotoagentur/Förster, 19.6 Wildlife/Hamblin, 19.7 L/Arcticphoto, 20 G/RH World Imagery/Gary Cook, 20/21 F1 online/Jan Byra, 21.1 FAN/ Achterberg, 21.2 G/The Image Bank/Hans Strand, 21.3 ifa/Aberham, 22 G/PC/Warwick Sweeney, 22/23 G/IB/Jan Tove Johannson, 24/25 ifa/F. Chmura, 25.1 G/Johner, 25.2 G/The Image Bank/Chad Ehlers, 26/27 F1 online/Johnér RF, 27.1 BB, 27.2 Blickwinkel/B. Zoller, 27.3 die bildstelle/Uwe Moser, 28 G/Panoramic Images, 28/29 L/Glaescher, 29.1 G/The Image Bank/Scott R. Barbour, 29.2 A/John Lens, 29.3 Visum/Alfred Buellesbach, 30 B/Felipe J. Alcoceba, 30/31 C/Philip Gould, 31.1 mauritius Images/Jose Fuste Raga, 31.2 C/Werner Forman, 32 A/imagebroker, 32/33 G/Stone/Cesar Lucas Abreu, 33.1 G/RH World Imagery/Jenny Pate, 33.2 A/Jon Sparks, 33.3 A/blickwinkel, 34.1 blickwinkel/K. Salminen, 34.2 A/Jef Maion/Nomads Land, 34/35 G/IB/Guy Edwardes, 35.1 A/blickwinkel, 35.2 A/Jef Maion/Nomads Land, 35.3 A/Interfoto Pressebildagentur, 35.4 G/IB/ Andy Rouse, 36/37 G/RH World Imagery/Reale Clark, 37.1 G/RH World Imagery/Gavin Hellier, 37.2 L/Kirchner, 37.3 G/De Agostini, 38/39 ALIMDI.net/White Star/Monica Gumm, 39 ifa/JA, 40/41 Bildagentur Huber/R. Schmid, 41 L/Eisermann, 42.1 A/Pawel Libera, 42.2 BB/Wolfgang Kunz, 42/43 C/Jim Richardson, 43.1 Zielske, 43.2 Zielske, Alt aus ETB: 44/45 Zielske, 45.1 Bildarchiv Monheim/Florian Monheim, 45.2 CARO/Ruffer, 45.3+45.4+45.5 Zielske, 46 Visum/Rezak, 46/47 A/Oleksandr Ivanchenko, 47.1 H/Ripani Massimo, 47.2 bridgemanart, 47.3 G/Panoramic Images, 47.1 A/Guy Edwardes Photography, 48.2 P, 48/49 A/David Noton Photography, 49.1 A/Nick Bodle, 49.2 S/RH, 49.3 Zielske, 49.4 B/artur, 49.5 L/Kuerschner, 49.6+49.7 Zielske, 50.1 B/Till Leeser, 50.2 B/Till Leeser, 51.3 LOOK/Holger Leue, 50/51 G/National Geographic/Richard T. Nowitz, 51.1 A/Guy Edwardes Photography, 51.2 G/Panoramic Images, 51.3 A/Trevor Smithers ARPS, 52.1 Zielske, 52.2 C/Listri, 52/53 Zielske, 53 Premium/ImageState, 54.1 A/David Chapman, 54.2 A/ImageState, 54.3 L/RAPHO, 54.4 L/Zielske, 54/55 G/The Image Bank/Travelpix Ltd, 55 G/The Image Bank/Guy Edwardes, 56 C/Reuters, 56/57 A/Jim Zuckermann, 57 Arco Images/NPL, 58/59 G/Andrew Ward/Life File, 59.1 G/Stone/Suzanne & Nick Geary, 59.2 Zielske, 59.3 B/Engler, 60.1 G/Stone/Joe Cornish, 60.2 G/Stone/Travelpix Ltd, 60.3 L/REA, 60.4 A/Francisco Martinez, 60/61 L/Babovic, 61.1 G/IB/Peter Adams, 61.2 Zielske, 61.3 LOOK/Laurence, 62.1 A/Skyscan Photolibrary, 62.2 C/Vannini, 62/63 C/Michael Freeman, 63.1 A/AA Worl Travel Library, 63.2 akg-images/Rabatti – Domingie, 63.3 Visum/Rezac, 63.4 Visum/Rezac, 63.5 Visum/Rezac, 64.1 Mauritius images, 64.2 A/Alan Novelli, 64/65 A/JA, 66.1 A/David Noble Photography, 66.2 Bildarchiv Monheim/ Florian Monheim, 66.3 LOOK/Ingolf Pompe, 66.4 A/Rod Edwards, 66.5 A/Jon Gibbs, 66.6 A/John Potter, 66.7 A/steven gillis hd9 imaging, 66/67 A/Jon Gibbs, 68 C/Sandro Vannini, 68/69 G/Stone/Mike Caldwell, 69.1 G/The Image Bank/Chris Simpson, 69.2 G/Iconica/Macduff Everton, 69.3 G/Stone/Crhis Simpson, 70.1 A/The Photolibrary Wales, 70.2 A/BL Images Ltd, 70/71 G/RH World Imagery/Roy Rainford, 71.1 A/David Noton Photography, 71.2 A/David Noton Photography, 71.3 G/The Image Bank/Guy Edwardes, 71.4 G/The Image Bank/Peter Adams, 72.1 G/Stone/Mike Caldwell, 72.2 G/The Image Bank/Kevin Schafer, 72.3 BB/Wolfgang Fuchs, 72/73 L/Hartmut Krinitz, 74.1 G/Panoramic Images, 74.2 Karl-Heinz Raach, 74.3 A/David Gowans, 74/75 A/Arco Images, 75.1 Premium, 76.2 A/RH Picture Library Ltd, 76.3 A/nagelestock.com, 76.4 A, 52.5 A, 76/77 Premium, 78.1 P/Images Colour, 78.2 P/Images Colour, 78.3 P/Mon Tresor/Woodfall, 78.4 P/Images Colour, 78.5 Karl-Heinz Raach, 78.6 A/ David Crossland, 79.1 Karl-Heinz Raach, 79.2 A/David Robertson, 79.3 Hartmut Krinitz, 79.4 LOOK/Wohner, 80.1 L/Jörg Modrow, 80.2 Hartmut Krinitz, 80.3 ifa/Panstock, 80.4 Martin Schulte-Kellinghaus, 81.1 ifa/Panstock, 81.2 P/Nägele, 82.1 C/WildCountry, 82.2 C/Clay Perry, 82.3 Martin Schulte-Kellinghaus, 82/83 P/ImageState, 84.1 L/Hartmut Krinitz, 84.2 Martin Schulte-Kellinghaus, 84/85 L/Jörg Modrow, 85.1 L/Hartmut Krinitz, 85.2 L/Hartmut Krinitz, 85.3 L/Hartmut Krinitz, 85.4 L/Jörg Modrow, 85.5 Ernst Wrba, 86/87.1 P/Stocklmage/B. Ancelot, 86/87.2 P, 87 A/Stephen Emerson, 88.1 G/Iconica/Macduff Everton, 88.2 A/Neil McAllister, 88.3 Brigitte & Emanuel Gronau, Weilheim, 88.4 G/Altrendo Panoramic, 88/89 H/Massimo Ripani, 89.1 A/Rough Guides, 89.2 A/Peter Mc Cabe, 90.1 G/Iconica/Macduff Everton, 90.2 A/Neil McAllister, 90.3 Brigitte & Emanuel Gronau, Weilheim, 90.4 G/Altrendo Panoramic, 90/91 Bildagentur Huber/Massimo Ripani, 91.1 A/Rough Guides, 91.2 Peter Mc Cabe, 92.1 P/ImagesColour, 92.2 ifa, 92.3 A/Paul Lindsay, 92.4 ifa, 93.1 G/Altrendo Panoramic, 93.2 G/IB/Don King, 93.3 G/National Geographic/Jim Richardson, 94.1 G/Photographers Choice/Tim Thompson, 94.2 Premium/ ImageState, 94.3 G/Panoramic Images, 94/95 A/Christopher Hill Photographic/scenicireland.com, 96.1 A/JA, 96.2 G/Riser/Ed Freeman, 96/97 P, 97.1 C/Richard Cummins, 97.2 G/PC/ Dennis Flaherty, 98.1 Ernst Wrba, 98.2 ifa, 60.3 Premium, 98.4 C/Richard Cummins,99.1 Premium, 99.2 C/Grehan, 99.3 ifa/JA, 99.4 ifa/Harris, 99.5 G/Altrendo Panoramic, 100/101 G/Digital Vision/RH, 101 G/Photographerẹs Choice/Harald Sund, 102.1 G/Stone/Jochem D. Wijnands,102.2 C/Bill Ross, 102/103 Schapowalow/RH, 104/105.1 Premium, 104/105.2 Premium, 106/107 LOOK/ Sabine Lubenow, 107.1 A/nagelestock.com, 107.2 Bildarchiv Monheim/Van der Voort, 107.3 G/Photographers Choice/ Glen Allison, 108 Premium, 108/109 A/Imagina Photography, 109 L/hemis, 110/111 Bildagentur Huber/Giovanni, 111.1 BB/ Dorothea Schmid, 111.2 BB/Dorothea Schmid, 111.3 BB /Dorothea Schmid, 112.1 BB/Dorothea Schmid, 112.2 akg-images, 112.3 Premium, 112.4 Schapowalow/Huber, 112.5 A/PCL, 112.6 A/ Mark Harmel, 112/113 Premium, 113.1 L/Meyer, 113.2 G/The Image Bank/Grant Faint, 113.3 L/REA, 114.1 BB/Dorothea Schmid, 114.2 L/Meyer, 114.3 L/Meyer, 114/115 BB/Dorothea Schmid, 115.1 BB/Dorothea Schmid, 115.2 A/D. Hurst, 115.3 A/JTB Photo Communications, Inc., 115.4 L/Meyer, 115.5 L/REA, 116.1 akg-images/Joseph Martin, 116.2 L/hemis, 116.3 L/hemis, 116.4 L/Gamma, 116/117 L/hemis, 117.1 A/JA, 117.2 L/hemis, 117.3 Mauritius-images/age, 117.4 L/hemis, 118.1 F1 online/Prisma, 118.2 L/hemis, 118/119 L/hemis, 119.1 L/hemis, 119.2 L/REA, 119.3 Bildagentur-online, 119.4 L/hemis, 119.5 BB/Andrej Reiser, 119.6 C/Sandro Vannini, 120 Premium, 120/121 Bildagentur Huber/G. Simeone, 121 ifa/Panstock, 122/123 ifa/JA, 123.1 ifa/JA, 123.2 artvertise, 123.3 A/JA, 124.1 P/Buss, 124.2 ifa/JA, 124.3 ifa/Panstock, 124/125 Bildarchiv Monheim, 125.1 L/hemis, 125.2 L/hemis, 125.3 BB/Thomas Ernsting, 125.4 BB/Thomas Ernsting, 125.5 L/Linke, 126 C/Gian Berto Vanni, 126/127 C/Vanni Archive, 127.1 L/hemis, 127.2 P/S. Roda, 127.3 Andia.fr/Boelle, 127.4 A/Mark Jones, 128.1 L/Kirchner, 128.2 G/The Image Bank/Travelpix Ltd, 128/129 BB/Berthold Steinhilber, 129.1 BB/Joerg Heimann, 129.2 L/Manfred Linke, 129.3 L/hemis, 129.4 L/Kirchner, 130.1 Bernd Ritschel, 130.2 L/Kürschner, 130/131 L/hemis, 132.1 S, 212.2 L/Krinitz, 132.3 L/Krinitz, 132/133 A/Rod Edwards, 134.1 G/RH World Imagery/Ruth Tomlinson, 134.2 G/Gallo Images/trafel Ink, 134/135 G/RH World Imagery/Ruth Tomlinson, 135.1 ifa/Panstock, 135.2 Visum/Cooperphotos, 136.1 L/Siemers, 136.2 LOOK/Karl Johaentges, 136.3 Schapowalow/RH, 136/137 Premium, 137 ifa/Panstock, 138.1 BB/Berthold Steinhilber, 138.2 L/Krinitz, 138.3 L/Hilger, 138/139 G/Time & Life Pictures, 139.1 L/hemis, 139.2 L/Krinitz, 139.3 L/hemis, 140 ifa/Diaf, 140/141 G/Photographerẹs Choice/Scott Stulberg, 141.1 G/The Image Bank/ Jeremy Walker, 141.2 G/Art Wolfe, 141.3 G/Purestock, 142 Blickwinkel/K. Thomas, 142/143 A/Images Etc Ltd, 144.1 B/Thomas Ernsting, 144/145 L/hemis, 145.1 L/hemis, 145.2 A/Andre Jenny, 145.3 A/David Noton Photography,146.1 IPN/Clay McLachlan, 146.2 L/hemis, 146.3 L/hemis, 146/147 Premium, 147.1 L/hemis, 147.2 Visum/ASK, 148/149 G/The Image Bank/David Madison, 149.1 Schapowalow/Sime, 149.2 A/JA, 149.3 Jahreszeiten Verlag/ Joerg Lehmann, 149.4 Schapowalow/Sime, 150 A/vario images, 150/151+151.1+151.2+151.3 Jürgen Richter, 152.1 G/Photonica/ Julio Lopez Saguar, 152.2 akg-images, 152/153 Dr. E. Rieber, München, 153 A/Luis Cuevas, 154.1 A/Chad Ehlers, 154.2 C/Riser/Anne Ripy, 154/155 G/IB/Allan Baxter,155.1 G/IB/Allen Baxter, 155.2 G/IB/Allen Baxter, 155.3 A/Alex Segre, 155.4 G/IB/Allen Baxter, 156.1 Jürgen Richter, 156.2 G/IB/Luis Castaneda, 156.3 H/Gräfenhain, 156/157 C/Jon Hicks, 157.1 S/H, 157.2 A/Jean Dominique Dallet, 158/159 C/Jon Hicks, 159.1 L/Eisermann, 159.2 ifa/Fried, 160.1 A/Melba Photo Agency, 160.2 L/Eid, 160/161 Jürgen Richter, 161.1+161.2 Martin Siepmann, 161.3 H/Gräfenhain, 161.4 LOOK/ Brigitte Merz, 162.1 L/Gonzales, 162.2 B&Y Photography, 162/163 H/Gräfenhain, 163.1 L/hemis, 163.2 L/Zuder, 163.3 G/Riser/Allan McPhall, 163.4 L/Tophoven, 163.5 G/RH World Imagery/Gavin Hellier, 164.1 Jürgen Richter, 164.2 G/Photographerẹs Choice/Peter Adams, 164.3 A/Peter Bowater, 164.4 A/PCL, 164/165 Bilderberg/Frieder Blickle, 165.1 G/RH World Imagery/Peter Higgins, 165.2 A/LOOK/Jürgen Richter, 165.3 L/Raach, 165.4 L/Cover, 166.1 G/The Image Bank/Peter Adams, 166.2 G/Axiom Photographic Agency/Anthony Webb, G/Photographerẹs Choice RF/Luis Velga, 166/167 Jürgen Richter, 167.1 Premium, 167.2 Pix/Silberbauer, 167.3 BB/Felipe J. Alcoceba, 167.4 BB/ Felipe J. Alcoceba, 168 Premium, 168/169 A/LOOK/Jürgen Richter, 169.1 G/Photographerẹs Choice/ Guy Vanderelst, 169.2 G/Photographerẹs Choice/Marco Cristofori, 169.3 G/Digital Vision/ Allan Baxter, 169.4 A/Peter Barritt, 169.5 G/Lonely Planet Images/Krzysztof Dydynski, 169.6 A/ LOOK/Franz Marc Frei, 170/171 ifa/K. Welsh, 171 C/Abilio Lope, 172 L/hemis, 172/173 Premium, 173.1 G/Panoramic Images, 173.2 G/The Image Bank/Luis Castaneda Inc., 173.3 G/Photographerẹs Choice RF/Allan Baxter, 173.4 G/The Image Bank/VisionofAmerica/Joe Sohm, 174 G/The Image Bank/Allan Baxter, 174/175 L/hemis, 175 L/Modrow, 176/177 ifa/Kanzler, 177.1 ifa/Lescourret, 177.2 Premium, 278.1 L/Selbach, 278.2 A/JA, 278.3 G/Christopher Pillitz, 278/279 P, 279.1 Arco Images/NPL, 279.2 G/Stone/Robert Frerck, 180.1 Jürgen Richter, 180.2 G/The Image Bank/Frank Seifert, 180.3 G/Stone/Manfred Mehlig, 180.4 L/H. & D. Zielske, 180/181 G/The Image Bank/Hans Strand, 181.1 L/Huber, 181.2 A/LOOK/Jürgen Richter, 181.3 Martin Siepmann, 181.4 Premium, 182.1 A/ Alandawsonphotography, 182.2 G/RH World Imagery/Marco Simoni, 182/183 Argus/Schwarzbach, 183 F1 online/Felix Stenson, 184 L/Tophoven, 184/185 G/IB/Bruno Morandi, 185.1 H/Schmid, 185.2 Jürgen Richter, 185.3 L/Tophoven, 186.1 G/Photographerẹs Choice RF/Guy Vanderelst, 186.2 G/Photographerẹs Choice RF/Guy Vanderelst, 186.3 G/Taxi/Guy Vanderelst, 186/187 L/hemis, 187.1 C/John and Lisa Merrill, 187.2 L/hemis, 188 C/Peter M. Wilson, 188/189 ifa/ JA, 189.1 C/Dennis Marsico, 189.2 G/PC/ Stuart Gregory, 189.3 C/Godong/Fred de Noyelle, 189.4 B/Felipe J. Alcoceba,190 L/Jerzy Modrak, 190/191 L/Zanettini, 191.1 G/The Image Bank/ Pauo Magalhaes, 191.2 L/hemis, 192.1 G/Stone/ John & Lisa Merrill, 192.2 G/Riser/Robert Frerck, 192.3 C/U. Schmid, 192.4 G/The Image Bank/Luis Velga, 192.5 G/Riser/Ed Freeman, 192.6 C/Grand Tour/Riccaardo Spila, 192/193 C/Jose Fuste Raga, 194.1 Biosphoto/Borrero Juan, 194.2 Biosphoto/Borrero Juan, 194.3 Biosphoto/ Borrero Juan, 194/195 A/photolocation 2, 196.1 L/Raach, 196.2 G/RH World Imagery/Bruno Barbier, 196.3 L/Raach, 196/197 A/Peter Mc Cabe, 198.1 H, 198.2 L/Heuer, 198/199 G, 199.1 L/Le Figaro Magazine, 199.2 L/Le Figaro Magazine, 199.3 L/Le Figaro Magazine, 199.4 L/Raach, 200 G/Stone/ Siegfried Layada, 200/201 G/Photographerẹs Choice/David Sutherland, 201 G/Photographerẹs Choice RF/Peter Adams, 202.1 G/The Image Bank/Siegfried Layda, 202.2 G/Photographerẹs Choice/ Travelpix Ltd., 202.3 G/The Image Bank/Wilfried Krecichwost, 202.4 L/Zenit/Langrock, 202.5 L/Plambeck, 203.1 G/The Image Bank/Joerg Greuel, 203.2 Zielske, 203.3 L/Zenit/Boening, 203.4 G/The Image Bank/Siegfried Layda, 204.1 L/Kreuels, 204.2 G/LOOK/ Konrad Wothe, 204.3 BB/S. Puschmann, 204/205 Premium, 205 G/LOOK/Karl Johaentges, 206.1 L/H. & D. Zielske, 206.2 F1 Online/Steiner,207.1+207.2+207.3+207.4+208.1 Zielske, 208.2 Schapowalow, 208.3 Zielske, 208/209 Zielske, 209.1 Premium/C. & R. Dörr, 209.2 Clemens Zahn, 210.1 L/Zenit/Boening, 210.2 L/Zenit/Boening, 210/211 EyeUbiquitous/Hutchison, 212/213.1 G/Panoramic Images, 212/213.2 G/The Image Bank/Siegfried Layda, 213 G/The Image Bank/Wilfried Krecichwost, 214/215 BB, 215.2 L/Linke, 215.3 L/Specht, 215.4 L/Specht, 216.1 C/The Gallery Collection, 216.2 Bildagentur Huber, 216.3 Das FotoArchiv, 216/217 Zielske, 218.1 ifa, 218.2 G, 218.3 Bildagentur Huber, 218/219 G, 219.1 L/Zenit/Boening, 219.2 C/Felix Zaska, 220/221 Zielske, 221.1 Schapowalow/Huber, 221.2 Mauritius, 221.3 Bildarchiv Huber, 222.1 A/Pat Behnke, 222.2 A/Rolf Richardson, 222/223 Corbis, 223.1 Bildagentur Huber, 223.2 Bildarchiv Monheim/Florian Monheim, 223.3 Bieker, 223.4 L/A. Hub, 224.1 transit/Thomas Haertrich, 224.2 BB/Zielske, 224.3 Bildagentur Huber/Schmid, 224.4 Zielske, 224.5 Bieker, 225.1 Bildagentur Huber, 225.2 Zielske, 225.3 Zielske, 225.4 Reinhard Feldrapp, 225.5 travelstock44.de/ Jürgen Feld, 224.6 Freyer, 226 Bieker, 226/227 Zielske, 227.1 Zielske, 227.2 Romeis, 228.1 Romeis, 228.2 Das Fotoarchiv, 228.3 C/Richard T. Nowitz, 228.4 ifa/Stadler, 228/229 Klammet, 229.1 Zielske, 229.2 Zielske, 230.1 ifa/Siebig, 230.2 L/Daniel Biskup, 230/231 LOOK/Ingrid Firmhofer, 231.1 Franz Marc Frei, 231.2 Schapowalow/Huber, 231.3 Romeis, 231.4 Zielske, 232.1 mediacolors/Bangerter, 232.2 F1 online/Prisma, 232/233 Visum/Alfred Buellesbach, 233.1 A/mediacolors, 233.2 Bildagentur-online, 233.3 alimdi.net/Michael Szoenyi, 233.4 L/Kirchgessner, 234.1 G/National Geographic/ Richard Nowitz, 234.2 Visum/Alfred Buellesbach, 234.3 fotofinder/Dirk Renckhoff, 234/235 Visum/Alfred Buellesbach, 235 G/Panoramic Images, 236.1 G/Stone/Siegfried Eigstler, 236.2 A/JA, 236/237 G/Photographerẹs Choice RR/Dan Tucker, 238 L/Christian Heeb, 238/239 A/mediacolors, 239 L/Specht, 240.1 A/JA, 240.2 a1PIX/ AAB, 240/241 L/Heeb, 241.1 F1 online/Prisma, 241.2 A/nagelestock.com, 242/ 243 mediacolors, 243.1 Schapowalow/Sime, 243.2 Schapowalow/Sime, 243.3 Schapowalow/Sime, 244/245 G/RH World Imagery/Jochen Schlenker, 245 G/Panoramic Images, 246.1 G/The Image Bank/Hans Wolf, 246.2 ifa/JA, 246/247 Schapowalow/ Huber, 247.1 Bildagentur Huber, 247.2 A/Wilmar Photography, 247.3 A/Interfoto Pressebildagentur, 248.1 L/Kirchgessner, 248.2 G/LOOK/Ingolf Pompe, 248/249 L/Galli, 249.1 G/Photographerẹs Choice/ Simeone Huber, 249.2 Iris Kürschner, 250.1 L/Kristensen, 250.2 G/Scott Barbour, 250.3 Anzenberger/Manfred Horvath, 250.4 mediacolors/vsl, 250/251 C/zefa/Fridmara Damm, 251.1 G/Panoramic Images, 251.2 BB/Berthold Steinhilber, 251.3 L/G. Huber, 252.1 Anzenberger/Carlos de Mello, 252.2 LOOK/Jan Greune, 252/253 Anzenberger/Yadid Levy, 253.1 L/Heeb, 253.2 L/Hahn, 254.1 mediacolors/vsl, 254.2 F1 online/Austrophoto, 254/255 Bildarchiv Monheim/Florian Monheim, 255.1 G/The Image Bank /dreamPictures, 255.2 L/Heeb, 256.1 Fan/Achterberg, 256.2 LOOK/ Andreas Strauss, 256.3 Bernd Ritschel, 256.4 LOOK/Ingolf Pompe, 256/257 Mauritius images/Ludwig Mallaun, 257.1 G/LOOK/Strauss, 257.2 G/Riser/Hans Peter Merten, 258.1 L/Caputo, 258/259 A/JA, 259.1 Schapowalow/Huber, 259.2 alimdi. net/KFS, 260.1 L/hemis, 260.2 Arco Images/ Usher, 260.3 Arco Images/Usher, 260.4 Arco Images/Usher, 260.5 Blickwinkel/H. Schulz, 260/261 A/Woodystock, 261.1 G/Altrende Panoramic, 261.2 Arco Images/Rolfes, 261.3 Premium/Minden P./Wisniewski, 261.4 Juniors Bildarchiv, 261.5 Premium/Schuyl/FLPA, 262 DFA/Riedmiller, 262/263 ifa/JA, 263 ifa/Lecom, 264/265 G/The Image Bank/Darryl Leniuk, 265.1 A/JA, 265.2 G/The Image Bank/ Walter Bibikow, 266.1 A/imagebroker, 266.2 Bildagentur Huber, 266/267 A/imagebroker, 267 F1 online/Prisma, 268.1 Udo Bernhart, 268.2 L/hemis, 268/269 Visum/Gerhard Westrich, 269.1 L/hemis, 269.2 Premium, 270.1 LOOK/Rainer Martini, 270.2 L/hemis, 270/271 L/Galli, 271.1 G/Taxi/Peter Adams, 271.2 L/hemis, 271.3 L/Galli, 272 ifa/Alastor Photo, 272/273 L/Galli, 273 L/Galli, 274.1 G/Photographerẹs Choice/Richard Elliott, 274.2 G/The Image Bank/Macduff Everton, 274/275 G/LOOK/Thorsten Rother, 275.1 G/The Image Bank/Macduff Everton, 275.2 G/The Image Bank/Macduff Everton, 276.1 L/Krinitz, 276.2 G/Hulton Archive/Imagno, 276.3 L/Kuerschner, 277.1 L/ Modrow, 277.2 L/Galli, 277.3 L/Kreuels, 277.4 Udo Bernhart, 277.5 A/Matteo Del Grosso, 277.6 L/Standl, 278/279.1 G/LOOK/ Jan Greune, 278/279.2 G/Panoramic Images, 280.1 G/Panoramic Images, 280.2 NN, 280.3 L/Caputo, 280.4 Mauritius images/age, 280/281 G/Axiom Photographic Agency/Chaelres Bowman, 281.1 G/IB/ Andrea Pistolesi, 281.2 bridgemanart.com, 282 C/Musico, 282/283 L/Eid, 283.1 S, 283.2 Mauritius images/Rene Truffy, 283.3 ifa/Aigner, 284.1 L/Le Figaro Magazine, 284.2 A/Art Kowalsky, 284.3 L/Galli, 284/285 ifa/JA, 285 G/Stone/Travelpix Ltd, 286.1 L/Zanettini, 286.2 Premium, 286.3 G/The Bridgeman Art Library/Leonardo da Vinci, 286/287 Premium, 288.1 L/Galli, 288.2 L/hemis, 288.3 Premium, 288/289 Axel M. Mosler, 289 L/hemis, 290/291 L/Zenit/Jan Peter Boening, 291 C/Sandro Vannini, 292.1 Ernst Wrba, 292.2 G/RH World Imagery/Bruno Morandi, 292/293 L/Celentano, 294 G/Iconica/Macduff Everton, 294/295 L/Celentano, 295.1 Axel M. Mosler, 295.2 A/M. Flynn, 296.1 L/Galli, 296.2 L/Zanettini, 296.3 L/Amme, 296.4 Axel M. Mosler, 296.5 C/David Lees, 296.6 Udo Bernhart, 296.7 BB, 296.8 AKG-images, 296.9 AKG-images, 296/297 L/Galli, 297.1 L/Ogando, 297.2 L/Galli, 297.3 L/Galli, 298.1 L/Galli, 298.2 L/Galli, 298.3 L/Galli, 298.4 L/Galli, 298.5 L/Galli, 298.6 L/Galli, 298.7 A/Alessandro Chiarini, 298.8 L/Galli, 298.9 A/Cuboimages srl, 298/299 BB, 299 G/The Image Bank/Macduff Everton, 300.1 Gerhard P. Müller, 300.2 BB, 300.3 G/The Image Bank/David Noton, 300/301 ifa/Aberham, 301.1 L/Celentano, 301.2 G/National Geographic/O. Louis Mazzatenta, 301.3 P/Image State, 302.1 Hubert Stadler, 302.2 BB, 302.3 Hubert Stadler, 302.4 Hubert Stadler, 302/303 Hubert Stadler, 303.1 G/The Image Bank/David Noton, 303.2 G/Taxi/David Noton, 303.3 Premium, 304.1 A/JA, 304.2 G/Photographer's Choice/Peter Adams, 304.3 C/Sygma/Fabian Cevallos, 304/305 G/De Agostini, 305 G/Photodisc/Stefano Stefani, 306.1 L/Zanettini, 306.2 S, 306.3 S, 306.4 G/Digital Vision/Allan Baxter, 306.5 L/Zanettini, 307.1 ifa, 307.2 L/Eligio Paon, 307.3 C/ Massimo Listri, 307.4 L/Celentano, 307.5 C/ Mimmo Jodice, 308.1 C/Jodice, 308.2 G/Stone/Sylvian Grandadam, 308.3 Mauritius, 308/309 L/Celentano, 309.1 A/Cuboimages srl, 309.2 L/Celentano, 309.3 BB/Walter Schmitz, 309.4 BB/Felipe J. Alcoceba, 310.1 L/Celentano, 310.2 ifa/Harris, 310.3 ifa/Harris, 310/311 Premium, 311 A/LOOK/Hauke Dressler, 312.1 G/The Image Bank/Andrea Pistolesi, 312.2 G/Stone/Duane Rieder, 312.3 L/Galli, 312/313 L/Galli, 313.1 L/Harscher, 313.2 L/Harscher, 314.1 G/Stone/Art Wolfe, 314.2 L/Celentano, 314.3 L/hemis, 314.4 L/Galli, 314/315 G/The Image Bank/David Trood, 316.1 L/Celentano, 316.2 A, 316.3 A/CuboImages srl, 316/317 ifa, 317.1 A/Blickwinkel, 317.2 A/F1 online, 317.3 L/Piepenburg, 317.4 Schapowalow, 317.5 L/Hauser, 318/319 L/Kirchner, 319.1 L/hemis, 319.2 A/JA, 319.3 L/hemis, 320.1 Bildagentur Huber/ Schmid, 320.2 Mauritius/Bibikow, 320.3 Das Fotoarchiv/ Müller, 320/321 Premium, 322.1 A/Bildagentur-online/ McPhoto-PMU, 322.2 ifa/Tschanz, 322.3 A/Mc-Photo, 322.4 A/Andreas Ehrhard, 322.5 A/Arco Images, 322.6 Premium, 322/323 L/Florian Werner, 323 P/Buss, 324/325 G/The Image Bank/Sigfried Layda, 325.1 BB/Ginter, 325.2 BB/Ginter, 326.1 BB/Blickle, 326.2 BB/ Peter Schröder, 326/327 AKG, 327.1 ifa, 327.2 Das Fotoarchiv, 328.1 L/Zanettini, 328.2 L/Zanettini, 328/329 A, 329.1 BB/Blickle, 329.2 BB/Modrak, 329.3 BB/Kalley, 329.4 BB/Madej, 329.5 Schapowalow, 330.1 alimdi.net/ Egmont Strigl, 330.2 alimdi.net/Egmont Strigl, 330.3 A/Beren Patterson, 330.4 alimdi.net/Egmont Strigl, 330/331 L/Henseler, 331.1 A/Steven Minle, 331.2 L/Henseler, 331.3 L/hemis, 331.4 L/Henseler, 331.5 L/Henseler, 332 Vario Images, 332/333 transit/Thomas Haertrich, 333 L/Westrich, 334/335 ifa/ Strobl, 336.1 L/ Barth, 336.2 Blumebild/Blume, 336.3 Visum/Peter Schickert, 336/337 Bildagentur Huber, 337 L/Kristensen, 338.1 L/Hahn, 338.2 L/Hahn, 338.3 L/Hahn, 338.4 L/Hahn, 338.5 L/Hahn, 338/339 L/Hahn, 339.1 ifa/ Panstock, 339.2 L/Hahn, 339.3 L/Hahn, 339.4 L/Hahn, 339.5 L/ Multhaupt, 340.1 A/archivberlin Fotoagentur/J. Fekete, 340.2 A/ imagebroker/Egmont Strigl, 340/341 A/imagebroker/Egmont Strigl, 341.1 A, 341.2 Bildarchiv Monheim, 341.3 Bildarchiv Monheim, 341.4 A/Peter M. Wilson, 342.1 Bernd Ritschel, 342.2 G/Photographerẹs Choice/Guy Edwardes, 342/343 G/ Photographerẹs Choice/Guy Edwardes, 343.1 L/Kristensen, 343.2 A/Simon Reddy, 344 L/Kuerschner, 344/345 BA-Geduldig, 346 C/Jose Fuste Raga, 346/347 L/ hemis/frank Guiziou, 347.1 L/Glaescher, 347.2 BB/Jerzy Modrak, 347.3 L/hemis, 347.4 L/Zanettini, 348/349 BB/ Wolfgang Kunz, 349.1 L/Heuer, 349.2 L/Zanettini, 349.3 L/Meazza/Amme, 350/351 G/Riser/Gary John Norman, 351.1 A/Globe Exposure, 351.2 L/hemis, 351.3 G/Photographerẹs Choice/Simeone Huber, 352/353 A/Sean Sprague, 353 L/IML, 534.1 transit/Peter Hirth, 354.2 AKG, 354.3 A/JA/Russell Young, 354/355 Still pictures/Dana Wilson, 355.1 L/Raach, 355.2 A/Gregory Wrona, 355.3 L/Raach, 355.4 A/Danita Delimont, 355.5 Avenue Images/Index Stock/David Ball, 356 Natrubildportal/Martin Zwick, 356/357 Naturbildportal/Martin Zwick, 357.1 Visum/Woodfall, 357.2 C/Sygma/Philippe Caron, 358.1 A/ Nikreates, 358.2 F1 online/Christian Bauer, 358/459 Mauritius/age, 360.1 AKG, 360.2 G/AFP/Johannes Eisele, 360/ 361 C/P. Saloutos, 361.1 L/Frank Heuer, 361.2 L/GAFF/ Adenis, 362/363 L/IML, 363.1 L/IML, 363.2 Mauritius/imagebroker, 363.3 L/IML, 364.1 BB/Wolfgang Kunz, 364.2 L/Harscher, 364/365 C/J. Hicks, 365.1 C/P. Souders, 365.2 C/Sandra Vannini, 366.1 G/Taxi/David Noton, 366.2 BB, 366.3 G/DEA/A. Garozzo, 366.4 A/David Crossland, 366/367 ifa/JA, 368 P/S. Bunka, 368/369 G/Stone/Simeone Huber, 369.1 L/IML, 369.2 L/Hilger, 370/371 L/hemis, 371.1 L/hemis, 371.2 G/Photographerẹs Choice/Darrell Gulin, 371.3 L/hemis, 372.1 Premium, 372.2 L/IML, 372/373 A/JA, 373.1 G/Taxi/Maremagnum, 373.2 L/Harscher, 374/375 L/IML, 375.1 L/Tophoven, 375.2 A/Jan Wlodarczyk, 375.3 G/National Geographic/ James L. Stanfield, 375.4 L/Huber, 376/377 Schapowalow, 377.1 A/Ian Dagnall, 377.2 Bridgemanart.com, 377.3 L/hemis, 378Premium, 378/379 A/Paul Carstairs, 380.1 L/Tueremis, 380.2 Schapowalow/SIME, 380.3 P/Fiala, 380.4 AKG, 380/381 C/Atlantide, 381.1 A/Images& Stories, 381.2 BB/Nar Photos, 381.3 A/Jean-Christophe Godet, 381.4 BB/Klaus Bossemeyer, 381.5 A/Images& Stories, 382.1 P, 382.2 LOOK/Konrad Wothe, 382.3 A/Images&Stories, 382/383 A/John Farnham, 383.1 A Blaine Harrington III, 383.2 mauritius images/Brand X Pictures, 383.3 ifa/JA, 384 A/ImageGap, 384/385 H/R. Schmid, 385.1 A/Alan Novelli, 385.2 L/Müller, 386.1 S/RH, 386.2 vario images, 386/387 G/RH World Imagery/Bruno Morandi, 387.1 G/IB/ Dario Mitidieri, 387.2 Caro/Riedmiller, 387.3 P, 388 L, 388/389 L/Raach, 390 Mauritius/Ferdinand Hollweck, 390/391 ifa/JA, 392 L/hemis, 392/393 A/JA, 393.1 ifa/JA, 393.2 L/Heuer, 393.3 ifa/JA, 393.4 L/Babovic, 394.1 C/Morton Beebe, 394.2 Schapowalow/Huber, 394.3 Premium/Buss, 394.4 C/W. Kaehler, 394/395 G/National Geographic/Dean Conger, 395.1 A/imagebroker/Ferdinand Hollweck, 395.2 Bildagentur Huber/Gräfenhain, 395.3 C/P. Turnley, 396.1 G/ Photographerẹs Choice/Fotoworld, 396.2 Mauritius/Ferdinand Hollweck, 396/397 G/National Geographic/Richard S. Durrance, 397 Bildagentur Huber/ Günter Gräfenhain, 398.1 Arco Images/Vnoucek, 398.2 BB/Russian Look/Vadim Nekrasov, 398.3 L/Hilger, 398.4 Bildagentur Huber/ Günter Gräfenhain, 398/399 L/hemis, 399 L/Galli.

This edition is published on behalf of APA Publications GmbH & Co. Verlag KG, Singapore Branch, Singapore
by Verlag Wolfgang Kunth GmbH & Co KG, Munich, Germany

Distribution of this edition:

GeoCenter International Ltd
Meridian House, Churchill Way West
Basingstoke, Hampshire RG21 6YR
Great Britain
Tel.: (44) 1256 817 987
Fax: (44) 1256 817 988
sales@geocenter.co.uk
www.insightguides.com

Printed in Slovakia

Original edition:
© 2009/2010 Verlag Wolfgang Kunth GmbH & Co. KG, Munich
Königinstr. 11
80539 Munich
Ph: +49.89.45 80 20-0
Fax: +49.89.45 80 20-21
www.kunth-verlag.de

Translation: Sylvia Goulding, Emily Plank, Katherine Taylor
Editor: Kevin White for bookwise Medienproduktion GmbH, Munich

The information and facts presented in this book have been extensively researched and edited for accuracy. The publishers, authors, and editors, cannot, however, guarantee that all of the information in the book is entirely accurate or up to date at the time of publication. The publishers are grateful for any suggestions or corrections that would improve the content of this book.